Attitudes to Psychological Stress Among Construction Professionals

Alan Patching

Attitudes to Psychological Stress Among Construction Professionals

palgrave
macmillan

Alan Patching
Faculty of Society and Design
Bond University
Robina, QLD, Australia

ISBN 978-3-030-93775-1 ISBN 978-3-030-93776-8 (eBook)
https://doi.org/10.1007/978-3-030-93776-8

This Palgrave Macmillan imprint is published by the registered company Springer Nature Switzerland AG
The registered company address is: Gewerbestrasse 11, 6330 Cham, Switzerland

I dedicate this book to Professor Michael Regan, who passed away just a few short weeks after providing his final comments on the research upon which this work is primarily based.

Contents

About the Author

Dr. Alan Patching is an experienced construction professional who also has formal qualifications and substantial clinical experience in counselling and psychotherapy practice. He began his career as a cadet quantity surveyor in the Queensland Government, before commencing his construction project management business, which quickly grew to four offices. His next position was as National Projects Director (Australia) in charge of a large portfolio of projects for a Japanese company. His last major project roles were as CEO of the owning entity of the Sydney Olympic Stadium, and Project Director for the design and construction of that venue—the largest Olympic stadium ever constructed—and as a phase project director and ministerial advisor for Suncorp Stadium in Brisbane.

Patching is a Professor of construction management and project management at Australia's Bond University, and Associate Dean of Engagement for the institution's Faculty of Society and Design. His research interests, which gave rise to this book, combine his interest and skillsets in construction project management and in aspects of human behaviour, and in particular attitudes to the avoidance and management of stress among construction professionals.

List of Figures

List of Tables

1

The Problem, the Questions It Raises, and the Path to Much-Needed Answers

Introduction

What This Book Is About

This book is about change. It is about why change is needed in an industry making up a substantial part of every western economy—not only why this change must be undertaken, but also about how government and industry leaders might initiate the long-overdue change required. In short, it is about necessary systemic transformation in the world's construction industries. My move from 'change' to 'transformation' was intentional. I regard change, when referring to business matters, as an adjustment to what a business does, while I see transformation as describing an adjustment to what a business is. In the context of this book, change is the minimum I hope to inspire, while transformation is the adjustment really required.

In project management (PM) parlance—the INITIATION phase
In psychotherapy parlance—the INTAKE session

A. Patching, *Attitudes to Psychological Stress Among Construction Professionals*,
https://doi.org/10.1007/978-3-030-93776-8_1

The construction of this book is detailed at the end of this chapter. I wanted its structure to be a metaphor for doing things differently. Accordingly, a somewhat different approach to this book was motivated by aspects of the phases involved in the two career areas to which I've dedicated much of my life—project management (PM) of major construction projects, and counselling and psychotherapy addressing stress-driven issues and their impacts on clients.

The first phase of PM is generically known as the initiation phase. During this phase information is gathered to prepare the technical and financial feasibilities for the project. The first phase in psychotherapy is similar. The therapist gathers relevant information about the client's background, needs, problem to address and what detailed information must be obtained in later phases to deliver the required objective.

There are some unlikely similarities between the professional processes of project management and psychotherapy. I have presented the stages of each set of processes for the respective practices at the commencement of each chapter to provide a sense of continuity to the work beyond the usual stages of the academic research process.

The initiation phase of a construction project often involves a client with very clear ideas about their needs and wants, and a project manager who, from (hopefully considerable) experience, simply knows some of those client's needs are probably unaffordable in the context of the current budget, or cannot be technically achieved, or would contribute substantially to cost but far less so to revenue generation, and so on. Success in this phase requires collecting, collating and examining data, usually via technical and financial feasibility analysis, and open and vigourous communication between relevant parties until a consensus is achieved regarding the content to be included in the project, and the way to deliver that content effectively. This latter task is a key focus of the detailed analysis of the second phase, which is project planning, something that simply cannot be effectively done without first collating the client's responses to the myriad questions asked in the initiation phase.

A similar circumstance exists for the psychotherapist. Let us name the characters of our psychotherapy-related storyline Will and Clare, whose relationship in many ways reflects that of some CPMs and their employers. That relationship can sometimes be somewhat bitter (even toxic) toxic, yet the resultant problems are seldom adequately addressed, often because each party believes the ineffective, not to mention upsetting behaviour of the other to be driven by well-meant intent. Neither seems to have awareness that the risk in such a scenario lies in the lack of focus on bringing underlying issues to light via effective and open communication and in not addressing the impact of risk that could extend to relationship or personal burnout.

In both the PM and the psych contexts, gathering and studying the correct information in the first phase of professional work pave the way for successful subsequent phases. It is to this objective this first chapter is dedicated, and to that effect, an introductory overview of the construction industry is warranted, as is an introduction to deeper aspects of Will and Clare's relationship, but we'll commence with the industry perspective.

Industry Overview

The Australian construction industry contributes 7.7 percent to Australia's Gross Domestic Product (GDP) and its 338,000 businesses employ over one million people, approximately nine percent of the entire workforce [1]. During 2010–2011 the industry recorded the fourth highest growth in contribution to GDP in Australia [2]. Construction is Australia's third largest industry, and 85 percent of its workers are employed full time, compared with 54 percent across other industries. Eighty-nine percent of workers are male, compared with 54 percent across other industries [1]. In February 2015, 15.8 percent of the construction workforce was 55 years of age of older. Thirty percent of the workforce was self-employed, compared with 8.5 percent across other industries, and 45 percent held a certificate 3 or certificate 4 vocational qualification, compared with 20 percent across other industries. However, only eight percent held a bachelor's degree or higher, compared with 28 percent across other industries [1]. Despite a quiet period in construction over several years, an anticipated growth in construction employment above employment growth across other industries up until 2019 was largely realised [1]. The industry represents a high-pressure work environment not only because of workloads, especially for industry professionals, but also environmental conditions, including noise, dust and weather [3].

Buildsoft, well-known for its construction quantity surveying software (and for being owned by MiTek Australia, a subsidiary of billionaire Warren Buffet's Berkshire Hathaway) rated construction as Australia's largest non service-related industry, contributing approximately AUD 134 billion to the economy. By comparison, the construction industry in the United Kingdom (UK) produces 6 percent of economic output and fills 7.1 percent of all UK jobs with 2.3 million people [4, 5]. The construction industry in the United States of America (USA) employs seven million people, is one of the largest customers for manufacturing, mining and services industries, and contributes USD 1.3 trillion to the economy annually [6]. When the health of the workforce of this industry is facing threat in any western country, the potential exists not only for a very large number of people to be negatively affected, but also for employers to experience substantial consequential loss of productivity and profitability.

In all examples above, the numbers quoted refer to contractor/tradespeople/building professionals employed in constructing buildings. Millions more people are employed in related employment, ranging from professional consultancies to products supply and general services provision. The primary research upon which the book is based focussed on the attitudes of professional Construction Project Managers (CPMs) to avoidance and management of psychological stress in their workplaces [7]. A CPM is defined for this book, as 'any professional who works in the management and coordination of the delivery of design, procurement and/or execution or construction of a construction project and who does not work as a tradesperson on such projects'. Accordingly, a CPM might be a project manager, contracts administrator, contracts manager or site manager. Interestingly, there is a strong theme regarding how these professionals become involved in construction, and to this theme I will now direct attention.

Relationship Awareness Theory posits an overdone or inappropriately applied strength becomes a weakness [8]. This proposition seems to fit CPMs more than other professions [9]. Construction project management has long offered young professionals interesting work, challenging opportunities, high levels of responsibility and subsequent career advancement. Many CPMs enjoy their work beyond simply having a job they love. Their job often has them, as it were. In situations where there is a balance between the demands of work and private life, this was not necessarily a negative phenomenon [9]. However, all-too-often work demands became unreasonable and, in keeping with the Relationship Awareness Theory premise, a strength of inappropriate commitment becomes a weakness of workaholism.

Strength also becomes a weakness when the matrix structure, via which project management was introduced into the corporate world, is controlled by managers who understand neither the concepts behind the approach, nor how effective and mature project management works. Matrix management has been a bigger problem for those involved in non-construction projects. However, in the modern business environment, it also affected construction-related organisations and thus demanded attention in this book.

Individuals who thrive on challenging work, yet have their projects fall behind deadlines because of the slow decision-making often found within matrix structures, discover their enjoyment from work quickly diminishes. It is common in such circumstances the employee's psychological experience of work changed from being motivating and satisfying to being stressful and debilitating [10–13]. Matrix organisations adopt a structure that combines the advantages of traditional functional organisational hierarchies and of the product or project producing organisational structure [14, 15]. It is ideally suited for projects-driven companies [14, 16]. Effectively, matrix management creates an approach wherein each employee has two jobs, one along vertical functional lines, and the second in a projects environment, to which personnel were appointed horizontally from across functions, based on project needs [14, 16].

Figure 1.1 presents a typical matrix organisational structure diagram. More senior personnel are sometimes subordinated to a hierarchically-junior project manager. This works efficiently in a mature projects environment established with well-defined structure and systems [16]. However, in an immature projects environment, the matrix structure

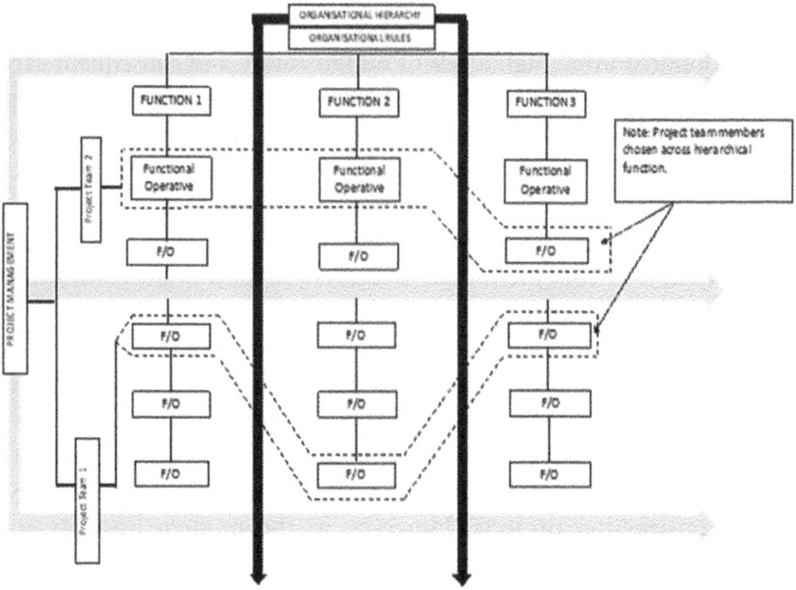

Fig. 1.1 Diagram of matrix organisational structure

is often stressogenic because of unnecessary power plays and, in crisis situations, even organisational anarchy [17–19].

When the disputation often prevalent in construction environments becomes part of a project's reality [20–22] or stakeholders with often contradictory demands insist on more active participation in the project [23, 24] the pressure upon CPMs quickly increases. When those CPMs begin to experience psychological stress, they find it difficult to extricate themselves from the environment that gives rise to it [25]. Furthermore, workplace culture aspects are often so powerful people who experience psychological stress impacts often are reticent to either take advantage of readily available workplace help, or to seek external assistance, despite knowing they should [25, 26].

This scenario is often a parallel of the relationships of people in the industry have with their life partners. Partners of CPMs who feel neglected by those CPMs seemingly prioritising work above family or partner might dispute that situation and it is almost inevitable the stress from such conflict is taken back to the work environment, triggering a destructive vortex of work pressure impacting private life pressure impacting work pressure. Uninterrupted and unmanaged, such a scenario can seldom lead to a positive outcome. Often, both Will and Clare are aware there is a problem, and have an idea of its genesis, but refrain from addressing it to avoid even more open life stress in an already uncomfortable situation. This attempt to avoid stress, ironically, often leads to the very increase in stress it seeks to avoid.

There are many more stress drivers than I've mentioned thus far within the construction environment and it is now important to gain a preliminary understanding of stress, its potential impacts, and how managing stress might need to differ within construction as compared with business at large.

The Concept of Stress and Its Drivers

Stress is not a new phenomenon. It had been used in medicine for centuries [27], and in 1624, Robert Burton identified social stress as a common cause of melancholy, today called depression. Workplace stress is a recent phenomenon developed from workplaces becoming aware of the impact of stress on productivity. Workplace stress giving rise to physiological, psychological and emotional outcomes is a post world war two concept [28].

Stress is seen as a psychological perception of pressure, and the body's response to it. This description is inadequate for deeper aspects of this work, and Chapter 2 investigates psychological and physiological effects of stress in greater detail. Bystritsky and Kronemyer [29] hinted at the serious nature of stress when they addressed it in terms of a reaction to abnormal and even catastrophic levels of stimuli experienced within the sufferer's environment.

In the USA, employment-related stress rates fifth of the top ten stressors, which includes the death of a loved one, divorce, financial issues, poor health, personal relationship issues and family illness issues [30]. While an Australian study revealed limited support for a causal relationship between workplace stress and physical aspects of work environments (e.g. noise, poor lighting) [31] it was reasonable to conclude psychological aspects of work environments (e.g. conflict, excessive workload, lack of appreciation or recognition) were likely causes of workplace stress for employees. A key purpose of this book was to understand how stress is perceived, caused, and managed within CPMs' workplace environments in Australia.

Stress and its effects have attracted exponentially increasing attention over recent decades, after their contribution to burnout and other problems involving serious physiological and psychological consequences became better understood [31–37]. The term burnout was attributed in the early 1970s to Freudenberger [37] and described by Burg-Brown [38, p. 49] as:

> *The point at which important and meaningful work can become unpleasant and unfulfilling. At this point, energy turns into exhaustion, involvement leads to cynicism and efficiency is replaced by ineffectiveness.* [39]

The World Health Organisation (WHO) [40] regards workplace stress as the second most frequent health problem in the European Union, affecting one third of workers. This is of great concern, but an even greater concern is only three percent of construction industry employers concur that work pressure causes serious health and safety problems [3]. Consequently, workers are expected to do increasingly complex work in decreasing periods of time [3]. Unless work environments change, it remains questionable whether any appreciable enduring benefits can be achieved [3, 41]. Albertson et al. [42, p. 82] also addressed workplace environment factors contributing to stress, referring to the 'concept of boundary-less work', and indicated role overload, especially in high job demand and low job control circumstances, is an important stressor. Interestingly, these authors disagree with Lingard and Francis [43] and Lingard and Sublet [44] and reported no effect of work circumstances on a range of issues including work-family conflict [42], a notable disparity that became one focus of this book.

Leadership attitude emerged as a major workplace stressor in construction environments, and continues to have powerful impact on industry professionals. The research this work explains revealed leadership issues are behind much stress among CPMs. In much the same way our friends Will and Clare each know there is a problem in their relationship, but simply choose not to address it (while waiting for the other to raise it for discussion) leaders within the construction industry appear to their CPM employees to be doing their best to win and deliver work in hard times and these CPMs tend to accept any impacts of whatever their leaders do to achieve that objective should reasonably be tolerated. The result of such an attitude is at least a continuation of unacceptable circumstances and impacts, and a lack of focus by industry leaders on what needs to be done to rectify the unspoken problem. I shall address that now.

Leadership Attitudes to Stress

Stress is not a disease, but rather a contributing factor to, or cause of, several diseases. It is now Australian law that business operators do whatever is reasonably practicable to eliminate or minimise risks to worker health and safety, including the risk of harm from work stressors [45]. This requirement is now common in many countries, necessitating business leaders to understand causes of work-related stress, including lack of role clarity and authority, high work demands, poor management support, low levels of recognition and reward, and exposure to bullying and harassment. Environmental factors including noise, temperature, humidity, lighting and air quality are also potential stressors.

A simple, well-recognised and broadly accepted definition of stress, providing insight into what workplace stress is and what causes it, is now relevant:

> *Work-related stress describes the physical, mental and emotional reactions of workers who perceive that their work demands exceed their abilities and/or their resources (such as time, help/support) to do the work. It occurs when they perceive they are not coping in situations where it is important to them that they do cope.* [45]

High workload and productivity expectations contribute to stress and burnout, but leadership acknowledgement and appreciation of effort, and feedback to employees their work is valued, partially alleviates effects of high job demands [37]. Van Der Molen and Hoonakker [3] found a low recognition by construction leaders of the link between high demand work environments and health and safety outcomes. The challenge for CPMs is to have their leaders better understand the relationship between increasing job demands and stress, especially in limited job control situations, and the correlation between stress and health and safety outcomes. Moreover, construction leaders should accept that improving working conditions to prevent stress should be prioritised above instigating stress management after stress effects manifest [45, 46].

The last decade has seen an increasing focus on serious effects of workplace stress, including burnout. Reports from Great Britain and other countries reveal substantial and concerning loss of productivity—13.8 million working days during 2006–2007 for Great Britain alone [47].

My research included reviewing the literature regarding the origins and development of workplace stress to assist construction industry leaders better understand the causes and extent of stress in their industry so they could improve working conditions, alleviate stress, and improve productivity and profitability. Important questions emerged that required answering if the above objectives were to be achieved:

- To what extent is workplace stress primarily generated within the workplace rather than by life outside of work and then displaced, in the Freudian sense, into the workplace? (Freud's concept of displacement involved the transfer of potentially high impact emotionality away from its perceived trigger and towards targets of less risk from an emotional perspective [48])
- To what extent does stress from private life exacerbate workplace-experienced stress?
- To what extent is workplace stress considered more a medical concept than psychological, and a consequence of deeper physiological problems, such as metabolic syndrome (addressed later) rather than a reflection of workplace environment and working conditions?

These are important questions, not only in relation to business at large, but also in terms of impact on CPMs. The parallel questions for a relationship such as Will's and Clare's might include:

- To what extent are their relationship challenges generated within the relationship rather than by life outside of the relationship and then displaced, in that Freudian sense, within the relationship?
- To what extent does stress from work exacerbate relationship-experienced stress?
- To what extent are relationship problems a consequence of deeper problems, such as lack of communication regarding work and other pressures on the relationship, rather than a reflection of problems within the relationship only?

For many, comprehending these relationship-oriented questions seems easier than getting a grip on the workplace stress issues. Perhaps this is due to a closer understanding of relationship issues than of work-related challenges. To begin to test this, a deeper understanding of the work of CPMs and of its effects on practitioners, is considered useful.

I found some answers to the work environment-related questions in a 2013 pilot study.

Pilot Study Overview and Key Findings

I commenced a pilot study in 2013 to ascertain interest level in researching stress among CPMs [9]. I collected data by survey-guided semi-structured interviews of CPMs ($n = 12$, age range 32–67 years, all male) from across a range of organisation sizes and focus areas. Purposive sampling facilitated identification of participants with information of interest who therefore could contribute to a more reliable study outcome [49, 50]. Eight were CPMs dealing with the preparation of contract documents, tendering and negotiating tenders. Four were involved with post-contract project delivery. All participants were senior personnel and two were Chief Executives.

The face-to-face semi-structured interviews involved participants answering 15 survey questions, primarily Likert type scale in form, and adding comments whenever they wished. Questions were presented within groups designed to determine:

1. Whether stress was primarily caused by work or home issues.
2. Whether participants considered their current workplace to be stressful, whether having stressed individuals within the workplace was of concern, regardless of the source of their stress, and whether stress contributed to absenteeism.
3. To what extent organisations trained leaders to identify symptoms of stress in themselves and others, and to what extent should they be so trained, if at all.
4. What participants considered to be an appropriate stress avoidance and management approach for their workplace.

Quantitative analysis revealed all participants either agreed or strongly agreed:

- Their work was stressful.
- Regardless of whether stress was caused more by work-related or non-work-related issues, it had a strong effect on performance at work.
- Stress was likely to result in reduced workplace productivity or increased risk of safety-related incidents.
- People were unlikely to attribute absenteeism to stress, for fear of appearing weak.
- Head office stress avoidance and management programmes seldom filtered down to site level. Where a site-based programme existed, it was likely to be the Mates in Construction suicide prevention programme [51].
- Stress symptoms identification training would be beneficial down to the hierarchical level of site project manager.

In addition:

- All feared training below that level might negatively affect productivity (workers' absenteeism under the guise of stress issues).
- All smaller organisation respondents opined stress was primarily a personal rather than organisational issue to be managed by individuals, not employers.

These points triggered concern, but other industry-specific issues from the pilot study motivated broader and deeper research. The most significant were:

- Often, construction organisations adopted stress avoidance techniques effective in other industries, including limiting hours worked per week, or hours driven without rest, or number of weekend days worked per month. These restrictions increased stress for CPMs, especially on projects delivered under lump sum, fixed price and fixed duration contracts.
- While reports of stress-related illness had increased in most industries, this was not so in construction. One explanation was CPMs were likely to be attracted to the 'tough' image/culture of construction. They expected to be less affected by stress than others or, more likely, were less inclined to report illness for fear of being branded unable to cope. This explanation aligned with the concept of psychological hardiness—an aspect of personality style typified by commitment, control and challenge [52]. This raised a question regarding whether CPMs accepted psychological hardiness often led to burnout, a point accepted across broader business since the nineteen seventies [53].
- Approximately half the participants reported their organisations had no stress avoidance or management procedures, and/or no Employee Assistance Programme (EAP).
- Over 80 percent of participants agreed stress management should not be a matter only for individuals, yet 50 percent believed an EAP to be a sufficient organisational response to workplace stress.

Perhaps the two most important conclusions I drew from the study, notwithstanding its narrow participant base, were:

- The strong construction industry emphasis on dealing with stress after the appearance of observable symptoms suggested a lack of management understanding of what constituted a comprehensive and well-structured organisational approach for dealing with stress effectively, and
- An industry wide education programme was necessary, and long overdue.

The Purpose of This Book

I commenced work on this book for several purposes:

- Firstly, to determine if the pilot study findings represented attitudes to psychological stress and its management across a broader representation of CPMs.
- Secondly, to determine if attitudes to and management of psychological stress among CPMs differed from those of other employees (e.g. administration personnel) in construction organisations.
- Thirdly, to determine whether attitudes to and management of psychological stress among CPMs differed from those of workers across other industry sectors.

To satisfy the three key objectives noted above, I undertook a comprehensive review of the literature, and identified a definite knowledge gap of significant importance to the broader construction industry. I formulated a series of questions that, if adequately answered, would substantially close that gap, and formulated hypotheses to test as a means of answering those questions. The answers the work sought would achieve certain important objectives after completion of the study. Those objectives would be achieved by the publication of this book, and other work to be progressed in parallel with the book publication:

- Educate industry regarding stress effects on its professionals
- Recommend procedural and systemic change to assist in the avoidance of stress, and

- Propose an approach by which individuals and organisations could work together to effectively manage workplace stress and its effects.

Stephen Covey, in *The 7 Habits of Highly Successful People* [54] advised commencing important work with the end in mind. The end in mind for the objectives above was to comprise publications, education disseminated via industry conventions, and preparation and distribution of a stress avoidance and management programme specifically designed for CPMs. It is now important to consider the approach by which production of this book was designed to produce the 'end in mind' summarised by the three points above.

Determining the Extent of the Problem of Stress Among CPMs

I consider it important to provide some '... account of how the research and analysis were undertaken' [55]. The purpose was to investigate attitudes among CPMs to psychological stress and its impacts, to determine any stress avoidance and management techniques they employed, and to assess whether their attitudes to psychological stress and its management differed from those across broader business.

This study was motivated by findings of the pilot study overviewed earlier, and the fact suicide rates for young men who worked in construction were 238 percent higher than for the nation as a whole [56]. These suicide statistics applied to industry tradespeople, rather than professionals, and the literature revealed no detailed study of attitudes to psychological stress and its management among CPMs specifically.

Questions That Demanded Answers

The knowledge gap broadly identified from the pilot study raised several questions that needed to be addressed:

1. What was the attitude to psychological stress and its management among CPMs and their employers, and did this differ from that of administration personnel (APs) in construction companies and/or professionals from the broader business community (BPs)?
2. What strategies were in place within construction organisations to assist in avoidance and/or management of psychological stress, and how did they compare with strategies used across business at large?
3. Were the main sources of stress (i.e. from work or from outside of work) the same for CPMs as for APs and BPs, and what were the effects of workplace-generated stress on CPMs' personal lives?
4. Was there a greater propensity among CPMs to either use no stress management, or to use maladaptive stress management, than there was for APs and BPs?
5. Did managers of construction firms provide stress avoidance and/or management programmes, and were CPMs aware of, and making use of any provided?

I initially identified these questions from the pilot study, and an extensive literature review endorsed their validity.

Finding the Answers to These Important Questions

Following are some of the hypotheses arising from the questions above and these informed the design of the research method. I have included only sub-hypotheses relevant to the content and context of this book:

First hypothesis: That CPMs would hold a different attitude towards the main causes of stress than would (APs) and (BPs), and specifically that:

- CPMs would believe stress was caused mainly by work-related factors, while APs and BPs would opine that stress was caused mainly by non-work factors.

- CPMs would consider their work to be stressful more so than APs and BPs.
- CPMs, more so than APs and BPs would agree, regardless of the cause of stress, it could have a significant impact on their performance at work.

Second hypothesis: That opinions regarding stress avoidance training, stress management training and the use of external EAPs or similar would differ substantially across role types, and specifically that:

- CPMs, more than APs and BPs, would consider their organisations did not train leaders, managers and other personnel to identify stress symptoms/effects in themselves and their employees.
- CPMs, more than APs and BPs, would believe that an EAP was all their organisation needed to address stress effects in personnel.

Third hypothesis: That CPMs would express significantly different attitudes from APs and BPs regarding what they believed organisations should offer by way of stress avoidance and management, and specifically:

- CPMs would report that stress should be a matter for individuals and not employers more so than would APs and BPs.
- All participants would report that a stress management programme should involve training of all leaders and managers, as well as all staff, in stress symptoms recognition.

Fourth hypothesis: That CPMs would be less knowledgeable than APs and BPs regarding what stress avoidance and/or management programmes their organisations had in place, and specifically:

- APs and BPs would be more aware of the existence of stress avoidance and/or management programmes in their organisations than would CPMs.
- CPMs would be less aware of existence of an EAP within their organisation than would APs and BPs.

Fifth hypothesis: That, regardless of workplace programmes, participants would personally engage in some form of stress management activity or technique but:

- CPMs would be less likely to do so than APs and BPs.
- CPMs would be less likely than APs and BPs to rate their chosen technique as effective.

I devised a research method to allow collection and analysis of data to facilitate the testing of these hypotheses [57]. I began with a strategy that overviewed the study stages, and then described the methodology steps for gathering and analysing data. The first phase of the strategy was to design the research method.

Research Method Design

The research tested the hypotheses and answered the questions giving rise to those hypotheses. The adopted approach was traditional and:

1. Gathered data using an appropriate research strategy [58, 59].
2. Analysed the data so collected and interpreted and discussed it with a view to drawing relevant conclusions [60].

I selected a mixed methodology research strategy involving the collection of data from three distinct groups of participants from three different sizes of organisation. The three different types of participants were CPMs, APs and BPs. I decided upon these three role categories not only so the research answered the questions presented earlier, but also to provide a solid basis for continuing work beyond this book. The three different sizes of organisation aligned with the approach used by the Australian Bureau of Statistics. This would facilitate useful comparison of findings with other research that adopted the same approach, when academic journal papers were published. The research findings relating to organisation size are not consistently relevant to this book. However, there are instances where relevant findings regarding organisational size are presented, and so it is important to understand the organisation sizes defined by the Australian Bureau of Statistics are:

1. A small organisation has up to 19 employees (SO).
2. A medium organisation has between 20 and 199 employees (MO).
3. A large organisation has 200 or more employees (LO).

Important aspects of the literature review presented in Chapter 2 include, inter alia, economic effects internationally of psychological stress. However, key questions were directed to better understand specific circumstances in the Australian context. Participants were sourced from within Australia, and so the findings of this study might reasonably be anticipated to differ somewhat from a similar study conducted in another country. In addition, I recognised that construction project management organisations that operated within only one type of contract delivery system, for example, negotiated contracts (wherein typically no competition would be involved) or design and construct (wherein CPMs might have more control over progressive quality and costs) might have produced study participants who provided significantly different data from those who won work only from the tendering process. Notwithstanding this, and because the majority of construction organisations in Australia use a variety of contract delivery approaches, I decided not to separate participants by their employer's preferred contract delivery type.

The mixed method research design involves both quantitative and qualitative components. I adopted an epistemological approach of positivism in relation to the data collected for quantitative analysis, collecting data from 489 participants via an online questionnaire, and analysed that data using statistical analysis [61, 62]. I collected qualitative data using semi-structured interviews to capture the narratives of participants, and analysed this data using recursive and reflective work. This did not fit the positivist definition (as did the majority of data collected for quantitative analysis) in that it failed to position me as researcher completely separate from the research process, and thereby opened the work to question concerning the extent, if any, to which my personal views might have affected interpretation of data [63]. A similar question might indeed be asked of any therapeutic intervention, including the metaphorical one we will develop regarding Will and Clare, but such a question does not undermine the inherent value of the work undertaken, especially if it is undertaken following appropriate and professionally recognised procedures. The approach of collecting qualitative data using semi-structured interviews parallels the clinical intervention approach and exemplifies a constructivist approach using ethnographic methodology, in that the data provided, while ontological, also collectively represents the reality of people from within a group who experienced common aspects of (organisational) culture [64]. It represents social construction by the participants of their reported experiences, and I needed to interpret the data provided by participants at times to gain a useful comprehension of underlying meaning [63]. That is one of the most difficult aspects of clinical intervention work—analysing client data provided to determine underlying meaning that can inform an effective intervention protocol. That was very much a key objective of the research—to analyse data to determine important underlying meanings and consider potential corrective recommendations. I considered it important the sample size calculation (addressed later), survey design and statistical analysis approach were sufficiently robust to determine the results of analysis provided a solid basis on which conclusions could be drawn regarding the research hypotheses [65].

A major concern for researchers using a mixed method approach is how questions should be framed [66]. The possibilities include a combination of separate quantitative and qualitative questions, or a single set of questions that incorporates approaches to eliciting both qualitative and quantitative responses [67]. Mertens [68] promoted a mixed approach whereby a transformative paradigm could emerge—one that effectively provided information not only about what was, but also about underlying factors that, if changed, could enhance human circumstances. I considered such an objective to be in line with the purpose of my research, in that it would not only provide statistical evidence of hypotheses and research questions, but would also provide reasons for the existence of what was found to be.

In that sense I agree with the position that qualitative research is for the discovery of reasons while quantitative determines causal relationships [69]. I also concluded a mixed methods approach was required to attain an internal triangulation of perspectives and provide deeper understanding of a problem that was complex [70].

In data collection design I followed the recommendation of several authors and combined overarching questions with specific questions [67, 68, 72]. Participants providing data for quantitative analysis responded to an online survey, answering questions via binary or Likert type scale response options presented in clusters relevant to each major hypothesis. Each cluster included an open question designed to gather more general data for qualitative analysis. Participants who preferred a semi-structured interview approach were able to use the online survey as a gateway into that process. The mixed methods research design served several other purposes, the most important being:

- Using two methods facilitated internal concurrent data triangulation. Data collected from one method either reinforced that collected by the other, or raised questions that needed to be answered, in order to maintain rigour in the work [72].
- Data collected using two separate methods, and separately analysed, provided a solid basis for discussion of research findings, and for relating those findings back to the study hypotheses [72–74].
- A multi-method approach was an effective means of countering biases that might have been inadvertently included in a single method design [61, 74].
- The mixed method approach made more data available and provided a deeper comprehension of all data, and thereby provided a better opportunity for more accurate testing of hypotheses [74, 75].
- The mixed method approach minimised weaknesses in any single method approach. (A quantitative approach, of itself, might have been weak in context comprehension, while a qualitative approach alone could have included biases and been less useful for generalisation of findings [72].)

Data Collection Strategy

Creswell [75] emphasised there is no limit to the number of questions that can be included in a survey document, but noted the time needed to complete the questionnaire should be considered, implying long questionnaires deterred participants [58]. I designed the questionnaire using a variety of proven presentation techniques within the Qualtrics research software [76] (chosen for its reputation and availability through my university's library) to ensure it was easy to use, and engaged participants until completion.

I wrote the survey questionnaire using closed questions, written in simple vocabulary following a logical flow, within groups. I avoided leading or sensitive questions [75, 77]. I invited participants to provide open comments at the end of each group of closed questions. Responses to these questions provided some triangulation of data collected for qualitative analysis using semi-structured interviews.

Closed questions facilitated comparisons and presentation of data after statistical analysis, but limited participants' ability to provide all information they had in relation to questions asked. This was a recognised limitation of quantitative statistics-based research [74, 75, 78]. The qualitative aspect of the research design balanced that weakness [78].

I used the internationally respected research software, Statistical Package for the Social Sciences (SPSS, version 24), for both descriptive and inferential statistical analysis of data, because of its reputation and the support available for its use at Bond University, from where I conducted the research.

Semi-Structured Interviews—Collecting Data for Qualitative Analysis

The semi-structured interview approach I chose for collecting qualitative data was appropriate given several participants would already have provided quantitative data via the online survey and volunteered for the semi-structured interview via that survey. However, I considered it essential to allow participants freedom to provide narrative they considered relevant and important, in whatever manner they preferred. I was concerned some participants might have been disinclined to provide valuable information if an overly structured approach was adopted in interviews [79]. On the other hand, a completely unstructured interview approach raised the risk of too much information being provided that might not be relevant [61, 79].

The shortcomings of the approach included the complexity and time-consuming nature of analysing qualitative data [61, 75]. The relative anonymity of the online survey facilitated engagement of potentially reluctant participants from the tough-culture construction industry [80]. The semi-structured approach provided the ability to keep interviews progressing within appropriate boundaries, and to collect detailed and deep information because both interviewer and interviewee were able to ask clarifying questions, and to explain meaning in great detail [75, 77].

Expert Agreement with Qualitative Research Approach and Findings

I obtained expert opinion regarding qualitative aspects of the research, and in particular the conclusions drawn from analysis of the qualitative data, to ensure the quality of data collection and analysis [81]. The first approach I considered to achieve this was the Delphi technique, a method of gaining expert consensus regarding complex topics [82]. The technique involves identification of the required experts and having them respond to a structured questionnaire, with repeated review of the responses until consensus is achieved. A key concern with using a Delphi approach is the lack of a universally recognised and accepted framework for its application [82]. A study by von der Gracht [83] of 114 articles about the use of Delphi concluded there were some 15 ways in which it could be applied. Fletcher and Childon [84] noted there is substantially less use of Delphi in qualitative research than in quantitative studies. Brady [85] emphasised that pragmatism and flexibility were core attributes of Delphi applications, and explained the technique can be used in a wide array of situations where expert opinion is required to confirm aspects of studies. However, Brady concurred with Skulmoski et al. [86] that the method does have gaps regarding consistency of application.

Skulmoski et al. [86] supported the use of modified Delphi approaches that involved adjusting the standard approach to one that facilitated achieving the result of gaining concensus in any particular application. I adopted a modified approach involving a discussion with three industry experts until consensus was reached regarding the types of questions to be asked and conclusions gained from the analysis of data collected.

Sample Size Calculation

I considered sample size to be very important, both to avoid allegations the sample was under-powered or over-powered, and because it observed ethical standards by avoiding unnecessary burden on participants through over recruitment [87, 88]. For the quantitative component of this study, the sample needed to be large enough and sufficiently representative of CPMs to enable assertion what was found to be true for the sample was expected to be true for the whole population within that profession [87–89].

Maxfield and Babbie [90] asserted a small sample was acceptable in research of this nature provided what interested that small sample also interested the broader population the sample represented. I was confident participants who volunteered to be interviewed in preference to, or in addition to completing the online survey, were committed to truthful responses to interview questions.

I completed several separate calculations to determine sample size. I took the largest size indicated by those exercises to be the minimum acceptable. The first calculation using the respected G*Power [91] programme for conducting power analysis and calculating sample size for research in the social and behavioural sciences [92, 93] determined a sample size of $N = 302$ would provide a power of 0.95. Using samples of these sizes provided a 95 percent certainty that both type 1 errors—observing a statistically significance when it did not exist, and type 2 errors—failing to observe a statistically significant difference when one existed [94] were avoided. Because some might regard this work as on the border between social science research and technical research the sample size was also calculated using a second method—the formula promoted by Smith [95]. That formula was as follows:

$$\text{RSS} = (z\ \text{score})^2 \times \text{Std. Dev.}(1 - \text{Std. Dev.})/M^2$$

where:
RSS was Required sample size.
Z score was the confidence level required where the most common confidence levels were:

- For 90 percent confidence—1.645
- For 95 percent confidence—1.96, and
- For 99 percent confidence—2.576.

Std. Dev. was the standard deviation, and since statistical analysis had not yet been conducted for this study, the accepted approach was to use a standard deviation of 0.50, which Smith regarded as providing a sufficiently large sample.

M was the margin of error, or confidence interval, which was commonly set at plus or minus five percent [95].

Using this formula, for a participant sample size calculation with a 95 percent confidence level, the calculation was as follows:

$$\begin{aligned} \text{95\% confidence participants numbers} &= (1.96)^2 \times 0.5(1 - 0.5)/0.05^2 \\ &= (3.8416 \times 0.25)/0.0025 \\ &= 384.16 \\ \text{Say,} &= 385 \text{ participants} \end{aligned}$$

Other well-known formulae produced sample size requirements of less than $N = 100$. I rejected those in favour of those calculated by more modern and broadly accepted approaches used in social science research. The outcomes of various modern approaches were participant sample sizes of 302, 251 and 385, and so the research targeted a minimum of 385 participants, which comfortably provided a 95 percent confidence level for the work.

Sourcing Participants

I considered several options for sourcing participants, and the final approach involved the following sequence:

- I approached two Professional Institutions and each sent two announcements to its members. The response totalled a disappointing 36 participants, with 15 of them completing all compulsory questions of the online survey.
- I approached a large national construction organisation that employed 550 professionals in research-relevant roles. The number who participated at some level was 279, or 50.73 percent. Participants who completed all compulsory questions of the online survey and were included in the final sample totalled 176, or 63.10 percent.
- A medium-sized construction organisation then agreed to be involved, and provided a list of 31 randomly chosen CPMs (17.40% of employees) all of whom agreed to partake in semi-structured interviews. The organisation agreed to provide the names of additional participants on request. Eight of the group completed the online survey questionnaire and underwent a semi-structured interview as well. Six others engaged in semi-structure interviews without completing the online survey. More were willing to undertake semi-structured interviews, but these were discontinued when saturation had been achieved.
- I emailed 36 people who had expressed interest in the research when I described it at annual conferences of professional institutions. This attracted a total of 29 responses of which 11 completed all compulsory questions on the online survey.
- Participant numbers were still below what was required so I conducted a Facebook advertising campaign, targeting CPMs with tertiary qualifications living and working in Australia. Expressions of interest were

encouraging (n = 41) and the majority continued to complete all compulsory questions on the online survey (n = 24 or 58.54 percent).

- Participant numbers remained below the requirement, so I engaged the Qualtrics organisation to present surveys and collect data. To complete the analysis required, 139 additional participants were sought. To maximise opportunities for publication of the work, I requested Qualtrics to source 250 additional participants in specified numbers from across the three role types stipulated for the research. The number of responses was 353. Of these, 253 (71.67 percent) completed all compulsory survey questions and their responses were included in the final data analysis.

Participant Sourcing Confirms the Industry Problem Being Investigated

The need to engage Qualtrics to source additional CPM participants demonstrates the importance of and need for this research. In the process of approaching industry contacts regarding involvement, I had consistently been told they were working huge hours each week, had no time to complete the survey, and they knew of no fellow CPMs who experienced less demanding work circumstances. These people explained they not only needed to work long hours, but also had very limited time to spend with their families because they had to attend to emails and write reports after hours. They had no time for private pursuits beyond family and felt there was no end in sight to the intensity of their workload. The disappointing response rate from professional institutions was probably another example of this limited spare time issue.

Notwithstanding the low response rate from professional institutions, it provided value as a triangulation resource, important because, if a proposition is confirmed by two or more independent (even imperfect) measurement processes, then any uncertainly of interpretation about that proposition was greatly reduced [96].

Table 1.1 provided an overview of participants who commenced responding to the online survey, and of participants who completed all compulsory questions.

Table 1.1 Make up of final participants sample ($N = 489$)

Source of participants	Initial number	Participants who completed all compulsory questions
Qualtrics	353	253
Large contractor	280	178
Medium contractor	10	8
Professional Institutions	37	15
Conferences	29	11
Facebook and general	41	24
Final total of participants	750	489

Note Eight additional participants from the medium contractor took part in semi-structure interviews because data collection via the online survey had been closed when they became involved

The Paramount Importance of the Mixed Method Approach to this Work

I identified one minor data collection concern. In data collection for quantitative analysis using survey questionnaires, the participants were remote and unidentified, whereas qualitative data collection using semi-structured interviews involved more personal interactions, with me and my recording equipment being embedded in the research situation. This tended to create a comfortable environment for participants before interviews proceeded, which could have been seen to create some reciprocal impact of the researcher on the researched [55, 97]. I nonetheless considered qualitative data collection via semi-structured interview to be of great importance to the work. Indeed, the clear insight provided by qualitative analysis into the causes of the problems revealed by the quantitative analysis endorsed that importance, despite the reality it involved the minority ($n = 35$) of participants for the entire study (7.16 percent).

Qualitative Approach Contributions—Determining Reasons for the Problems

Denzin and Lincoln [98] posited humans understood their world through the medium of stories they told about it. I thematically analysed the narratives of participants who engaged in semi-structure interviews and gained deep understanding of the participants' experience of events which constituted an important part of their work experience. To achieve this, I used words as data, identifying not only patterns and interactions within participants' statements [99] but also emphasis they placed within their phraseology. This provided a starting point to uncovering what participants considered to be major contributors to workplace stress. I then further reflected upon themes so identified and analysed and defined categories into which these themes most appropriately fitted. I undertook this analysis separately and with a different mindset from the quantitative analysis, in concurrence with the recommendation of Atkinson and Delamont [100] that interpretive research was not always to conform with inappropriate definitions of scientific research from the quantitative domain. This approach to qualitative data collection and analysis was also in agreement with Wadick [101] that new knowledge can be created only when one permits old certainties to be challenged.

Put another way, I used a quantitative approach to data collection and analysis to determine personal and organisational attitudes and actions in relation to psychological stress and its management. Where I sought a deeper understanding of differences between the development and manifestation of stress for participants, and the perceived reasons for the stress experienced, I adopted a qualitative approach.

To optimise the value of semi-structured interviews data, I posed the questions from a partnership approach, with no superior—subordinate context between myself as researcher and the participants. This approach provided the best environment from which deep meaning from participants' experience could be understood. This approach aligned with core concepts of designing qualitative research compiled by the African Medical and Research Foundation [102].

Summarising the Mixed Method Approach

Trochim [103] asserted all research was positioned on a continuum between fully quantitative and fully qualitative, and from an extreme quantitative position, some draw the conclusion qualitative data simply does not exist, while from a fully qualitative position, all data, including qualitative, had a quantitative grounding. This attitude was endorsed by the fact qualitative data can be quantitatively coded with a binary approach to thematic analysis, for example, using zeros and ones. In a parallel manner, data considered to be completely quantitative in nature often derived from an ontological or strongly qualitative base as is often the case when research participants respond via a Likert type scale [103].

This insight qualitative and quantitative data are, at some level, inseparable, and neither is totally devoid of the other was significant in my decision to embrace the combined approach to data collection and analysis. I tested theories and hypotheses using both deductive and inductive processes. I adopted a mixed methodology approach in full commitment to the proposition quantitative and qualitative research philosophies 'are neither mutually exclusive (i.e. one need not totally commit to either one or the other) nor interchangeable (i.e. one cannot merge methodologies with no concern for underlying assumptions') [104, p. xi].

I sought statistics regarding participants who held a particular attitude to individual survey questions, but also sought to understand social phenomena in work and other environments that contributed to a participant's personal experience of psychological stress [105]. I collected data using a survey that utilised questions in groups or domains and so alpha Cronbach testing was often not required because individual component responses, rather than only the collective response to the overall group of questions, were used to test hypotheses.

I designed the qualitative component of the research to gather information from participants regarding the causes of stress and their attitudes to its management in their workplaces [105] and, in the case of participants who provided personal experience narratives of workplace stress, I sought to gain insight into how they constructed their perception of that stress experience [106, 107].

The final approach was I analysed data from Likert type scale-based responses using quantitative methods, while I analysed narrative data from semi-structured interviews, which were principally ethnographic in nature, using qualitative techniques, commencing with a thematic analysis, within an overarching hermeneutic approach. In gathering and analysing data using these techniques I considered it crucial to observe and document participants' voice tonality and choice of words. In other words, 'The emotional tone of the participants' talk and of the researcher's reactions' [108, p. 16] were important factors to observe and reflect upon during qualitative analysis. The empathy I experienced and emotions I noticed when collecting qualitative data opened the opportunity for a deeper understanding of participants' experiences and aligned with Bahn and Weatherill [109] regarding the way collecting sensitive data affected researchers.

Despite attempts to minimise researcher effects, especially in relation to the qualitative component of the research, these could not be eradicated, but this fact did not negate the value of qualitative data collected nor of the analysis outcomes achieved. This was especially the case where I took all reasonable steps to ensure interview techniques used were of the highest quality. This maximised the likelihood responses recorded could be regarded as representative of typical examples of interaction between people and circumstances in the population from which the participants were drawn. This enhanced the likelihood the perspectives of the participants would prevail in a similar but broader sampling of the subject community [110]. This approach to data collection and analysis facilitated maintenance of process rigour and ensured a more flexible methodology emphasis that embraced the needs and experiences of a broad range of individual participants [65].

I discussed the online survey with experienced colleagues who reviewed it prior to distribution. In addition, the survey questions were subjected to ethics review and approval at Bond University. Participants' experiences of stress-related disorders were discussed within time and context, not regarding symptomology but to satisfy the dual ethnographic aspects of obtaining a portrait of the world view of participants who had experienced either the negative effects of stress or the positive effects of a stress management programme [111, 112]. Importantly, interpretive phenomenological analysis (IPA) enabled the participants' narratives to be explored from the perspective of being within each respondent's particular circumstances [113].

The ethnographic character of the qualitative aspects of the study provides a solid basis for future research for the benefit of CPMs, and the community at large [114]. This possibility provides gravitas because such a programme would sensibly be refined based on findings from this research, in particular from the narratives of participants' experience of workplace stress [115]. This potential future use of participants' lived experience added a valuable dimension of phenomenology to the qualitative aspects of the research [114].

Particularly Important Aspects of the Research Methodology

At the heart of this research was the gathering and analysis of the quantitative data that allowed core study questions to be answered and hypotheses to be tested, while the purpose of qualitative analysis was to understand those answers to a greater depth and from a humanistic perspective. It was important that qualitative data collection followed a rigourous framework, but one that facilitated an authentic and relational interaction with participants.

Writing about qualitative research in education, Denzin [116, p. 145] noted that Feuer, Towne and Shavelson [117] stated, 'when problems are poorly understood, and plausible hypotheses are scant, qualitative methods such as ethnographies are necessary to describe complex phenomena, generate theoretical models and reframe questions'. While the quantitative approach to this study provided rich information, the unexplained lack of increase in reported stress-related illness in the construction industry despite a contemporaneous increase in industry suicides among young men demanded the inclusion of some ethnographic aspect within the research methodology. This ensured the narratives of those most affected by stress were heard and better understood.

The ethnographic component provides insights into how attitudes to causes of workplace-generated stress in construction must change to benefit CPMs and other industry professionals [114]. I concur with Madison [115] that benefit can only be realised when change is motivated by authentic insights from the experiences and emotions of the research participants as distilled from their narratives. The open-question approach adopted sought to elicit the requisite deep and strong responses from participants [61].

Importantly, when participants' experiences had emotional impact, my clinic experience allowed quick change from a position of being affected by the narrative to one of maintaining empathy and unconditional positive regard for the participant [118], with the positive outcome participants felt sufficiently comfortable to take their narrative to deeper and more meaningful levels. The literature recognised this approach for dealing with researcher emotions during qualitative data collection [119, 120].

Saturation Point in Qualitative Research

Saturation in qualitative research is the point beyond which interviewing additional participants is unlikely to provide additional information. It is reached when there is sufficient information to establish confidence the study could be replicated for a similar participant base [121] and when further coding was no longer feasible [122]. Data saturation is not about numbers of participants but rather about the depth of the data collected [123]. This research reached a saturation point where no new data was emerging from interviews and so it was pointless to continue interviewing [124]. Importantly, semi-structured interviews were conducted with participants from the large construction organisation ($n = 15$) contemporaneously with interviews with other participants ($n = 14$) from across other construction organisations across a broad range of sizes. Common themes were identified and saturation reached both within each group and across the entire participant base. The total number of participants in semi-structured interviews was 35, including participants ($n = 6$) from business at large who elected to partake in semi-structured interviews. However, as quantitative data collection progressed in parallel with semi-structured interviews, I concluded there was no point continuing with participants from business at large because they did not significantly serve the objectives of this aspect of the research in that it was clear, unlike for CPMs, there was little similarity in responses from the different participants in that group. Also, I concluded any findings from this aspect of the study would not contribute significantly to the long-term industry and community benefit programme the research was intended to inform.

Rewards for Participants

By way of incentive, and in appreciation of participation, I offered participants the following rewards for their contribution to the study:

- I offered individual participants from large and medium organisations copies of my psychotherapy-based programmes 'You CAN Enhance your Relationships' and 'You CAN Sleep Better'.
- I offered senior managers who organised their company's involvement, in additional to the above, my digital business programme entitled, 'How to be a world class consultant and service provider', together with permission to distribute within their organisations.
- I offered the large and medium organisations that promoted involvement in the research a one-day workshop for as many staff as wanted to attend, on the organisation's choice from a range of possible topics. Neither organisation accepted the offer, one stating they were pleased to see the opportunity for some progress in an important area for the industry, and the other preferring an anonymous report of findings from participants from their organisation, and recommendations regarding what they should do about them.
- Participants sourced and managed by Qualtrics were rewarded by Qualtrics in accordance with its terms of service.

I ensured all participants were advised of the rewards when invited to participate. The incentives were designed to attract participation from people who were known to have extremely busy working lives. I do not believe participants' responses were affected by the incentives. However, for research rigour and objectivity, I must state there was no way to be certain this was the case.

Research Rigour and Triangulation

I ensured anonymity and confidentiality were maintained regarding participants involved in the quantitative component of the study by asking each to use a five-character code made up of the first three letters of his or her mother's maiden name, and the last two digits of the participant's year of birth. Any participant who opted to be involved in a semi-structured interview provided his or her name and contact details to enable the interview to proceed.

I considered it important the research did not lack rigour and therefore, validity and reliability—even credibility. In order to adequately address these concerns, I adopted the following countering mechanisms:

- I conducted expert colleague debriefings regarding research process and progress to ensure maintenance of satisfactory quality.
- I ensured triangulation was undertaken regarding process and findings including reviews of terminology used by peer researchers, and by an experienced researcher knowledgeable in the human behaviour aspects of this work.
- The Chartered Institute of Building (CIOB) conducted detailed research into the state of wellbeing in the construction industry in 2016 and released a report in 2017. Permission was received from the CIOB to reference the report and use it in triangulation for this study.
- I undertook these actions to endow the work with the transparency of process that would ultimately enhance its trustworthiness [125].
- In finalising the participants sample for the qualitative aspects of the research, and in arranging triangulation, I sought to understand the degree to which participants' responses were typical examples of interaction. A high probability of being typical would give greater credibility to the likelihood of the perspectives provided by the research participants prevailing in a similar but broader sampling of that community—in this case, CPMs as a profession [110].

I progressed all semi-structured interviews following the noticing, collecting and thinking model [126]. I concluded the material distilled from recorded semi-structured interviews represented typical responses from the types of participants involved. Accordingly, there was a high probability the perspectives expressed would prevail in a similar but broader sampling of the community; in this case, the subject profession as a whole [110].

Researcher Effects

I consider it important to reveal certain facts that, unstated, might have potential to take from the rigour of process and so devalue findings. Important among these are:

- I felt the need to remain aware that any personal experience of work-related anxiety and depression might add to a hermeneutic cycle of data interpretation as participants as narrators and myself as researcher interpreted through the lens of our own values and experience and subsequently risked adding unintended unconscious meaning to the data and analysis of it.
- The more that I felt familiarity with participants' perspectives, the more aware I was of possibly reaching conclusions too quickly and accordingly, I made a concerted effort to systematically think about all data before drawing conclusions.

I accepted the ontological reality, despite the best attempts to minimise researcher effects, they could not be eradicated. Notwithstanding this, data from interviews could be regarded as typical examples and therefore treated as credible perspectives reasonably expected to prevail in a similar but broader example of community [110]. In summary regarding research subjectivity and rigour:

- Quantitative aspects of the study followed generally recognised principles for rigour in sampling, testing, data collection and data analysis.

- Qualitative aspects of the study achieved credibility and dependability, the qualitative research equivalents of internal validity and reliability, respectively, as previously described.
- The study included referential adequacy, thus ensuring transferability, the qualitative research equivalent of external validity [127].

Ethics

Bond University Human Research Ethics Committee (BUHREC) gave ethics approval for this research and the study complied with the BUHREC ethics policy. The ethics approval number for the work was RO1697. I clearly advised all participants involved in semi-structured interviews of their right to add to the material they provided, or to change it, and informed them they were free to withdraw from the study at any time.

I also advised participants, if it was considered any information provided might lead to unwanted conclusions regarding their identity, that information would not be included in written research documents.

Weaknesses in the Study

It is crucial I make study limitations transparent to ensure the research is regarded as rigourous, and to avoid allegations of weakness in any circumstance where future research of a similar type within a similar population reveals different findings [128]. In keeping with this crucial component of solid scientific research, I identified the following potential weaknesses, together with steps I took to remedy the weaknesses, where possible:

- I held a qualitative analysis concern that repeated:
  - reviews of recordings
  - reading of transcripts, and

  - checking of coding and cross coding all necessary because of the rich complexity of emotional layers within the data, eventually might lead to a feeling some of the later collected qualitative data all too conveniently fitted the already broadly identified themes and categories.
- Critical thinking about this point revealed researcher bias was possibly at play.
- I took a one-month break from qualitative data analysis—and discussed the matter with a peer researcher.
- After the break, I found I was able to revisit the data with greater clarity of mind and a sense of freedom from bias.
- I coded qualitative data immediately after it was recorded and transcribed, but ensured at least one week passed between data coding and data analysis. This prevented data coding and analysis inadvertently leading to new data analysis being conveniently fitted to established themes.
- This approach facilitated open-minded awareness of new emerging themes and overcame bias-driven fitting of new data to pre-established themes.
- In the areas of quantitative data collection and analysis, offering rewards to participants of higher value than usual raised concern. However, I recognised that CPMs worked long hours including weekends and this necessitated offering attractive rewards to engage participants and interest them in partaking in the study.

The Book Structure

This book contains five chapters. In this first chapter I provide an overview of aspects of the construction industry relevant to the book's topic, explain the content and purpose of the book, and introduce the concept of psychological stress and its impacts on construction professionals. I address the findings of the pilot study that motivated extensive research upon the findings of which this book was conceived. I discuss aspects of leadership in the context of attitudes to psychological stress effects within the construction industry and then describe the mixed quantitative and qualitative method I adopted for the research about which the book is written and explain the reasons for that approach. I also provide an overview of the epistemological underpinnings of the study central to the book's content. I explain the positivist approach used for collecting quantitative data using an online survey questionnaire, and for analysing data so collected using statistical techniques. I also describe the constructivist ethnographic approach of using semi-structured interviews to collect narrative data from participants for qualitative analysis using an interpretive thematic technique. I address triangulation within the study, as well as my approach to maintaining validity and credibility of the work. I also address the determination of the sample size to achieve a minimum power of 0.95 for the work, and the way participants were approached and engaged in the research and what rewards I offered for involvement. Finally, I note potential weaknesses of the study, and address researcher effects and ethics approval.

I presented the material above in the context of metaphors of the Initiating Phase of the classic phases of project management and the Intake Session of the Psychotherapeutic process.

In Chapter 2, I present material in the context of the metaphors of the second phase of both project management and psychotherapy—the Planning Phase and Determining the Extent of the Problem respectively. I direct the writing to provide a useful depth of understanding of psychological stress, with particular emphasis on defining terms, and discussing both the potential psychological and physiological impacts of stress. I address aspects of stress particular to the construction industry, before reviewing some of the basic science behind stress, especially in relation to health conditions prevalent today. I next discuss strategies for avoiding or managing stress, before reviewing the impacts of workplace stress on the Australian and international economies. I describe the psychological concept of locus of control in the context of managing stress, with particular emphasis on how this concept exists among CPMs generally, before addressing a potential major impact of stress for female CPMs.

I present Chapter 3 in context of metaphors of the third phase of both project management and psychotherapy—The Implementation/Execution Phase and Intervention Strategy Formulation phases respectively.

I begin the chapter with an analysis of what needs to be known by industry professionals for the problem of stress impacts on CPMs to be effectively alleviated. This analysis primarily focusses on differences in attitudes to the avoidance and management of stress among CPMs as compared with APs and BPs. I seek answers to questions that resolve the first hypothesis presented earlier in this chapter and its sub-hypotheses.

I next investigate attitudes regarding avoiding and managing stress effects within construction organisations, as compared with within business at large, by seeking answers to questions that resolve the second hypothesis presented earlier in this chapter and its sub-hypotheses.

Having determined attitudes to how stress is currently being managed within construction and other organisations, the next matter I address is attitudes of CPMs regarding how stress should be managed within their organisations, as compared with the attitudes of APs and BPs. In this section I seek answers to questions that resolve the third hypothesis presented earlier in this chapter and its sub-hypotheses.

In addition to the above sets of questions, I pose others to gain a broader and deeper understanding of the problem. The objective is dealing with the problem systemically, organically, and thoroughly rather than via reaction to spasmodic news of serious negative impacts of stress on people in construction that amounts to little more than bandaid therapy in terms of making valuable long-term difference. The main questions in this category include:

- How popular are stress avoidance programmes among CPMs?
- How broadly used are stress management programmes among CPMs?
- How broadly do confidential EAPs, at employer expense, exist and to what extent are they used by CPMs?
- To what extent is absenteeism among CPMs attributable to stress effects?
- What are CPMs' stress levels over a typical month?

- What do CPMs use/do to manage stress, and how effective do they consider their chosen approach to be?

Chapter 3 concludes with a summary of quantitative research findings.

Chapter 4 is dedicated to determining the main causes of psychological stress among CPMs. I approach the chapter through the metaphors of Phase 4 of the classic PM processes model, and the fourth stage of the psychotherapeutic intervention process—implementation/monitoring and control and Monitoring patient progress and observing for co-morbid issues phases respectively.

I address the approach by which the main categories of causes of stress among CPMs were identified, and by which particularly significant individual stressors evolved from the data and were articulated. Following are the main categories of causes of psychological stress that I address by investigating themes and details in Chapter 4:

- Effects of major life experience.
- Specifically work or employer contributors to stress.
- Work–life balance issues.
- Locus of control aspects of stress.
- Industry contributors to stress.

I dedicate Chapter 5 to defining active steps to commence a long-overdue transformation within the construction industry. I consider it impossible to engender change without strong support from government, professional institutions, and senior industry leaders. This being the case, I approach this final chapter with the intention that the content can be used as a core component of a major 'white paper' addressing the problems that exist, their causes, and a way forward for dealing with the identified issues and taking the construction industries that are so important to the economies of so many countries to a new and superior level of performance, not only from technical, contractual and general performance perspectives, but also, perhaps most importantly, from a perspective of compassion for and commitment to matters of individual human importance, not the least being long-term health and wellbeing.

Revisiting the Phase Parallels

At the end of the initiation phase of a project, much overview consideration and feasibility analyses have been completed, and certain key questions have been raised that can only be answered by some further detailed design and analysis. As this process progresses during the (following) planning phase, a clearer direction for the project is determined, and this is reflected in designs and specifications for inclusion in contract documents. This research work was conducted as a project, complete with schedules, risk analysis and communications plan (of which this book is part) and so the alignment of the project management process with research work should be easily discernible. The parallel with the psychotherapeutic process, as exemplified by the metaphorical couple, Will and Clare, will require further progressive development to be of optimum value. To that end I will now begin to develop their story. I suspect you will find it something that easily parallels the experience of several relationships with which you are familiar. I trust you will also see its strong parallel with the scenario unveiled by my research, and from the progressing metaphor, gain insights into the importance of addressing a currently significant and rapidly growing challenge for the construction industry.

Our couple is quite typical of double income—two kids professional families, with one working a few days a week with regular hours and the other a senior CPM finding it difficult to achieve any real normality in working hours due to responsibilities extending beyond the working week well into the weekend. The pressure of work, especially from unexpected contractual issues, simply consumes weekday time, leaving no option but to catch up on emails and essential administration after hours and on the weekend. Even when physically with the family, the construction professional is often mentally at the office, and if office matters are occasionally under control, any free time is often spent sleeping off oncoming burnout.

Of course, neither the party experiencing the work stress nor the one carrying the bulk of home and family duties wants to discuss the issues. This might be because of concern for their partner, perhaps because they do not wish to appear ungrateful for the work their partner is doing for the benefit of the family, or it might be one of the pair is highly stressed and the other certainly does not want to risk inflaming that situation to flash point. No, better not inspect the growing wound—far better to leave well enough alone and simply wait until things improve. But is that likely to happen? I will address this in later chapters, as our storyline develops, along with our research findings.

From the perspective of the first phase of project management process, we have an overview understanding of our project, primarily presented in the form of this book's structure. From the psychotherapy process perspective, we have an overview understanding of our metaphorical couple. It is now time to progress to gathering a deeper understanding of the problem this book addresses.

References

1. AI Group 2015, 'Australia's construction industry: profile and outlook', cdn.aigroup.com.au/Economic_Indicators/Construction_Survey/2015/Construction_Industry_Profile_and_Outlook.pdf. Published July 2015. Accessed on 4th April 2018.
2. ABS 2007, *National survey of mental health and wellbeing: summary of findings*—Cat. no. 4326.0, Canberra, Australian Bureau of Statistics.
3. Van der Molen, H & Hoonakker, P 2000, 'Work stress in the construction industry: causes and measures', *Proceedings of the Human Factors and Ergonomics Annual Meeting*, vol. 5, pp. 651–657.
4. Buildsoft, n.d., '10 statistics defining the Australian Construction Industry', buildsoft.com.au/blog/10-statistics-defining-the-Australian-construction-industry. Accessed on 26th April 2020.
5. Green, B for The Chartered Institute of Building, 'The real face of construction 2020: socio-economic analysis of the true value of the built environment', policy.ciob.org/wp-content/uploads/2020/02/The-Real-Face-of-Constructioon-2020.pdf. Accessed on 26th April 2020.
6. AGC, n.d., 'Construction data', The Association of General Contractors' of America, agc.org/construction-data. Accessed on 26th April 2020.
7. Patching, A 2019, 'Attitudes to psychological stress awareness, avoidance and management in organisations engaged in construction project

management—a comparison with business at large', PhD Thesis, Gold Coast, Australia, Bond University.

8. Porter, E 1973, *Relationship awareness theory-manual of administration and interpretation*, Carlsbad, USA, Personal Strengths Publishing.
9. Patching, A & Best, R 2014, 'An investigation into psychological detection and management in organisations operating in project an construction management', *Procedia—Social and Behavioural Sciences*, vol. 119, pp. 682–691.
10. Patching, A & Best, R, 'An investigation into psychological detection and management in organisations operating in project an construction management', *27th IPMA conference, finding balance and moving forward*, Dubrovnik, Croatia, 30th September–3rd October 2013.
11. Leung, M, Chan, Y-S & Olomolaiye, P 2008, 'Impact of stress on the performance of construction project managers', *Journal of Construction, Engineering and Management*, vol. 134, no. 8, https://doi.org/10.1061/(ASCE)0733-9364(2008)134:8(644). Accessed on 2nd August 2016.
12. Leung, M, Chan, Y-S & Yu, J 2009, 'Integrated model for stressors and stresses of construction project managers in Hong Kong', *Journal of Construction, Engineering and Management*, vol. 135, no. 2. ascelibrary.org/doi/abs/10.1061/(ASCE)0733-9364(2009)135:2(126). Accessed on 6th April 2017.
13. Leung, M, Chan, Y-S & Cooper, C 2015, *Stress management in the construction industry*, West Sussex, UK, Wiley Blackwell.
14. Stuckenbruck, L 1979, 'The matrix organization', *Project Management Quarterly*, vol. 10, no. 3, pp. 21–33. https://www.pmi.org/learning/library/matrix-organization-structure-reason-evolution-1837. Accessed on 12th October 2017.
15. Kerzner, H 1989, *Project Management: a systems approach to planning, scheduling and controlling*, New Jersey, Wiley, cited in Patching, A & Waitley, D 1996, *The futureproof corporation*, Singapore, Butterworth-Heinemann Asia.
16. PMI, 2013, *A guide to the Project Management Body of Knowledge (PMBOK Guide)* (5th ed.), Newtown Sq. PA, Project Management Institute.
17. Davis, S & Lawrence, P 1978, 'Problems of matrix organizations', *Harvard Business Review*, https://hbr.org/1978/05/problems-of-matrix-organizations. Accessed on 12th October 2017.
18. Schnetler, R, Steyn, H & van Staden, P 2015, 'Characteristics of matrix structures, and their effects on project success', *South African Journal of*

Industrial Engineering, vol. 26, no. 1, pp. 11–26, www.scielo.org.za/pdf/sajie/v26n1/03.pdf. Accessed on 28th January 2018.
19. Patching, A & Waitley, D 1996, *The futureproof corporation*, Singapore, Butterworth-Heinemann Asia.
20. Watts, V. 1998, in Fenn, P, O'Shea, M & Davies, E (eds.) 1998, *Dispute resolution and conflict management in construction—an international review*, Milton Park, UK, Taylor and Francis.
21. UK Essays, 2013, *Management of conflict and dispute resolution construction essay*, https://www.ukessays.com/essays/construction/management-of-conflict-and-dispute-resolution-construction-essay.php?cref=1. Accessed on 28th January 2018.
22. Sudhakar, G 2015, 'A review of conflict management techniques in projects', *Brazilian Journal of Operations and Production Management*, vol. 12, pp. 214–232.
23. Olander, S 2006, 'External stakeholder analysis in construction project management', PhD thesis, Lund, Sweden, Lund University, citeseerx.ist.psu.edu/viewdoc/download?doi=10.1.1.452.728&rep=rep1&type=pdf. Accessed on 28th January 2018.
24. Pandi-Perumal, S, Akhter, S, Zizi, F, Giradin, J-L, Ramasubramanian, C, Freeman, R & Narashimhan, M 2015, *Project stakeholder management in the clinical research environment: how to do it right*, Frontiers in Psychiatry, https://www.ncbi.nlm.nih.gov/pmc/articles/PMC4434843/. Accessed on 25th March 2017.
25. Yip, B & Rowlinson, S 2006, 'Coping strategies among construction professionals: cognitive and behavioural effects to manage job stressors', *Journal of Education in the Built Environment*, no. 2, pp. 70–79. www.tandfonline.com/doi/pdf/10.11120/jebe.2006.01020070. Accessed on 13th October 2017.
26. O'Brien, R, Hunt, K & Hart, G 2005, 'It's caveman stuff- but is, to a certain extent, how guys still operate: men's accounts of masculinity and help seeking', *Social Science and Medicine*, vol. 61, no. 3, pp. 503–516. www.sciencedirect.com/science/article/pii/s0277953605000031. Accessed on 25th March 2017.
27. Hobfoll, S 1998, *Stress, culture and community: the psychology and philosophy of stress*, New York, Plenum Press.
28. Baur, N, in Jackson, M (ed.) 2015, *Stress in post-war Britain, 1945–85: studies for the society for the social history of medicine; Vol. 23*, New York, Routledge, https://www.ncbi.nlm.nih.gov/books/NBK396509/. Accessed on 29th October 2018.

29. Bystritsky, A & Kronemyer, D 2014, in Kirsch, D & Woodbury-Farina, M (eds.) *Clinics review articles from psychiatric clinics in North America—stress in health and disease*, Philadelphia, Elsevier.
30. HCCUA 2007, 'Top ten causes of stress', www.hccua.org/health/healthandwellness.cfm?id=348 (article no longer available on this site). Accessed on 24th May 2018.
31. Shea, T, Pettit, T & De Cieri, H 2011, *Work environment stress: the impact of the physical work environment on psychological health. A snapshot review*, Melbourne Monash University, Business and Economics, https://www.iscrr.com.au/workplace-health-and-safety/maintaining-mental-health-and-wellbeing/monitoring-mental-health-at-work. Accessed on 31st March 2017.
32. Moore, H 2004, '10 Proven antidotes for workplace burnout', *Vibrant Life*, vol. 20, no. 2, pp. 12–15.
33. Williams, P 2005, 'Design/construction consultant offers tips to prevent occupational burnout', *Daily Commercial News and Construction Record*, vol. 78, no. 22, p. 7.
34. Lingard, H & Francis, V 2006, 'Does a supportive work environment moderate the relationship between work-family conflict and burnout among construction professionals?' *Construction Management and Economics*, vol. 24, no. 2, pp. 185–196.
35. ABS, 'Employee earnings and hours, Australia, May 2016', Canberra, Australian Bureau of Statistics, http://www.abs.gov.au/ausstats/abs@.nsf/0/27641437D6780D1FCA2568A9001393DF?Opendocument. Accessed on 6th April 2017.
36. Epstein, G, Halper, J, Barrett, E, Birdsall, C, McGee, M, Baron, K & Lowenstein, S 2004, 'A pilot study of mind-body changes in adults with asthma who practice mental imagery', *Alternative Complementary Medicine*, vol. 10, no. 4, pp. 66–71.
37. Waite, A 2012, 'Battling workplace burnout', *OT Practice*, vol. 17, no. 17, pp. 9–12.
38. Burg-Brown, S 2013, 'Work-life balance', *Journal of Property Management*, vol. 78, no. 4, pp. 48–53.
39. Ericson-Lidman, E & Strandberg, G 2007, 'Burnout: co-workers' perceptions of signs preceding workmates' burnout', *Journal of Advanced Nursing*, vol. 60, no. 2, pp. 199–208.
40. World Health Organisation, 'Global burden of mental disorders, and the need for a comprehensive, coordinated response from the health and social sectors at the country level', cited by Varvogli, L & Darviri, C

2011, 'Stress management techniques: evidenced-based procedures that reduce stress and promote health', *Health Science Journal*, vol. 5. no. 2, pp. 74–89.
41. Haynes, N & Love, P 2004, 'Psychological adjustment and coping among construction project managers', *Construction Management and Economics*, vol. 22, no. 2, pp. 129–140.
42. Albertsen, K, Rugulies, R, Garde, A & Burr, H 2010, 'The effect of the work environment and performance-based self-esteem on cognitive stress symptoms among Danish knowledge workers', *Scandinavian Journal of Public Health*, vol. 38, no. 3, pp. 81–89.
43. Lingard, H & Francis, V 2009, *Managing work—life balance in construction*, Milton Park, Australia, Spon Press.
44. Lingard, H & Sublet, A 2010, 'The impact of job and organisational demands on marital or relationship satisfaction and conflict among Australian civil engineers', *Construction Management and Economics*, vol. 20, no. 6, pp. 507–521.
45. WorkSafe Queensland, n.d., *Overview of work related stress*, https://www.worksafe.qld.gov.au/injury-prevention-safety/mentally-healthy-workplaces/guidance-and-tools/work-related-stress. Accessed on 29th May 2018.
46. Limm, H, Gundel, H, Heinmuller, M, Martin-Mittag, B, Nater, U, Siegrist, J & Angerer, P 2011, 'Stress management interventions in the workplace improve stress reactivity: a randomized controlled trial', *Occupational and Environmental Medicine*, vol. 68, no. 2, pp. 126–133.
47. HSE, *Annual Statistics Report for 2011–2012*, London, Health and Safety Executive, http://www.hse.gov.uk/statistics/overall/hssh1112.pdf. Accessed on 18th August 2016. Cited in Jackson, M 2016, *Stress in post-war Britain*, London, Routledge.
48. Chalquist, C, 'A glossary of Freudian terms', www.terrapsych.com/freud.html. Accessed on 12th October 2017.
49. Guarte, J & Barrios, E 2006, 'Estimation under purposive sampling', *Communication in Statistics—Simulation and Computation*, vol. 35, no. 2, pp. 277–284.
50. Tongco, M 2007, 'Purposive sampling as a tool for informant selection', *Ethobotany Research and Applications*, vol. 5, pp. 147–158, https://scholarspace.manoa.hawaii.edu/bitstream/10125/227/4/I1547-3465-05-147.pdf. Date accessed not recorded.

51. BERT 2008, 'About Mates in Construction. Building Employees Redundancy Trust', http://www.bert.com.au/Media/Default/Forms/AboutMatesInConstruction.pdf. Accessed on 3rd August 2016.
52. Lambert, V, Lambert, C & Yamase, H 2003, 'Psychological hardiness, workplace stress, and related stress reduction strategies', *Nursing and Health Sciences*, vol. 5, no. 2, pp. 181–184.
53. Kobasa, S 1979, 'Stress life events, personality and health: an inquiry into hardiness', *Journal of Personality and Social Psychology*, vol. 37, no. 1, pp. 1–11, cited in Lambert, V, Lambert, C & Yamase, H 2003, 'Psychological hardiness, workplace stress, and related stress reduction strategies', *Nursing and Health Sciences*, vol. 5, no. 2, pp. 181–184.
54. Covey, S 1989, *The 7 habits of highly effective people*, New York, Simon and Schuster.
55. Lyons, E & Coyle, A 2007, *Analysing qualitative data in psychology*, London, Sage.
56. Keegel, T, Ostrey, A & La Montagne, A 2009, 'Job strain exposures versus stress-related workers' compensation claims in Victoria, Australia; developing a public health response to job stress', *Journal of Public Health Policy*, vol. 30, no. 1, pp. 17–39.
57. Kelley, K, Clark, B, Brown, V & Sitzia, J 2003, 'Good practice in the conduct and reporting of survey research', *International Journal of Quality in Health Care*, vol. 15, no. 3, pp. 261–266.
58. Rolstad, S, Adler, J & Ryden, A 2011, 'Response burden and questionnaire length: is shorter better? A review and meta analysis', *Value in Health*, vol. 14, no. 8, pp. 1101–1108, https://www.sciencedirect.com/science/article/pii/S1098301511015245. Accessed on 10th April 2018.
59. Novikov, A & Novikov, D 2013, *Research methodology: from philosophy to science to research design*, Boca Ratan, FL, CRC Press, cited in Al Hasani, M, 'An investigation into risk management in construction projects within the UAE', PhD thesis, Gold Coast, Australia, Bond University.
60. Ratner, C 1997, *Cultural psychology and qualitative methodology: theoretical and empirical considerations*, New York, Plenum Press.
61. Gardner, R & Coombs, S 2010, *Researching, reflecting and writing about work*, East Sussex, Routledge.
62. Mills, J & Birks, M 2014, *Qualitative methodology: a practical guide*, Melbourne, Sage.
63. Darlaston-Jones, D 2007, 'Making connections: the relationship between epistemology and research methods', *The Australian Community Psychologist*, vol. 9, no. 1, pp. 19–27.

64. Taber, K 2014, 'Methodological issues in science education research: a perspective from the philosophy of science', in Matthews, M (ed.) *International handbook of research in history, philosophy and science teaching*, Netherlands, Dordrecht, Springer, vol. 3, pp. 1839–1893.
65. Smith, S, *Determining sample size: how to ensure you get the correct sample size*, https://www.qualtrics.com/blog/determining-sample-size/. Accessed on 5th February 2018.
66. Creswell, J & Plano Clark, V 2007, *Designing and conducting mixed methods research*, Thousand Oaks, CA, Sage.
67. Creswell, J & Tashakkori, A (eds.) 2007, 'Exploring the nature of research questions in mixed methods research', Editorial for *Journal of Mixed Methods Research*, vol. 1, no. 3, pp. 207–211.
68. Mertens, D 2010, 'Transformative mixed methods research', *Qualitative Inquiry*, vol. 16, no. 6, pp. 469–474. journals.sagepub.com/doi/pdf/10.1177/1077800410364612. Accessed on 2nd June 2018.
69. Shavelson, R & Towne, L (eds.) 2002, *Scientific research in education*, Committee on Research Principles for Education Research, Washington, DC, National Research Council, cited in Mertens, D & Hesse-Biber, S 2012, 'Triangulation and mixed method research: provocative positions', *Journal of Mixed Methods Research*, vol. 6, no. 2, pp. 75–79. journals.sagepub.com/doi/pdf/10.1177/1558689812437100. Accessed on 2nd June 2018.
70. Flick, U 2018, *Doing triangulation and mixed methods*, Thousand Oaks, Sage.
71. Christ, T 2007, 'A recursive approach to mixed methods research in a longitudinal study of postsecondary education disability support services', *Journal of Mixed Methods Research*, vol. 1, no. 3, pp. 226–241, http://journals.sagepub.com/doi/10.1177/1558689807301101. Accessed on 19th December 2017.
72. Mahmood, K n.d., *Mixed methods research: Centre for Innovation in Research and Teaching*, USA, Grand Canyon University, https://www.slideshare.net/kmahmood2/mixed-methods-research. Accessed on 5th February 2018.
73. Almalki, S 2016, 'Integrating quantitative and qualitative data in mixed methods research: challenges and benefits', *Journal of Education and Learning*, vol. 5 no. 3, pp. 288–296.
74. Moss, M 2017, 'The advantages and disadvantages of mixed methodology research', https://penandthepad.com/advantages-disadvant

ages-mixed-methodology-research-4263.html. Accessed on 5th February 2018.
75. Creswell, J 2013, *Research design: qualitative, quantitative, and mixed methods approaches*, London, Sage Publications.
76. Qualtrics, 'ESOMAR 28: 28 questions to help research buyers of online samples', https://www.esomar.org/what-we-do/code-guidelines/28-questions-to-help-buyers-of-online-samples. Accessed on 14th February 2018.
77. Denscombe, M 2014, *The good research guide: for small scale social research projects* (5th ed.), Berkshire, England, McGraw-Hill Education (UK).
78. Amaratunga, D, Baldry, D, Sarshar, M & Newton, R 2002, 'Quantitative and qualitative research in the built environment: application of mixed research approach', *Work Study*, vol. 51, no. 1, pp. 17–31.
79. Stuckey, H 2013, 'Three types of interviews: qualitative research methods in social health', *Journal of Social health and Diabetes*, vol. 1, no. 2, pp. 56–59, http://www.joshd.net/article.asp?issn=2321-0656;year=2013;volume=1;issue=2;spage=56;epage=59;aulast=Stuckey. Accessed on 15th February 2018.
80. Kajewski, S & Weippert, A 2001, *Industry culture: a need for change*, Brisbane, Australia, The Australian Cooperative Research Centre for Construction Innovation, www.construction-innovation.info/images/pdfs/Research_library/ResearchLibraryA/Project_Reports/Industry_Culture_A_Need_for_Change.pdf. Accessed on 5th February 2018.
81. Gibbs, G & Lewins, A 2011, 'Quality of qualitative analysis: the debate about criteria for good quality', QDA, http://onlineqda.hud.ac.uk/Intro_QDA/qualitative_analysis.php. Accessed on 27th July 2014.
82. Habibi, A, Sarafrazi, A & Izadyar, S 2014, 'Delphi technique in theoretical framework in qualitative research', *International Journal of Engineering and Science*, vol. 3, no. 4, pp. 8–13. Theijes.com/papers/v3-i4/Version-4/B03404008013.pdf. Accessed on 4th June 2018.
83. von der Gracht, H 2012, 'Concensus measurement in Delphi studies: reopinions and implications for future quality assurance', *Technological Forecasting and Social Change*, vol. 79, pp. 1525–1536.
84. Fletcher, A & Childon, G 2014, 'Using the Delphi method for qualitative, participatory action research in health leadership', *International Journal of Qualitative Methods*, vol. 13, pp. 1–18, http://ejournals.library.ualberta.ca/index.php/IJQM/article/view/19025/16138. Accessed on 27th September 2017.

85. Brady, S 2015, 'Utilising and adapting the Delphi method for use in qualitative research', *International Journal of Qualitative Research Methods*, vol. 14, no. 5, http://journals.sagepub.com/doi/full/10.1177/1609406915621381. Accessed on 22nd January 2017.
86. Skulmoski, G, Hartman, F & Kran, J 2007 'The *Delphi* method for graduate research', *Journal of Information Technology Education*, vol. 6, no. 1, p. 21, http://www.jite.org/documents/Vol6/JITEv6p001-021Skulmoski212.pdf. Accessed on 4th June 2018.
87. McCrum-Gardner, E 2010, 'Sample size and power calculations made simple', *International Journal of Therapy and Rehabilitation*, vol. 17, no. 1, pp. 10–14. https://www.uv.es/uvetica/files/McCrum_Gardner2010.pdf. Accessed on 5th February 2018.
88. Martinez-Mesa, J, Gonzalez-Chica, D, Bastos, J, Bonamigo, R & Duquia, P 2014, 'Sample size: how many participants do I need in my research', *Epidemiology and Biostatistics Applied to Dermatology*, vol. 89, no. 4, pp. 609–615, https://www.ncbi.nlm.nih.gov/pmc/articles/PMC4148275/pdf/abd-89-04-0609.pdf. Accessed on 17th April 2018.
89. Runeson, G & Skitmore, M 1999, *Writing research reports*, Canberra, Australia, Deakin University Press.
90. Maxwell, M & Babbie, E 2012, *Research methods for criminal justice and criminology*, Stanford CT, Cengage Learning.
91. G*Power 2017, 'G*Power manual', http://www.gpower.hhu.de/fileadmin/redaktion/Fakultaeten/Mathematisch-Naturwissenschaftliche_Fakultaet/Psychologie/AAP/gpower/GPowerManual.pdf. Accessed on 14th February 2018.
92. Erdfelder, E, Faul, F & Buchner, A 1996, 'G*Power: a general power analysis program', *Behavior Research Methods, Instruments and Computers*, vol. 28, pp. 1–11.
93. Faul, F, Erdfelder, E, Lang, A-G & Buchner, A 2007, 'G*Power 3: a flexible statistical power analysis program for the social, behavioural and biomedical sciences', *Behaviour Research Methods*, vol. 39, pp. 175–191, http://www.psycho.uni-duesseldorf.de/abteilungen/aap/gpower3/download-and-register/Dokumente/Gpower3-BRM-Paper.pdf. Accessed on 5th February 2018.
94. Berkeley, 'Multiple hypotheses testing and false discovery rate', https://www.stat.berkeley.edu/~hhuang/STAT141/Lecture-FDR.pdf. Accessed on 14th February 2018.
95. Smith, J 2008, *Qualitative psychology: a practical guide to research methods*, London, Sage.

96. Webb, E, Campbell, D, Schwartz, R & Sechrest, L 1996, *Unobtrusive measures*, Chicago, Rand McNally.
97. Willig, C 2013, *Introducing qualitative research in psychology*, Buckingham UK, OUP.
98. Denzin, N & Lincoln, Y 2005, 'Part IV: methods of collecting and analysing empirical materials', in Denzin, N & Lincoln, Y (eds.) *The Sage handbook of qualitative research* (3rd ed.), Thousand Oaks, CA, Sage (pp. 641–650).
99. Braun, V & Clarke, V 2013, *Successful qualitative research: a practical guide for beginners*, London, Sage.
100. Denzin, N 2009, 'The elephant in the living room: or extending the conversation about the politics of evidence', *Qualitative Research*, vol. 9, no. 2, pp. 139–160, http://qrj.sagepub.com/content/9/2/139. Accessed on 6th August 2016.
101. Wadick, P 2011, 'Constructing the safe workplace: the dance of subjectivity, power and agency in the performance of OHS', PhD thesis, Melbourne, Monash University.
102. Nigatu, T 2009, *Qualitative data analysis*, http://amrefetmer.wikispaces.com/file/view/Qualitative+data+analysis.pdf (Note: site closed by Wikispaces in 2018). Accessed 22nd April 2014.
103. Trochim, W 2006, *The qualitative-quantitative debate*, Research Methods Knowledge Base, http://www.socialresearchmethods.net/kb/qualdeb.php. Accessed on 17th August 2016.
104. Newman, I & Benz, C 1998, *Qualitative-quantitative research methodology—exploring the interactive continuum*, Carbondale and Edwardsville, Southern Illinois University Press.
105. Pope, C & Mays, N 1995, 'Reaching the parts other methods cannot reach: and introduction to qualitative methods in health and health services research', *British Medical Journal*, vol. 311, no. 6996, pp. 42–45.
106. Schwandt, T 1994, 'Constructivist, interpretivist approaches to human inquiry', in Denzin, N & Lincoln, Y (eds.) *Handbook of qualitative research*, Thousand Oaks, CA, Sage.
107. Frost, N 2011, *Qualitative research in psychology*, Maidenhead, OUP/McGraw-Hill Education.
108. Willig, C & Stainton-Rogers, W 2013, *The Sage handbook of qualitative research in psychology*, London, Sage.
109. Bahn, S & Weatherill, P 2012, 'Qualitative social research: a risky business when it comes to collecting "sensitive" data', *Qualitative Social Work*, vol. 11, no. 4, pp. 431–444.

110. Sandal, V 2013, 'An exploration of the role and relationship of school counsellors within the independent sector', MA dissertation, Bath Spa UK, Bath Spa University.
111. Johnson, R, Onwuegbuzie, A & Turner, L 2007, 'Toward a definition of mixed methodology research', *Journal of Mixed Methods Research*, vol. 1, no. 2, pp. 112–133.
112. Johnson, N 2009, 'The role of self and emotion within qualitative sensitive research: a reflective account', *Enquire*, no. 4.
113. Smith, J & Osborn, M 2003, 'Interpretive phenomenological analysis', in Smith, JA (ed.) *Qualitative psychology: a practical guide to methods*, London, Sage.
114. Ebrahim, G & Sullivan, K 1995, *Mother and child health research methods*, London, Book Aid Publishing.
115. Madison, D 2005, *Critical ethnography: methods, ethics and performance*, Thousand Oaks, CA, Sage, cited in Denzin, N 2009, 'The elephant in the living room: or extending the conversation about the politics of evidence', *Qualitative Research*, vol. 9, no. 2, pp. 139–160.
116. Denzin, N 2009, 'The elephant in the living room: or extending the conversation about the politics of evidence', *Qualitative Research*, vol. 9, no. 2, pp. 139–160.
117. Feuer, M, Towne, L & Shavelson, R 2002, 'Science, culture and educational research', *Educational Researcher*, vol. 31, no. 8, pp. 4–14.
118. Joseph, S 2012, 'Unconditional positive regard: if you think it's smiling and nodding, you're doing it wrong', *Psychology Today*, https://www.psychologytoday.com/blog/what-doesnt-kill-us/201210/unconditional-positive-regard. Accessed on 6th February 2018.
119. Beale, B, Cole, R, Hillege, S, McMaster, R & Nagy, S 2004, 'Impact of in-depth interviews on the interviewer: roller-coaster ride', *Nursing and Health Sciences*, vol. 6, pp. 141–147.
120. Mitchell, W & Irvine, A 2008, 'I'm OK, You're OK. Reflection on the wellbeing and ethical requirements of the researchers and research participants in conducting qualitative fieldwork interviews', *International Journal of Qualitative Methods*, vol. 7, no. 4, pp. 31–44.
121. O'Reilly, M & Parker, N 2012, 'Unsatisfactory saturation: a critical exploration of the notion of saturated sample sizes in qualitative research', *Qualitative Research Journal*, vol. 1, no. 8, https://doi.org/10.1177/1468794112446106 cited in Fusch, P & Ness, L 2015, 'Are we there yet: data saturation in qualitative research', *The Qualitative Report*, vol.

20, no. 9, pp. 1408–1416. tqr.nova.edu/wp-content/uploads/2015/09/fusch1.pdf. Accessed on 6th February 2018.

122. Guest, G, Bunce, A & Johnson, L 2006, 'How many interviews are enough? An experiment with data saturation and variability', *Field Methods*, vol. 18, no. 1, pp. 59–82, cited in Fusch, P & Ness, L 2015, 'Are we there yet: data saturation in qualitative research', *The Qualitative Report*, vol. 20, no. 9, pp. 1408–1416, tqr.nova.edu/wp-content/uploads/2015/09/fusch1.pdf. Accessed on 6th February 2018.
123. Burmeister, E & Aitken, L 2012, 'Sample size; how many is enough?' *Australian Critical Care*, vol. 25, pp. 271–274, cited in Fusch, P & Ness, L 2015, 'Are we there yet: data saturation in qualitative research', *The Qualitative Report*, vol. 20, no. 9, pp. 1408–1416. tqr.nova.edu/wp-content/uploads/2015/09/fusch1.pdf. Accessed on 6th February 2018.
124. Rubin, H & Rubin, I 2012, *Qualitative interviewing: the art of hearing data* (3rd ed.), Thousand Oaks, Sage.
125. AERA 2006, *Standards for reporting on empirical social science research in AERA publications*, American Education Research Association (as quoted in Denzin 2009—no longer available on line).
126. Seidel, J 1998, *Qualitative data analysis—the Ethnograph manual (v5)* (Appendix E) [Date viewed not recorded], http://www.qualisresearch.com.
127. Taylor, C & Gibbs, G 2010, 'What is qualitative data analysis—QDA', http://onlineqda.hud.ac.uk/Intro_QDA/what_is_qda.php. Accessed on 22nd February 2016.
128. Puhan, M, Aki, E, Bruant, D, Xie, F, Apolone, G & ter Riet, G 2012, 'Discussing study limitation in reports of biomedical studies—the need for more transparency', *Health and Quality of Life Outcomes*, vol. 10, no. 23, https://www.ncbi.nlm.nih.gov/pmc/articles/PMC3305390/pdf/1477-7525-10-23.pdf. Accessed on 10th February 2018.

2

Coming to Grips with, and Getting to Understand the Problem

Introduction

In the first chapter, I introduced the research about which this work is written, explaining how it evolved from the results of a pilot study, and relating that to the initiation phase of project management and the intake session of psychotherapy. In this chapter, I progress the work of better understanding the problem via a literature review, using the second phase of project management as a parallel and the second phase of psychotherapy practice as a useful explanatory metaphor.

The second phase of Project Management (PM) is the Planning phase, wherein project teams develop client requirements from the concepts described in the project brief (from the Initiation Phase) to detailed designs and specifications. They subject the developing documents to critical thinking and challenging aspects of technical and financial feasibility to ensure meeting quality standards, budget limitations and schedule requirements. When this process has progressed to a level of

In project management (PM) parlance—the PLANNING phase.
In psychotherapy parlance—the DETERMINING THE EXTENT OF THE PROBLEM session.

A. Patching, *Attitudes to Psychological Stress Among Construction Professionals*,
https://doi.org/10.1007/978-3-030-93776-8_2

completion satisfactory to the various client, financing and advisory parties, the documents can be collated, tenders called and evaluated and a contract awarded in final preparation for the project implementation phase. In a way, this is not overly dissimilar from the research process. From a project perspective that involves progressing from determining a gap in the literature on a particular topic (initiation of the research) to determining and planning the steps required (planning the research approach or method) before moving to implementation phase—gathering and analysing data to close that knowledge gap identified during the initiating phase.

The second phase of the psychotherapy process is similar in concept but potentially more complex in application. It involves summarising client issues described at the intake session to ensure accuracy and thoroughness, before confirming an intervention strategy based on presenting problems and desired outcomes. After explaining the planned intervention strategy, the issue for that session is addressed in depth, using a range of intervention techniques. In both project management and psychotherapy contexts, appropriate strategy formulation paves the way for success in ensuing phases.

Before I direct the principles described above to defining what is known, and what is not, about the concerning topic of attitudes to the avoidance and management of stress impacts on CPMs, let's take a moment to review where we stand with Will and Clare. I have described their relationship circumstances in Chapter 1. In this chapter, I'll address the important step of determining the real extent of the problem, and possible underlying causes. Before we can usefully understand the impact of stress in the couple's relationship, we first need to understand stress and its effects as medical and psychological concepts.

The Nature of Psychological Stress

Psychological stress affects people in both their working and private lives in a variety of ways, with the underlying common factor they experience changes in emotional and physical responses that can lead to disease [1]. Stress is not a disease, but the literature reveals it is a contributing factor to several diseases [1, 2]. Recognising the importance of stress, the Australian Government issued a comprehensive document addressing stress avoidance and management in the workplace [3].

Stress is the most significant cause of illness affecting both workers and workplaces, with the potential to inflict extensive consequences on both [4]. Organisations often initiated stress management practices and encouraged employees to exploit them, but contemporaneously escalated use of practices that cause stress. Even organisations embracing stress prevention were often slow acknowledging the high impact of working conditions on employees' health and productivity [4].

Stress acts in difficult-to-detect ways before physical or psychological responses become apparent. One example is stress impacts on women who undergo In Vitro Fertilisation (IVF) when having difficulty becoming pregnant. This field attracted increasing scientific attention as people in Western society worked longer in stressful occupations before beginning families. In 2014, an American team [5] determined stress in women increased both fecundity and time to pregnancy. This is an important consideration for research targeting stress impacts in any profession attracting increasing numbers of women, including construction project management [6–8].

People subjected to stress might be psychologically well-adjusted, with minor deviation between their data and normative data [9, 10 (in 11), 12 (in 13)] This sounds counter-intuitive but is an important concept to grasp to understand why much stress goes unreported. It is explained by the medical concept of heterostasis, addressed later.

"Psychologically well-adjusted" does not mean free of stress at a level that could have an impact on psychological or physiological wellbeing. Average scores used in much scientific research often mask individual participants with high distress levels in specific problem areas [12]. Seven to 16 percent of cardio-vascular disease among men is attributable to high-demand work wherein they have little job control [14].

Stress and the General Adaption Syndrome

The concept of psychological stress dates back to the work of Hungarian medical doctor and organic chemist, Hans Selye. He noticed, despite suffering different diseases, patients generally had a common look—one of being sick—and he referred to this as stress [15]. Selye later admitted he used the word erroneously due to confusion from speaking eight languages, and stated he should have used strain. Nonetheless, stress is still used to describe what Selye detailed in both his book and his published work [16, 17].

Selye discovered and described the General Adaption Syndrome (GAS), which explains stress-induced autonomic hormonal responses, which, over time, led to several serious medical conditions. GAS is still used to describe a three-stage reaction to stress [18]. Selye labelled the first stage the alarm stage. The brain's limbic system (discussed later) discerned an environmental experience as either safe or a threat and, if the latter, immediately activated a limbic system response [16, 19]. Selye's alarm stage is synonymous with fight or flight response, a term attributed to Walter Cannon in 1915. This response activates the release of the stress hormones adrenaline, noradrenaline and cortisol, essential to escape danger or fight to survive, but harmful if frequently released in circumstances the brain incorrectly perceives to be physically threatening [18, 20, 21].

In the second phase, stress levels reduce and the body directs energy to repairing tissues strained or weakened by first-phase hormones. The body is weaker in ability to react effectively to stressors during this phase. This weakness is prolonged by perception a threat persists, because a state of heightened alertness is maintained to best respond to new threats. The more the threat perception prevails, the more the body's ability to deal with manifesting real threat is reduced [16, 21, 22].

The third and final phase in Selye's GAS sequence is exhaustion. This occurs after perceived stress prevails for a lengthy period. With adjustment energy nearing depletion, the body loses its response effectiveness to combat perceived threats and exhaustion ensues [16, 22]. Exhaustion is the precursor to burnout, which triggers serious health problems if not quickly addressed [23]. Figure 2.1 diagrammatically presents Selye's GAS phases.

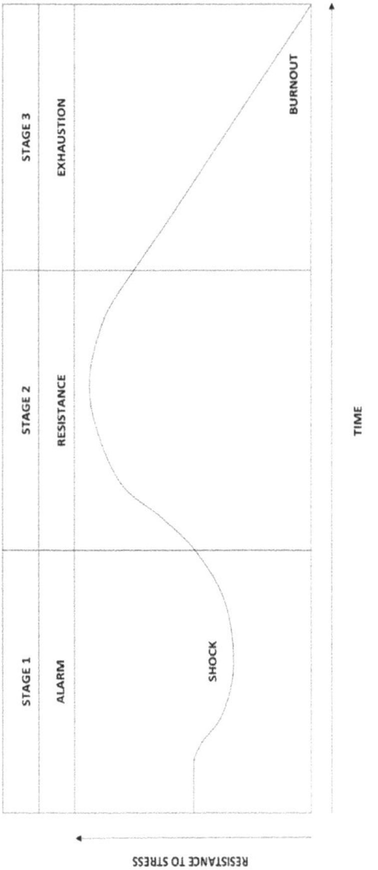

Fig. 2.1 Diagram of the three stages of the GAS

Sources of Stress in the Construction Environment, and Effects on Relationships

Relentless exposure to uncertainties regarding employment, contractual deadlines, project size and complexity, economic environment and perception of one's ability to deal with one's responsibilities are all significant contributors to stress and potential burnout among construction professionals [7, 24, 25]. In 2003, Lingard [7] posited stress could not be attributed to workplace factors only. In 2010, Lingard and Sublet [26] noted the spill-over effects stress had from home into work. Job satisfaction is negatively affected when work interferes excessively with family life, and an important factor in determining work effects on personal relationships is the number of hours worked.

The pilot study described in Chapter 1 revealed whether stress originated primarily in the workplace or in the private arena, its effects are seen in reduced productivity and profit reduction at work [27]. Family conflict is also strongly associated with hours worked, and both stress levels and conflict increase with longer hours worked [28–30].

Regardless of whether stress initiates at work or home, undetected stress affects productivity and profit for the employer and contributes to disease for the employee [31, 32]. The business world has addressed workplace stress for some time (via EAPs) [33]. However, the literature revealed scant material on the subject for CPMs specifically.

The pilot study described in Chapter 1 revealed differences in attitudes to stress avoidance and management between CPMs and managers across broader business. To understand those differences, a deeper understanding of stress is helpful.

Defining Stress

Health is a state of complete physical, mental and social wellbeing, not just the absence of disease [34]. Workplace stress results from various combinations of job design, workplace setting, workplace relationships and job demands [35, 36]. When workplace stress exists, management effort is required to address it, and that effort is significantly higher than it was seven to ten years ago [37]. Managers need to understand workplace stress and its impacts. A good place to begin is with definitions of stress.

The Diagnostic and Statistical Manual of Mental Disorders—Fifth Edition (DSM 5) [38] explains stress as the consequence of exposure to actual or threatened death, serious injury or sexual violence, or experiencing repeated exposure to negative aspects of traumatic events. This seems more appropriate to medical environments than general workplaces. The definition of acute stress disorder in the previous edition, the DSM-IV [39], was simply psychosocial factors affecting general medical conditions.

Byrtritsky and Kronemyer [40] paraphrased the DSM-5 [38] definition indicating stress was caused by catastrophic stimuli resulting in mental disorders and psychiatric breakdown. They noted there were numerous ways to experience a stress response other than the experience of catastrophe, and offered a more realistic definition for workplace situations wherein stress was:

> *...caused by or results from abnormal or catastrophic levels of environmental stimuli.* [40]

The DSM-5 differentiates between stress and anxiety, but medical practitioners and the general public tended to understand patients' awareness of stress often preceded manifestation of anxiety symptoms, but not always. For that reason, this study did not differentiate between the terms. The following paraphrased summary of the DSM-5 [38] table of similarities and differences between stress and anxiety is relevant:

- The symptoms of stress include increased arousal, strain and tension; those of anxiety included hyper-vigilance, worry and expectation of threat
- With stress, the autonomic nervous system triggers increase in heart rate, blood pressure and muscle tension, whereas irregular breathing, heart palpitations and increases in blood pressure and muscle tension are symptomatic of anxiety

- A stress response follows stimulus provocation. With anxiety, stress has the effect of combining with cognitive, affective and environmental variables which then affect the initiating stress response, and continue the cycle

It was little wonder that Byrtritsky and Kronemyer [41] concluded:

> *To a large extent these divisions are artificial because stress and anxiety overlap and enhance each other.*

Anxiety is experienced when stress forces neural networks into highly activated unstable states, in which dysfunctional beliefs and unregulated emotions seem to take executive control [38]. This often leads sufferers to adopt maladaptive coping strategies, common among construction workers experiencing stress impacts. The important question is, 'To what extent did this apply to professionals as well as tradespeople?'.

Henceforth, differentiation between 'stress' and'anxiety' is made only where necessary to maintain the accuracy of writing. Any other approach would necessitate a level of language use that would add nothing to the quality of the data collected [42]. Most important, and to be avoided, was the risk of collecting invalid data by confusing participants with overly technical terminology [42].

Psychological and Physiological Aspects of Stress

The National Institute of Occupational Safety and Health (USA) viewed workplace stress as harmful physical and emotional responses that occurred when job requirements did not meet the capabilities, resources or needs of the worker [43]. There are two main stress types. Eustress or positive stress is experienced when doing well in some important endeavour, such as completing an important task on time [44]. Distress was the negative stress addressed in this research [45].

Hanson [46] and Cooper and Baglioni [47] emphasised stress is situational and an individual reaction. Hanson [46] noted stress can be fantastic and fatal, and described a critical line between eustress and distress about which people should remain aware—and avoid crossing. Colligan and Higgins [45] posited, regardless of whether an individual was exposed to eustress or distress, he or she experienced a cognitive, behavioural-emotional and physical response directly related to coping capacity.

Mohsin and Wahab [48, p. 165] defined stress as, 'an outer force that has a command over inner feelings' and explained stress occurred when perception of danger arose as a person came to realise a lack of personal resources to deal with a situation. Mohsin and Wahab [48] also described stress in terms of the fight or flight response initiated by the release of epinephrine and norepinephrine when the amygdala of the Limbic Hypothalamic System (LHS) registered threat or fear in the environment [49, 50]. However, with the increase in work-related stressors [51, 52], the up-to-date expression of fight, flight or freeze response [53] was more appropriate. Freezing describes reaction to situations that quickly overload the autonomic nervous system and is most easily understood in the context of small reptiles remaining still and camouflaged under threat to avoid detection. Adrenal fatigue or burnout, addressed later herein, is like the freeze response and prevents the body from moving in an extremely stressful situation in order to survive [54].

These considerations give rise to the important question, 'how much stress is it acceptable for a person to experience?' Hanson [46] stated the awareness required to adequately address this question was well-served by asking whether the added stress of new responsibility was expected to increase or decrease one's efficiency. This had value in the context of slow-degeneration diseases associated with the Western lifestyle, including diabetes and metabolic syndrome, being caused or made worse by stress [55, 56].

Medical and psychotherapeutic professions broadly accept that acute stress and post-traumatic stress are disorders that originate with exposure to traumatic or stress-inducing life events [38] and were diagnosed from easily observable symptomology including hyper-vigilance, poor sleep patterns, flashbacks, avoidance of trigger circumstances and heightened irritability. Sapolsky [56] referred to a more sinister origin of psychological stress disorders, one widely prevalent among CPMs—a gradual increase in stress-inducing triggers until a stress-related psychological disorder was experienced.

Another simple but important definition of stress is:

> *Stress is a living thing's response to changing circumstances in its immediate environment. It is a "sense-analyse-decide-respond" system that is necessary for survival.* [18, p. 10]

An interesting aspect of stress aligning with Porter's [57] view of an overdone or misapplied strength becomes a weakness was found in the proposition stress arises from too fast or too slow achievement of success, achieving the wrong type of success, or from becoming stuck in an endeavour [58]. Another sinister stress source is envy, common in workplaces, and an emotion with potentially destructive aspects [59]. In developed, wealthier societies, envy prevailed as a competitive desire to excel to prove value. At its extreme, envy motivated people to seek high salaries not for survival and growth, but as a symbol of success [59].

I considered it important to compare increases in stress-related health disorders across business at large and within construction. A 2016 WorkCover Western Australia statistical note reported construction as the top industry in terms of total claims made, but not among the top three industries for stress-related claims, despite burnout being a serious problem for the construction industry [60]. Explanations are required.

Particularising Stress to the Construction Professions Environment

If my introductory comments were filtered through Sapolsky's [56] proposition and the Yeung et al. [18] definition, the following statement might result:

> *People were attracted via the often euphoric eustress promised by the profession of construction project management, took on more and more responsibility, driven by eustress, until they crossed that critical line proposed by Hanson* [46] *and their load then moved them from a psychological state of eustress to one of*

distress, wherein the person's efficiency diminished, often significantly, resulting in increasing distress, until, quite often, the result was serious physical or psychological illness.

Patching and Best [27] saw this as accurate, and it is well-supported in the literature [60–62]. A Scottish study concluded that often, 'the greatest sources of stress are also the greatest sources of satisfaction' [63, p. 126]. Social Exchange Theory [64] and Effort Reward Imbalance (ERI) theory [65] posit there is a point where the pressure of a situation overcame rewards gained from it and stress was the consequence. These theories raise several questions:

- What is the science behind stress and its effects on people in various situations and contexts?
- Is there clear delineation between workplace and general life stress and their respective effects?
- Are there differences between how stress develops and is managed among CPMs and across broader business?
- To what extent do general life stressors manifest as workplace stress?

At this point, there is value in reviewing the circumstances of our metaphoric couple, Will and Clare, especially in the context of the second and fourth bullet points above. We know that Will is extended at work and experiences stress from not being with the family as often as he would like, and not paying full attention to family matters even when he is at home, because of his excessive workload. We get the impression he would like to clear the stress to a significant degree but cannot see a way clear to doing that. We know that Clare is feeling the stress of having to manage home and family in Will's absence but is reticent to raise the question in order to investigate solutions, fearing it might indicate a lack of appreciation for his efforts. In terms of the points above, while it might be clear where the stress of each party originated, it is probably now fair to recognise there is little delineation between sources of stress for each of them. Will's work pressures are having an impact on Clare's home life, and if the truth be known, the pressure he is feeling because of that is probably beginning to add to his already high-stress levels. After all, the major project he is managing still has a year to run, and it does not look like there will be time for a holiday anytime soon. Again, in terms of the points above, to what extent, if any, has Will's additional stress at home affected his performance at work?

Clearly, there are many questions for Will and Clare to answer in order to get a well-structured solution to their stress-driven relationship issues. However, to properly formulate those questions, it is imperative we first gain an even deeper understanding of stress, how it functions and what its effects are. The fact that the negative impacts of psychological stress increase over time emphasises the urgency of better understanding the problem and finding an effective solution to stress [66, 67].

Basic Science Behind Psychological Stress

Stress is governed by the limbic hypothalamic system (LHS) at the base of the brain, comprising the hippocampus, hypothalamus and amygdala. The LHS deals with emotion, controls certain metabolic processes of the autonomous nervous system, regulates responses to strong emotions including aggression and fear, and regulates the brain's pain and pleasure centres, important aspects of a person's perception of stress [18, 21]. The LHS filters sensory information out of conscious awareness, and categorises the result into a sense of being either safe or threatened [21]. The sense of safety or threat is based on emotion associated with whatever happened. Another idiosyncrasy of the LHS is state dependent memory (SDM) which notices how a person survives a 'threatening' situation (e.g. public speaking) and automatically replays that survival programme in similar situations in future [21]. In other words, this automation, variously called a survival response, imprint, or fight, flight or freeze response causes hypersensitivity to future similar 'threatening' circumstances [18, 67, 68].

In stress-related situations, each activation of SDM response causes the release of epinephrine and norepinephrine from the adrenal gland [18]. When those stress responses are of a certain frequency or intensity (which differs between individuals) communication between the amygdala and hypothalamus stimulates the release of corticotrophin-releasing hormone (CRH) [18]. This, in turn, signals the pituitary gland to release adenocorticotrophic hormone (ACTH) and travels down the adrenal cortex, producing cortisol, the stress hormone [18]. Cortisol is a glucocorticoid, or steroid hormone. It increases glucose availability to provide energy to service the fight, flight or freeze response. Contemporaneously, it negates the effects of insulin produced to neutralise over-production of glucose. This leads insulin resistance and triggers type 2 diabetes [69]. In stressogenic environments, the often almost-constant release of adrenalin (epinephrine) and cortisol leads to an almost inevitable series of body chemistry reactions contributing to acute and chronic illness [69]. Workplace stress and associated elevated blood cortisol levels [1, 14, 18, 70] are strongly correlated with depression, cardio-vascular disease and cancer.

Modern medicine has confirmed stress contributions to illness [71, 72]. It is appropriate to identify the health impacts correlated with stress levels and a stressogenic working environment:

- Psychological effects, together with reduced production of serotonin essential for feelings of wellbeing
- Heart disease due to repeated increases in the pumping force of the heart contemporaneous with restriction of arteries, increase in blood viscosity and blood inflammatory markers and increase in the risk of heart arrhythmias
- Increased risk of stroke due primarily to significant increases in blood pressure
- Increased susceptibility to infection due to suppression of the body's immune response
- Potential effect on cancer sufferers. A causal relationship between stress and cancer has not been proven but there is medical opinion stress has an impact on life duration beyond cancer
- Obesity due to overeating in response to increased cravings for sugary and fatty foods when the body needs glucose to fuel energy to manage situations perceived as stressful
- Exacerbation of existing type 2 Diabetes
- Pain, especially some joint pain and headaches
- Insomnia
- Sexual dysfunction and reproductive dysfunction [5]

- Skin disorders, gum disorders and increase in maladaptive use of alcohol and recreational drugs

Our sympathetic nervous system controls the stress response automatically and subconsciously and our parasympathetic system mediates a sense of calmness, and could work in opposition to the stress-response triggering sympathetic system [56]. This opposing operation is important in maintaining homeostasis, a term coined by American physiologist, Walter Cannon [20] describing the body's internal equilibrium maintenance process [18, 73]. The operation of the sympathetic and parasympathetic nervous systems inspired an anxiety management technique that involves sufferers breathing in fully and out slowly until they relax. This exercise engages the parasympathetic nervous system longer than the sympathetic, and triggers anxiety reduction [74]. The technique was initially called seven-eleven breathing because teachers advised breathing in gently but fully for a count of seven before breathing out slowly for a count of 11 at the same rate of counting [75].

Coronary heart disease has long topped the list of stress-exacerbated health problems with depression in second place [76]. Often, in a parallel of the stress-feeds-anxiety-feeds-stress cycle discussed earlier, stress, depression and risk of coronary disease are engaged in an interconnected cyclical dance of increasing negative effect on health [18, 76]. The effect is often regarded to be a work-stress phenomenon [77] but some debate any depression—coronary disease link. Interestingly, despite rejecting a depression—coronary link exists, Steptoe and Whitehead [77] concluded with a reference to Lane et al. [78] and Lane et al. [79, 80], who stressed the importance of continuing studies into links between stress, depression and coronary heart disease to develop a model for effective mediation. This was an important insight, given depression's association with inflammation and other contributors to heart failure.

Excessive exposure to chronic stress is toxic and can result in long-term emotional, physiological and behavioural responses that cause serious disease, especially depression, auto-immune and coronary disease [1, 18, 69, 72]. 'Chronic' stress should be understood in the context the scientific community recognises three levels of stress:

- Acute stress, experienced when demands and pressures trigger levels of arousal beyond the suffering individual's threshold of adaptability
- Episodic stress, which includes acute levels of arousal experienced frequently and consistently in multiple episodes, and
- Chronic stress, incurred from accumulation of the effects of persistent stresses [45]

Some research indicates serious levels of stress contribute to the initiation and growth of cancers by affecting deoxyribonucleic acid (DNA) repair and cellular ageing [1]. However, the evidence stress causes cancer is weak, and it is more likely stress motivates people to adopt maladaptive stress management techniques that contribute to cancer (smoking, drinking to excess, overeating) [81]. Moreover, while one individual might experience no stress reaction from exposure to a particular stressor, others exposed to the same stressor might experience high levels of stress [82]. For example, some studies found that some female project managers felt increased stress from striving to out-perform male colleagues to maintain technical competence and earn respect [82, 83].

Stress and Sleep

Sleep patterns are closely related to stress intensity, especially for sufferers approaching burnout [84]. Duration of sleep consistently achieved is important [21] but depth of sleep is of at least equal importance for stress avoidance and management [85]. Yeung et al. [18, p. 7] summarised the point well:

> *.... stress impedes the capacity to enjoy restorative sleep, and without this, one's daily stress response will have a tendency to skyrocket.*

The sleep cycle comprised five stages of varying depth until the American Sleep Association removed one stage and re-described the remaining stages in 2007, with stages 3 and 4 labelled deep sleep [86]. Of significance to this book are:

- During sleep we experience dreams, and
- When we fail to resolve stress during the day, we could experience an increase in dream activity during sleep as our brains act to neutralise that stress

The Human Givens Institute (HGI) in the UK confirmed dreaming reduces already accumulated stress effects [87]. The HGI posits repetitive, intense dreaming required to neutralise stress reduces time available for deeper, restorative sleep [87]. This results in sufferers waking tired, which often leads to an increase in stress during that day. If this cycle continues it can extend beyond being stress–inducing and become depressogenic [87–89].

Stressed people often undertake more than their share of work, prioritise little and experience a sense of burden, yet they work harder to disguise their symptoms and appear strong, productive and independent. They lack awareness that doing so is a strong precursor of increasing stress, anxiety and/or depression taking them rapidly towards burnout [7, 25, 84, 90, 91]. These characteristics typify many CPMs, perhaps including Will.

Daytime anxiety and stress increase sleep arousal levels [85, 87, 88]. Subsequent increased levels of sleep deprivation and decreased stress resolution lead to more stress [87, 88]. The consequence is often a negative effect on metabolic and endocrine functions that eventually contributes to serious disease, including type 2 diabetes, cancer and coronary heart disease [18, 92, 93].

The HGI's work is valuable, and patient recovery rates considerably exceed the National Health Service's cognitive behaviour therapy (CBT) based targets when Human Givens therapy is used [94, 95]. I considered it imprudent to omit discussion of the hypothalamus–pituitary–adrenal (HPA) axis in overviewing important scientific aspects of psychological stress.

Stress and Metabolic Syndrome

Selye, in addition to the GAS, posited a process of heterostasis, by which the body changed the benchmark state to which homeostasis sought to return it. People become so familiar with repeated exposure to stressors and their reactions to them that reactions reduced and a new benchmark for triggering a significant stress reaction is set [19, 44]. In ideal circumstances this builds resilience, a well-affirmed counter to psychological distress effects [18, 96–99]. However, if heterostasis produces too many new and higher benchmarks too quickly, some threshold to stress-related illness could be crossed. This risked taking an affected person beyond the relative stability of heterostasis-induced resilience into extreme sensitivity to all manner of psychological and physical ailments.

It would be extraordinary oversight to investigate stress and its effects without discussion of the modern-day phenomenon of metabolic syndrome [18, 100]. Metabolic syndrome comprises an integrated collection of related risk factors for cardio-vascular and other diseases. In 1920, Swedish physician, Kylin, proved the association between hypertension, hyperglycaemia and gout. In 1947, Vague linked visceral obesity with cardio-vascular disease. In 1965 Avogaro and Crepaldi linked hypertension, obesity and hyperglycaemia with cardio-vascular problems. In 1988, Reavan presented Syndrome X, a cluster of integrated risk factors for diabetes and cardio-vascular disease, but failed to include visceral obesity as had those studying the phenomenon before him. In the 1990s, visceral obesity was re-included, and several name changes ensued before the International Diabetes Federation coined the name metabolic syndrome in 2005 [101]. The symptoms of metabolic syndrome parallel stress-induced symptomology [100], and that makes it important to address.

Some definitions of metabolic syndrome include references to inflammation and thrombosis [18, 102–104]. The latter is an elevation of blood lipids and/or cholesterol often caused by factors including too little physical activity and too high sugar intake, common in stressed individuals, and it has been linked to insulin resistance; it is a significant precursor to diabetes [18, 56, 104–107].

Of significant importance to CPMs exposed to incrementally increasing workloads and stress levels is medical research has shown most people diagnosed with metabolic syndrome had no symptoms, apart from an abnormally large waist circumference, before the underlying integrated components of the disorder led to serious illnesses including cancer, cardio-vascular disease and diabetes [102, 104, 107].

Workplace Stress Specifically

Work is not the only cause of stress for most people [108] despite Nakao [32] emphasising work-related problems are the most frequent stressors. Regardless of where stress initiates, it impacts the workplace [27]. Furthermore, private life-initiated stress is often exacerbated by workplace stress. Both the previous statements are salient to Will's circumstances, but we will investigate that further in the following chapter. It makes sense employers act to manage stress impacts in the interests of a more harmonious work environment, which is expected to contribute to workforce stress reduction and enhanced productivity [109–111]. Of course, that did not occur in Will's situation, and as you will soon discover, this research revealed that in the construction industry, it happens all too seldom. If Will's workplace had considered his mounting stress and its impacts on his work and private life, management might have been prompted to make some much-needed adjustments, and these might well have resulted in some very positive changes for the better for Will and Clare. At this point, you might well be asking, 'Why did Will not discuss the pressure he was experiencing with his manager?' My research revealed the reasons many CPMs do not do this, and I address this in Chapter 4. For now, let us return to the literature.

The literature endorses Nakao's view most stress initiates at work [2, 25, 112, 113]. Continued exposure to occupational stress gives rise to cumulative trauma, for which there has been an increase in claims in the USA. The UK has also seen an increase in successful claims [114].

A correlation identified between hours worked and ill health is unsurprising [112] as is evidence the worst cases of stress led to physical and psychological health issues of clinical significance [114].

While claims in Australia for workplace physical injury have decreased across all industries, claims for mental stress increased 83 percent between 1996–1997 and 2003–2004. Despite this, no elevated job stress effects were reflected in claims patterns from the construction industry [14]. This raises two important questions:

1. Why is that the case? Is the tough industry culture preventing employees from reporting stress-related symptoms?
2. Given that Keegel et al. [14] stated workers' compensation claims were an inadequate basis for developing government policy regarding job stress, should the message for construction organisations be stress management programmes should not be based only on reported stress-related illness?

All references to stress in this book refer to distress, and not eustress (the positive, motivating type) [45]. Stress reactions differ between individuals. Stress is experienced when responsibilities faced are beyond one's perception of one's ability to manage. Accordingly, a low/medium level of strain for one person might be perceived as a very high level of pressure by another [115].

Late last century, distinctions were made between mental load and psychological stress. Gaillard concurred [116, p. 991]:

> *High workload is regarded as an important but not critical factor in the development of stress symptoms. It is quite possible to work hard in difficult and complex tasks, even under unfavourable conditions, without cognitive strain, psychosomatic complaints, or adverse physiological effects. High task demands can be met by mobilising extra energy through mental effort. This 'trying harder' reaction is a normal and healthy coping strategy to adapt to situational demands. In contrast, stress is regarded as a state in which the equilibrium between cognitive and energetic processes is disturbed by*

ineffective energy mobilization and negative emotions. Stress typically is characterized by inefficient behaviour, over reactivity, and the incapacity to recover from work. Stress is regarded as a state in which the physiological system is disorganized, which results in decreased well-being, sleeping problems, psychosomatic complaints, and increased health risks.

Workplace stress not only affects individuals, but also family members, in ways more serious than tolerating the behaviour of the stressed person [117, 118]. A complex cycle was identified in the work–home life balance scenario [119]—it was often not work stress taken home, but rather an addiction to work causing problems that led to stress.

One example of accumulated work and home stress on a person's life is women undergoing In Vitro Fertilisation (IVF) [13]. Gonadotropin-Releasing Hormone (GnRH) releases Follicle Stimulating Hormone (FHS) and Luteinising Hormone (LH) from the anterior pituitary gland during the follicular phase of the female fertility cycle, and inhibited GnRH pulsatility has been linked with reproductive disorders in women [120] and with the stress-regulating LHS [121]. The adrenal steroid hormones, or glucocorticoids, secreted in response to stress, suppress reproductive ability [5, 122, 123]. Women have reported experiencing stress related to additional work pressure after being promoted into senior organisational positions during their mid to late thirties—a time when chances of falling pregnant reduce naturally [5, 124]. This is one of many stress-circuits at play between family/private environments and workplaces [5, 124].

Early stress management approaches focussed on sufferers' coping rather than organisation-initiated stress avoidance and management programmes. Coping is a person's cognitive and behavioural efforts to manage when demands exceeded their resources [125].

Recent studies focussed on the benefits of EAPs [33] and coping with perceptions of job insecurity [126]. This latter point is becoming crucial because workplace stress/insecurity is now the biggest factor influencing people's decisions to leave workplaces [66, 127].

Most employees see pressure as organisational rather than task-generated [66]. This conflicted with research [27] which indicated limiting work hours as a project approaches a contractual deadline increases rather than reduces stress for CPMs. Perhaps a Coffey, Dugdill and Tattersall [66, p. 99]. study aligns with CPM's experience that employees see difficult aspects of their work as 'too much to do in too little time and with too few staff'.

When construction work environments are typified by extreme pressure, relentless and often-changing demands and ruthless attitudes and behaviour, they become toxic workplaces, wherein employees operate consistently in fear, paranoia and increased anxiety states [45, p. 93]. This, and Nakao's [32] work differed from the finding of Albertson et al. [113, p. 82] that 'recent studies have found no effect of influence at work on outcomes such as long-term sickness absence and work-family conflicts'.

In a changing social environment, workplace-generated stress has a negative impact on the very place that generates the stress. For example, with more women becoming CPMs, stress concerns emerge when women feel under pressure to out-perform male colleagues to earn respect, and females feel inclined to adopt male colleagues' life patterns to fit the profession [82, 128, 129].

Alhaug and McLaughlin [82, p. 149] concluded work for women in predominantly male construction project management is hazardous and the women in their study were 'just coping'. Gender aside, Albertsen et al. [113, p. 86] concluded, 'it seems likely that people who have a high need to perform well at work and whose self-esteem is highly dependent on performance and success may run an increased risk for overload and accordingly, increase cognitive stress symptoms'.

Stress prevails across broader business. Varvogli and Darviri [130] reported a World Health Organisation (WHO) statistic work-related stress impacted one-third of European Union employees and was the second most prevalent health problem. Focus on the extent of stress among CPMs is not intended to diminish its impact elsewhere. Rather, it is an essential step in determining the extent to which members of specific professions experience and manage stress differently from those in broader business. I considered if questioning contributors to stress was normative, questioning various possible contributors to its avoidance or resolution made perfect sense. This is important because stress both triggers health risks for sufferers and increases the risk of mistakes and safety breaches in the construction environment [131] and contributes to burnout [7, 24, 25].

Waite [25] described burnout as emotional exhaustion, and emphasised leadership 'giving positive feedback keeps employees happy and feeling like their work is valued' [25, p. 11]. This raised the question whether effects of contractual and other pressures of construction environments were likely to be allayed by leaders acknowledging stress existed, as Waite [25] recommended. Leadership action of the type Waite [25] described had been shown, a decade earlier, to enhance job engagement and reduce absenteeism [132]. Nonetheless, while leaders acknowledging workplace stress exists is of value, I doubt it would reduce absenteeism caused by intense stress impacts.

There had been little increase in reported stress-related illness in the construction industry at the end of the first decade of the twenty-first century [27] despite industry suicide rates [133] having motivated the Mates in Construction [134] suicide prevention programme. A study by Action Alliance [135] suggested a cultural element was involved. Suicide was the second-highest cause of death for men between the ages of 25 and 54 and men in construction outpace women in suicide deaths by four to one. Construction workers in high skill—high risk jobs such as supervising heavy construction equipment operations had the highest suicide rates. Construction and extraction (mining) industries reported the highest female suicide rates across all professions. Construction workers generally were in the top nine professions at risk of suicide [135]. These statistics made sense because stress-related illness in workplaces had increased significantly over recent years across the industry at large [136]. Unfortunately, the literature addressed the construction industry as a whole, and little specifically addressed stress effects on CPMs.

The problem is exacerbated by some leaders' ignorance of its existence, despite job stress being recognised internationally as a growing concern by working people, employers, regulators and insurers [14, 137]. Only three percent of construction industry employers understand work stress leads to serious health problems, and they continue to give employees increasingly less time to do increasingly complex work [6].

Despite technology being introduced to alleviate the workload, the opposite effect eventuated. The simple tasks of answering business-related phone calls and emails during non-work hours create for the average American worker, more than a month and a half of unpaid overtime work annually [138]. Burg-Brown proposed workers must dedicate private time to cut all business connectivity and give 100 percent attention to family or private pursuits [138]. It is difficult to accept this being achieved in the hard-dollar contracts environment of the construction industry.

Porter [57] proposed a strength overdone or misapplied becomes a weakness, and his theory relates closely to people becoming engaged with work for positive reasons, but over-applying strength of work enjoyment to the extent they suffer stress effects. Money has been recognised as not the main reason people work. Work also provides a sense of purpose and contributes to a person's identity perception [58, 139]. Therein lay a potential problem of major concern.

In extreme cases of this work-forming-identity phenomenon, the outcome was death from overwork, so common in Japan it was given a name—Karoshi, translated as 'overwork death' [58, 140]. Japan also has a word for overwork-driven suicide—karojisatsu [141]. A balancing philosophy emerged from American author, Dr. Wayne Dyer who said at the 1994 National Achiever's Congress in Singapore, 'be careful allowing what you do to become who you are. If what you do is who you are, then when you don't, you're not!'.

Knez [139] presented a credible model for work-based identity, made up of emotional and cognitive components, and based on ontological and epistemological considerations that include connections with psychology's attachment and belonging theory, among others. Construction culture generally attracted tough people [142, 143] and the possibility that psychological stress in that profession had its roots in attachment theory-related issues (for example, lack of early years maternal connection being compensated by connection to work and colleagues) is a bold and thought-provoking proposition.

Profile of the Australian Construction Industry

The Australian construction industry contributes 7.7 percent to Australia's Gross Domestic Product (GDP) and its 330,000 businesses employ over one million people, approximately nine percent of the workforce [144]. During 2010–2011 the industry recorded the fourth-highest growth in contribution to GDP [145]. Construction is Australia's third-largest industry, and 85 percent of its workers are employed full time, compared with 54 percent across other industries, with 89 percent of those workers being male, compared with 54 percent across other industries [144]. In February 2015, 15.8 percent of the construction workforce was 55 years of age or older, 30 percent of the workforce was self-employed, compared with 8.5 percent across other industries and 45 percent had completed a certificate 3 or certificate 4 qualification compared with 20 percent across other industries. Only eight percent held a bachelor's degree or higher, compared with 28 percent across other industries [144].

Actions, Taken and Required, by the Australian Construction Industry

The industry responded to the high suicide rate among workers with the Mates in Construction suicide prevention programme [146] which introduced the important concept that 'suicide is everyone's business' and not a matter for individuals and health professionals only. The programme operates independently of the employers and unions which promote its expansion throughout the industry. The programme was motivated by a Queensland report showing construction industry suicide rates to be higher than the national average, and youth suicide to be 2.38 times higher for young men in construction than for other young Australian men [147]. These findings chronologically aligned with broader workplace claims evidence showing virtually no increase in claims for stress-related illness in the construction industry across Australia [14]. Whether a similar situation existed for industry professionals as for tradespeople was of interest to this study.

Workplace stressors causing poor health cannot be dealt with easily by direct action [31]. This inspired the research question, 'what, if any, stress avoidance measures were adopted by CPMs?' Mates in Construction trains workers to recognise depression symptoms and suicide ideation in themselves and others, and to begin a dialogue when symptoms are noticed. Across a broader industry base, there is strong acceptance of programmes focusing on stress avoidance, stress management and EAPs [33, 148–150]. The important aspect is that all three phases are addressed, whereas the pilot study discussed in Chapter 1 revealed construction-related organisations are more likely to focus on the third stage, and to a lesser extent the secondary, with few organisations covering all three phases. Figure 2.2 overviews the three phases.

Some recent literature focussed on managers assuming a counselling role somewhere between the Mates in Construction colleague and the external professional counsellor [151]. The Australian government's recently published a template for managers and leaders to deal with workplace mental health issues from avoidance, detection, management and recovery support perspectives [152] sets the benchmark for dealing

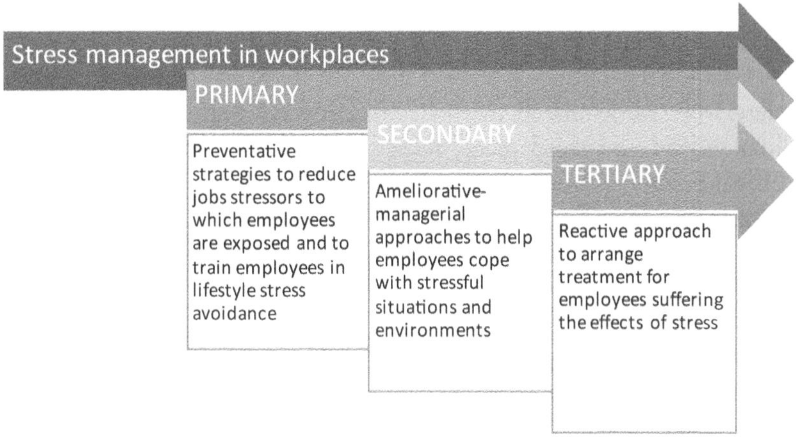

Fig. 2.2 The three phases of stress management—after Cooper and Cartwright 1997

with workplace mental health in this country. The following quotation from the document provides insight regarding the way forward:

Leaders and managers must build their levels of confidence around mental health issues to better include people with mental ill health in our teams, and to enable appropriate support of employees during illness and recovery [152, p. ii].

Beyond that government template one bold suggestion is to conduct stress audits to understand vulnerability to stress impacts across an organisation, and to formulate appropriate responses.

While the literature contains studies of differences in aspects of stress between business owners and non-owners [153, 154] and on stress within project management [155, 156] and construction [157–159] no studies were found that compared impacts of stress and attitudes to it between CPMs and BPs. It is now appropriate to address deeper aspects of how which CPMs differ from APs and BPs in avoidance and management of psychological stress.

The Impact of Workplace Stress

Nakao [32] described psychological stress as the body's physiological and/or psychological reaction to circumstances that required behavioural adjustment. Some 49 percent of Japanese aged 23 years or older experienced daily stress in their lives and the most frequent stressors in Japanese society were work-related, with health concerns and financial pressures taking second and third place, respectively [32]. Nakao [32] presented no breakdown of data by industry or profession when he reported the Japanese government, as early as 2004, took workplace stress very seriously, and urged all Japanese employers to implement a four-faceted mind–body approach to stress management. Those facets were:

- Focussing on individuals
- Utilising supervisory lines
- Enlisting company health care staff
- Referring to external medical services when necessary

This approach aligns with Western models apart from the third point. The focus seemed to be on stress impacts on individuals without consideration of causal effects of working conditions [4]. Ideal strategies for stress management focus on both job demands and the extent to which the psychosocial organisational and environmental contexts in which the job is performed constitute serious stressors [32, 70, 109, 111, 160–162]. Even these need to be addressed ontologically—with each individual's perception of the fabric and structure of his or her subjective workplace experience considered [163].

The Japanese researched the impact of stress on the economy. Apart from the effects of acute epidemics, stress-related chronic non-communicable diseases pose the greatest dangers to our overall health and economies [18]. Interestingly, impacts on business are felt even before the stress-related illness is experienced physically [31]. Job function errors increase, decision-making quality decreases, job satisfaction decreases and loyalty and creativity diminish, and these factors directly impact business even if employees are unaware of stress effects on themselves [31].

A survey of stress and wellbeing in Australia for 2015 [164] reported, inter alia:

- 35 percent of Australians experienced significant levels of stress
- 26 percent experienced above normal levels of anxiety (the highest ever for the survey)
- A similar percentage suffered moderate to severe depression
- Workplace stress was not among the top 5 stressors, whereas finance, family and personal health were major stressors for between 44 and 49 percent of participants.

An extensive meta study by Harvey et al. [165] revealed:

- Mental disorders are now the leading cause of sickness, absence and long-term work incapacity in most developed countries, and
- The most common workplace mental illnesses are stress-induced anxiety and depression

Among those with the highest levels of anxiety and/or depression symptoms:

- Between 61 and 66 percent drink alcohol to relieve symptoms
- Between 41 and 46 percent smoke and
- Between 38 and 47 percent take recreational drugs

These are maladaptive stress management techniques [164]. It was reasonable to assume maladaptive management techniques contributed to rather than reduced effects of workplace stress [166, 167]. A 2016 report by WorkCover Queensland [168] indicated alcohol consumption by construction workers in Queensland was a factor most likely to cause harm—50 percent of adult workers and 60 percent of apprentices drank alcohol at a level that put them at risk, and 25 percent of workers had used either cannabis or methamphetamine in the past year. The report presented no separate data for industry professionals. There were clearly serious industry impacts of stress at play, but the question remained, 'What were the economic impacts?'.

Impact of Stress on International Economies

Workplace stress costs the Australian economy $14.81 billion per year [169]. Stress-related absenteeism and presenteeism (attending work while ill) comprised $10.11 billion of that amount, with an average of 3.2 days per worker across the Australian workforce lost through workplace stress [169].

One in five Australians experience mental health problems annually, but half of senior managers believe none of their employees suffer mental health issues at work [170, 171]. This raised the question, 'were managers unaware of the symptoms of stress/mental health problems, or were workers disguising symptoms?'.

Australians have amassed an average of 21 days of accumulated leave per person across the workforce, a total of 124 million days, and an increase of 24 million days since 2006 [172]. These statistics make little sense—people experience increasing stress effects but fail to take time off. Williams [24] emphasised, with increased workloads and project commitments, a flexible attitude to time off is critical in preventing burnout.

Interestingly, construction was one industry that took vacations, probably because of the across-the-industry end-of-year closedown, necessitated by the inability to obtain supplies because manufacturers also close during that period.

Guthie Chiccarelli and Babic [173] listed ten emerging psycho-social risk factors for work-related stress identified by The European Agency for Safety and Health at Work. These include concerns with employment contracts and job security, longer working hours and job intensification. The literature reveals a change of attitude among employers regarding management of workplace stress, but the extent to which that prevailed within construction was not reported. Points that are clear from the literature were summarised as follows [173, p. 113]:

> *The incidence and prevalence of stress claims since the introduction of (stress claims) exclusions suggest they contribute little to the prevention and management of stress among workers.*

and

> *The continued increase in the costs and incidence of so-called stress claims indicate that there is an asymmetry between the state of knowledge in relation to the prevention of poor mental health which indicates that attention should be directed at interpersonal relations and organisation relations within the workplace.*

Debate concerning whether stress was caused within the workplace did little to alleviate stress effects in the workplace. A change of focus towards stress recognition, avoidance and management was in the interests of all involved [173].

Anxiety, to which stress contributes, increased in Australia between 2011 and 2015 [164], but work was not one of the top five causes of stress identified by an APS survey—it held sixth position. Work was reported a significant contributor to stress by 32 percent of participants, six points less than for the fifth of the major stressors, which was concerns for the health of a close one, reported by 38 percent of participants [164].

Long working hours have had a major impact on Japanese workers. In 2015, some 55.7 percent of Japanese workers reported being severely troubled by workplace conditions and stress [141].

Hassard et al. [174] reported the cost of work-related illness in the European Union was between 185 and 289 billion euros per year, and a cost of at least 20 billion euros was attributed to work-related stress [175, 176]. A more detailed calculation of the cost of work-related depression in Europe by Matrix [177] revealed a more dramatic cost exceeding 616 billion euros annually, comprising 272 billion euros absenteeism and presenteeism, 242 billion euros productivity loss, 63 billion euros health care costs and 39 billion euros disability benefit payments.

These figures are difficult to comprehend in the Australian context. Accordingly, a look at the figures for individual European countries is appropriate to provide context. A 2005 study in France estimated the effects of job stress at between 1.17 and 1.97 billion euros per year [178], including sick leave and medical costs, and loss of productivity. Depression due to high work demands and work-stress-related cardio-vascular disease cost between 650 and 752 million euros and between 388 and 715 million euros, respectively [178]. A more recent study estimated the annual cost of job strain to France's economy in 2007 at between 1.9 and 3.0 billion euros [179].

Between 1.199 and 2.399 billion euros were lost to Germany's economy annually, but workplace stress-related losses were not specified [180]. Between 11 and 27 percent of mental disorders in Spain were attributed to working conditions, and the direct health cost of mental and behavioural disorders due to workplace stress was estimated at up to 372 million euros in 2010 [180]. In Spain, 2.78 million sick days were taken due to temporary mental illness related to work environment during 2010, at a cost to the economy of 170.96 million euros [181]. In addition, stress effects of harassment were once estimated at 52 million euros [182] and that figure increased to 62 million euros in a later study [183].

Stress effects cost Switzerland CHF 4.2 billion annually, and only 4.6 percent of study participants attributed stress effects to non-work stressors [184]. In 1996, the total effect of job strain on the economy was ECU 450 million [176]. In 2016, a trade union survey revealed sick leave taken per thousand employees doubled between 2010 and 2016, with the professions most affected predominantly occupied by women, albeit men in the same professions also suffered from stress [185]. The author of that research argued a clear link between working conditions and stress-related sick leave days.

The literature reveals a range of statistics for the UK but they contain inconsistencies. However, even the lower statistics confirmed that stress substantially impacts the British economy. The cost of stress, depression and anxiety was estimated at 3.6 per billion pounds per annum with 222,000 cases reported [186]. During 2011–2012 financial year, stress was present in 428,000 cases of work-related illness—40 percent of reported cases—at a cost of 13.4 billion pounds to the British economy, and 10.4 billion days were lost due to work-related stress [187] and that increased to 12.5 billion days during the 2016–2017 financial year [188].

The number of cases wherein stress was present in work-related illness increased to 488,000 in 2015/16, and a total of 11.7 million working days were lost to stress-related sick leave. For 2015/2016, stress accounted for 37 percent of all work-related ill health cases and 45 percent of sick leave days [189].

In the USA, three out of four workers described their work as stressful and in the late nineteen nineties stress cost the USA economy $200 billion, with 60 percent of lost work days each year attributed to stress effects [190, 191]. In 2015 that stress-related figure increased to between US$125 and US$190 billion [192]. When the cost of health care to cover organisations for the risk of workplace stress was included, the annual cost of workplace stress in the USA was approximately US$300 billion [193].

In the USA construction was sixth on a list of industries wherein employees stated there were 14 days or more during the previous month on which they perceived their mental health to be poor, and the construction figure of approximately eight percent of employees compared with seventeen percent and thirteen percent for the top two industries, which were retail and transportation/public utilities, respectively [194]. Mitchell and Bates [195] supported the cost to the USA of lost days due to illness but did not specifically target stress-related illness.

Workers suffering from depression missed 68 million days of work due to sick leave more than their non-depressed counterparts [196], and to mid-2013, 12 percent of all workers had been diagnosed with depression at some point during their lifetime, and half of that number had been treated. The literature confirms psychological stress had a significant impact internationally. I shall now address the situation in Australia.

The Cost of Workplace Stress in Australia

Safe Work Australia [197] estimated that AUD 5.3 billion was the annual cost of work-related mental stress. During 2009–2010, Safe Work Australia paid 6,480 claims for mental stress related to work. The median claim value was AUD 12,700, compared with AUD 2500 for all other claims received and paid [197]. Of the claims made, 33 percent related to stress from work pressure, 22 percent related to stress from harassment or bullying, 21 percent relates to exposure to workplace violence and 14 percent to other stress-inducing factors [197]. In 2009, Keegel, Ostrey and La Montagne reported that between 1996–1987 and 2003–2004, physical injury claims in the workplace were decreasing but mental stress-related claims increased by 83 percent. Around the same time, Medibank Private reported an economic impact to Australian employers of $14.81 billion [169].

The cost to Australia of job stress-related depression was AUD 730 million annually and the cost of depression over the sufferers' lifetimes would amount to AUD 11.9 billion [198]. That study included presenteeism as well as absenteeism costs and concluded that $14.81 billion was lost per annum for all stress-related disorders, and not just diagnosed depression. In a rare example of detailed industry statistics, one study reported 285 claims for stress-related illness for construction over a year, as compared with 3065 from education and 4380 from healthcare [51]. That report did not break the construction figures into professional versus trade employees [51].

More recent figures are intriguing. The Safe Work Australia [199] report for 2014–2015 indicated that labourers, technicians and tradespeople accounted for 40 percent of all serious claims, despite making up only 23 percent of the workforce. On the positive side, claims by technicians and tradespeople between 2001 and 2014 reduced by 40 percent, second only to managers at 43 percent. Construction rated third in serious claims with 12 percent of the total, behind health care and social assistance at 16 percent, and manufacturing at 13 percent. Mental illness or disorder made up 5.7 percent of all claims, with 3.7 percent and 9.4 percent of claims made by men and women, respectively. The increase in time lost for mental illness was the second-highest over the study time frame at 38 percent, behind cancers at 44 percent, and mental illness recorded the fourth-highest increase in the median amount of claim at 80 percent increase over the study time frame. These figures provided no information concerning CPMs specifically.

Having identified in the literature data regarding the extent and economic effects of stress-related illness, it was appropriate to compare both prevalence and impact of stress-related disorders, and attitudes to stress and its management, between business-at-large and construction project management [4, 200]. Work-related stress had a significant impact on both the stressed person and his or her employer, but one extreme alternative was equally unattractive. Evidence consistently showed unemployment was associated with increased morbidity and mortality [201, 202].

Stress Effects from Long Working Hours

People worked for numerous reasons other than financial. Work provided people with satisfaction of their sense of purpose, sometimes to the extent that it became part of their identity [58]. Baruch insightfully stated that:

> *Stress is sometimes the price many people are happy to pay for a successful career. It is also a factor that sends successful careers to their downfall.*
>
> Baruch [58, p. 197]

And,

> *In extreme cases, overwork can lead to the ultimate outcome – death due to hard work – known as karoshi in Japan, where it becomes an unfortunate phenomenon in a culture of high stress work environments.*
>
> Baruch [58, p. 200]

Japan was one of several countries that legislated to limit maximum hours worked each week without paying overtime. France led by reducing hours, firstly voluntarily and in 2000, compulsorily, with the objective of reducing unemployment [203]. Japan set its limit at 40 hours [204]. In 2017 the Japanese government reacted to extensive overtime being demanded of workers. A leading Japanese newspaper article opened with:

> *The government has begun making arrangements to set the upper limit for overtime working hours at 720 hours per year, or 60 hours, on average, per month.*
>
> (Yomiuri Shimbun 2017 in The Japan News 2017)

This 'limit' embraced permission for workers to be expected to contribute the equivalent of one and a half additional working weeks per month on average and provided for that figure to be extended to 100 hours for a month on the condition that average overtime hours worked did not exceed 80 hours per month over two consecutive months [205]. The intended legislation was expected to allow additional overtime (over and above the hours stated herein) by special agreement (Sabu Roku Kyotei) between management and labour [205]. The transport and construction industries were not initially covered by the Labour Standards Law, but by separate intended new regulations, after a grace period [205]. Despite what appeared to be faux limitations on working hours, the Japanese took these new regulations seriously, with the administering authority to be chaired by Prime Minister, Shinzo Abe [205].

Japan was not alone in facing the crisis effects of excessive working hours. Burg-Brown [138] found that the average American put in more than one and a half month's unpaid overtime each year because they took phone calls and answered texts and emails after hours [206]. Burg-Brown [138, p. 50] also stated that:

> *It is interesting to see that the more technology people drag into their working day, the more they end up doing. While using technology to stay connected is not all bad, problems arise when people feel obligated to stay connected to their smartphones and emails after work, feeling compelled to respond to instant messages and texts.*

The contemporary organisation was markedly different from that of the late twentieth century. As Weinberg, Sutherland and Cooper 2010 [207, p. 11] succinctly put it:

> *Advances in New Technology and globalisation have ushered in endless possibilities for changes in work environment*

And,

> *So, survival of the fittest becomes the name of the game, and the pace and speed at which the key players can adapt to the continually changing environment is the factor that will determine this survival.*
>
> (Weinberg et al. [207, pp. 21–22])

There is little evidence technology contributed to fewer working hours. Some 16 percent of full-time employees in Australia worked between 50 and 59 hours per week, against the typical standard—37.5 hours [208]. This tendency for Australians to work more than statutory hours was common, with the average additional hours across all full-time workers being 4.9 hours per week in 2005, an increase of 1.7 hours since 1985 [145]. In 2005 males worked 43.2 hours [145], which was significant in what still are predominantly male construction project management environments. However, recent national research showed that full-time construction workers averaged 42.1 hours per week (males = 42.2 hours and females = 41.3 hours) [209]. These hours were insufficient to predict psychological stress. The Chartered Institute of Building (CIOB) in 2006, showed that job demands, poor communications, environmental factors, lack of training and job insecurity were more likely triggers of psychological stress effects within relatively constrained working hours, such as those reported by the ABS research. The stressors quoted in the CIOB research [209] were similar to those for broader British business [189] but ten years after the CIOB study, 'violence threats or bullying' was noted as a significant stressor in the broader business study.

Some researchers strongly believed that the major contributors to stress were non-work factors [7, 108]. Others concurred that such factors contributed to total stress but emphasised the most frequent stressors were work-related [2, 25, 32, 113, 210]. A common stressor among work-related problems was the perception of high job demand but low job control, and studies have found interaction effects between these and adverse health outcomes in occupational groups (construction was not represented) [211, 212].

When research attention focussed on managerial and/or professional groups within a workforce, hours worked and job demand factors were shown to significantly increase, and along with them, stress impacts [209]. In support of this assertion for construction professionals, were the following CIOB findings:

- All respondents were industry professionals with 63 percent being CPMs
- 41 percent of participants were full-time employees in organisations with more than 500 staff
- 82 percent were aged between 26 and 55
- 93 percent were male
- 68.2 percent of respondents had experienced stress, anxiety or depression as a result of working in the industry but only 26.6 percent had sought medical advice
- Only 17.3 percent of those who suffered anxiety sought professional help
- Only 5.9 percent of those who experienced occupational stress took time off from work for that reason, and of those who did, 74 percent were off work for one week or less

These figures raise concern, especially when statistics for the broader UK show the prevalence of work-related stress, anxiety and depression across all workers across all industries was just 1.2 percent from 2013/14 to 2015/16, and the corresponding figure for professionals was 2 percent [189], substantially lower than the CIOB findings [209]. The literature generally recognised increased stress, anxiety and depression had at least a correlative relationship with the performance of CPMs [213–215]. Nothing was found in the literature with similar detail as the CIOB's 2006 report, but specifically relating to CPMs in Australia. The question now to mind was, 'what was the profession, and the construction industry at large doing about the problem and how did that action, if any, compare with action taken within business at large?' [216]

The Extent of Problem Recognition, and Action Being Taken Within Construction at Large

Awareness and recognition of stress impacts on CPMs have become more commonplace because the problem became significant [197] as an increasing number of industry professionals experienced burnout [194, 217]. Burnout typically is caused by the continual stress of maintaining tight schedules and keeping costs within budget [217]. These pressures are exacerbated with downturns in economic cycles. Gonzales [217] reported the global financial crisis saw a reduction of some 23.8 percent in employment of construction workers between 2008 and 2009.

Smith, Bruyns and Evans [218] noted project managers with prior experience of a problem they eventually solved demonstrated learned mastery and showed increased resilience when facing similar future challenges. The Director of Safety, Environment and Education Services for Idaho Associated General Contractors once opined that the construction professionals most at risk of suffering burnout were CPMs, and he added that, for these people, when the phone rings, it was never something good [219].

Organisational leadership for effective utilisation of all workplace resources, minimised workplace stress [220]. However, the nature of the subject industries, which used sub-contracted human resources within rigid contractual frameworks, prevented them from benefitting optimally from this factor [27].

Working conditions are stressful for CPMs not only because of tight budgets and deadlines, but also from environmental stressors including noise and danger [197, 209]. Limm et al. [221] reported the importance of improving working conditions as a primary goal of stress management, but recognised this was often difficult to achieve in practice. It was as if they had CPMs in mind in making this observation, given the noise and other stress-inducing environmental factors within those professions [222].

Problem awareness certainly has increased. The Australian National Survey of Health and Wellbeing [223] found a prevalence of 12-month depression of 3.89 percent for the working male population and 8.41 percent for employed women. Disturbingly, the same study revealed that only 35 percent of people with any mental disorder consulted professional help during the previous year. By 2004, payouts for stress claims were double those for physical injuries in Victoria, representing 83 percent increase between 1996–1997 and 2003–2004. Keegel et al. [14] reported job strain effects were higher among women than men and higher for lower occupational skill levels.

The highest basis of the claim for mental health effects in Australia between 2008–2009 and 2010–2011 was work pressure, which constituted 33 percent of all mental stress claims [197]. Professionals made 26.5 percent of all claims, while associate professionals were in third place at 19.6 percent [197]. Safe Work Australia [197] found construction workers did not rate in the top 15 high-risk occupations for males, and that raises a question. It was important to know whether cultural pressures continued to prevent construction employees from reporting stress from job pressure or if those workers are very adept at heterostasis, without crossing stress limits into the ill-effects of distress. The construction industry rated 12th in number of mental stress claims made in Australia between 2008–2009 and 2010–2011 [197]. The SWA [197] report failed to separate between professionals and tradespeople in industries.

There were large differences between stress reported by CIOB [209] which directly surveyed construction industry professionals, and the statistics from the Safe Work Australia 2013 survey. The CIOB found that 68.2 percent of respondents experienced stress, anxiety or depression and 17.3 percent sought professional help, whereas Keegel, Ostrey and La Montagne [14] reported claims for mental stress compensation in Australia underestimated the actual extent of job strain attributable to depression by a factor of at least 30-fold. In short, the construction industry is one wherein the presence of elevated job strain is not always reflected in actual claims patterns [14]. Claims data in Australia were not a sufficient basis for formulating comprehensive strategic responses to job stress [14, 224] and direct industry survey data, such as obtained by CIOB [209] were preferred.

Compared with available data for business at large the literature is scant regarding stress-effect statistics for CPMs. A review of several models relating to organisational project management maturity led to the conclusion that:

> *The inherent assumption is that perceived maturity levels are as powerful on the individual psyche as actual project management maturity levels.*
>
> Aitken [225, p. 50]

Aitken concluded project managers who perceived they controlled stress triggers within organisations of varying levels of project management maturity experienced 'similar effects as when subjects have actual control' [225, p. 50]. While Aitken's comment seemed superfluous given the substantial literature that addressed the locus of control principle at its core [226, 227], it did provide insight into a mental state that might reduce stress effects in CPMs as it had in non-construction project managers. Aitken's work also inspired this study to avoid looking for connections that could reasonably be assumed to exist and did not need proving beyond the support of the literature available [228]. As McLeod [229, p. 94] stated, '...a key criteria of research quality is the extent to which a theory supplied a complete and coherent account of the data', and qualitative researchers should be aware of likely criticism if they use methods that 'merely finds what they already know'.

Stress and CPMs

The literature covers stress effects identified and coping strategies promoted in professions such as nursing [230], general medical and dental [231], law enforcement [232] and military services [233]. Studies commonly address physiological outcomes of inadequate stress management, such as elevated blood pressure and increased anxiety. The literature also addresses increases over recent decades in anxiety and depression symptoms because of workplace-related stress [76, 234].

There was an increase in studies of the effect of culture and/or a personality on stress impacts [235] and of gender-based perceptions of stress impacts [140, 236]. The literature contains few studies of project managers in general, with the work of Sommerville and Langford [237] and Gällstedt [155] being the best respected. CPMs were recognised as having better expertise in handling stressful situations than employees in consultancy practices or government [158]. Lingard (in Yip and Rowlinson [238]) noted site-based contractors are exposed to different, arguably more extreme stressors than office-based personnel.

Yip and Rowlinson [238] highlight the construction industry's tendency to be cost-driven and to accept the lowest bidder for work despite strong criticism of this practice. They also highlight the impact of this practice on CPMs forced by low-bidding practices to embrace multi-dimensional responsibilities and often conflicting expectations of multiple stakeholders [238].

CPMs face high job demands and low job control when tightly-costed contracts are involved [239], but often do not realise the necessity to have support from supervisors and co-workers if they are to avoid stress [51]. The sources of stress appeared to differ substantially between BPs and CPMs. Kowalski et al. [240] reported 26 percent of respondents to a workplace survey reported aggressive acts, mostly verbal and passive, were the main cause of their workplace stress.

Informal investigation revealed CPMs expressed disbelief at those findings, possibly revealing more about the level of stressor regarded as acceptable within construction than about research participants in Kowalski et al.'s study [241].

The Kowalski et al. study [240] concludes that less stress and aggression leads to better employee satisfaction and better business results, something few CPMs would debate. In contrast to Kowalski et al. [240] is Yip and Rowlinson's [238] assertion that burnout is widespread in construction, and the industry risked a reduction in efficiency that could impact the long-term competitiveness of the sector. In 2005, McCormick [242] recognised people can work intensely for short periods without ill-effect, but continuing at high levels of output, common within construction, led to burnout. Yip and Rowlinson [238] and Gonzalez [217] agree that long working hours, concerns about job security and role conflict and ambiguity are key factors behind alarmingly high burnout levels among CPMs. Both managers and employees should recognise burnout is sinister and does not appear quickly, rather taking the path of a gradual process of response to exposure to stress over time [217, 238]. Burnout comprises three diagnostic characteristics—exhaustion, cynicism (leading to irritability and withdrawal) and inefficacy (reduced sense of accomplishment and an inability to cope) [243].

CPMs might make light of what appeared to members of their tough culture as soft nonsense causing stress for people in general business [240]. They would be better off accepting they too are affected more than they might admit by work practices more and more regarded as a sure path to burnout [131, 166, 238]. Thankfully, there is increasing recognition of the problem, which probably began when Lingard [7], Densten [244] and Maslach, Schaufeli and Leiter [243] developed models to comprehend modern industry burnout, rather than rely on the older three-factor models based around emotional exhaustion, cynicism and reduced professional efficacy [238]. Maslach, Schaufeli and Leiter [243] developed an Organisational Check Up Survey to assess work overload, lack of control, insufficient reward, breakdown of community, absence of fairness and value conflict.

Two points of interest emerged from this finding:

1. Karasek et al. [239] and Siegrest et al. [245] Kristensen [246] developed similar models for detecting strain and burnout
2. I found several burnout indicators in the models prevalent among CPMs

We must recognise high levels of stress also apply Among APs and BPs, with withdrawal behaviours and increases in workplace accidents and staff turnover often the consequences [247].

One stressogenic factor common to CPMs and BPs was job insecurity [248]. Job insecurity motivates employees to work harder than required to gain favour from managers in critical job reduction/redundancy situations [248]. This leads to stress that contributes to simple but often costly mistakes, decreases efficiency and increases illness and absenteeism, often resulting in the outcome the employee sought to avoid [248]. Coping with multiple demands leads to stress overload that causes people to act without thinking, often with serious effects [249].

It seems appropriate today to follow advice from 2005:

> *It's a timely thing for construction companies to look at the long-hours culture, both in the office and on the site.*
>
> Renshaw in McCormick [250, p. 25]

The impact of psychological stress on job performance is well-documented [45, 66, 221, 251, 252]. Decrease in job performance of CPMs has serious potential impact due to the inherently dangerous nature of construction work. Also, behaviours ranging from inferior work and stealing from employers to various types of white-collar crime have been linked with workplace stress [251]. Workplace stress often occurs when there is a lack of reciprocity between the effort workers perceives they contribute and the rewards they receive, and a potential link exists between that and employee actions (e.g. stealing) to balance perceived inequities [253].

Returning to our metaphoric couple, we find Will has received no assistance in regard to his mounting stress from work pressure, but my research revealed even when assistance in the form of EAPs and the like are offered by employers, CPMs are reticent to take advantage of them for fear of appearing weak to their managers. I address this topic in some detail after research findings are presented.

It might well be that Will's employers have some impression of the pressure their staff are under. However, in the economic circumstances existing in South East Queensland at the time of writing, construction-related organisations are having great difficulty employing well-qualified and experienced professional staff at anything like the usual levels of salary for the positions in question, and employers perceive they have little choice but to continue to allocate the most complex work to their most experienced employees and hope that all will be well.

Clare continues to run home and family, as well as attend her own work, but her concern for Will's situation is now leading to her being even less inclined to raise the matter and discuss it with Will, for fear of adding to his already heavy burden of pressure. Both parties know they need to do something about their circumstances, but each feels lost for action to take. They might well be experiencing what is known in psychology as 'locus of control' problems, and so I will address those now.

Support and Locus of Control Impacts on Stress

The psychology concept of locus of control proposes stress is often dependent on not only job demands, but also the employees' perception of their level of control over delivering what is expected [239, 254–258]. This is especially true for CPMs facing immovable contractual deadlines. Reticence by senior managers to delegate authority as well as responsibility establishes among CPMs a perception of low control [259], often worsened by employees' perceptions of economy-related job insecurity [254].

The literature is somewhat inconsistent on this point. Davidson and Sutherland [256] identified site CPMs facing strong deadlines reported the highest levels of stress, but Djebarni [157] posited moderate workplace stress, and not low levels of stress, was the ideal for site CPMs.

A point of significant interest for CPMs arose from social capital [260], the links between an individual and supportive resources within private networks at work. Higher levels of social capital result in lower stress levels and effects [260]. There is a strong case for social capital connections within workplaces when one in ten workers in the USA experienced depression and 200 million working days were lost annually at a treatment cost of $30–$44 billion [260].

Construction industry mateship in Australia effectively constituted the social capital promoted by Gächter et al. [260] It is so well recognised within the industry the Mates in Construction organisation used it as a promotional theme for a recent campaign under the banner, 'Mateship Matters' [115]. Interestingly, a study by Crawford [261] (of organisational project managers) indicated management attitudes contributed to an unhealthy tendency to suppress reporting stress effects triggered within their work environment [261].

Gächter et al. [260] investigated social support as a means of ameliorating stress effects but did not investigate CPMs specifically. They found women had higher stress levels than men but use social support, which buffers individuals against both acute and chronic levels of stress, more than men. They also highlighted a key cause of perception of low social capital is feeling oneself to be an outsider.

The literature showed no clear distinction between stress triggered at home and that triggered within the workplace for BPs. Lingard and Sublet [26] found that was also the case for CPMs, confirming each of home and work lives are adversely affected by stress triggered in the other [26] However, it is more likely workplace factors are likely to be the major stressors for CPMs [27] and the methodology for this study includes a means of testing this hypothesis.

Lingard and Sublet [26] also found a high quality of family and marital life moderates for the better the impact of career role quality on an individual's state of psychological distress. They found a link between remuneration level and hours at work, and that the most important factor in participants' home relationship quality was hours worked [26]. Interestingly, Alhaug and McLaughlin [82] found female managers struggled to balance family and work commitments and this struggle especially in predominantly male professions. Among predominantly male CPMs, women felt under pressure to work longer hours to achieve respect [82].

Organisations that expect CPMs to manage increasing stress in the absence of stress avoidance and management training and support effectively abdicate responsibility, and possibly elevated their workplace to something fitting the Colligan and Higgins [45, p. 93] description of toxic, wherein, '…relentless demands, extreme pressure, and brutal ruthlessness' are prevalent, and wherein employees, '…operated consistently in fear, paranoia, and increased anxiety states'.

Knowledge Gap

This literature review facilitated identification of gaps in knowledge regarding aspects of stress among CPMs, the key components of which can be identified in the following:

- Organisations overloading CPMs without affording them control or authority to refuse additional work could constitute a risk to their health, and those CPMs might not report stress experienced fearing they would look weak, or risk losing their jobs
- CPMs might experience stress differently from APs and BPs
- It is not certain whether construction industry culture and processes contribute to the stress of CPMs, or if their stress is caused more by work factors or personal factors
- It is not clear to what extent construction organisations utilise stress avoidance or management techniques, or to what extent CPMs use maladaptive stress management techniques
- It is suspected but not clear whether locus of control issues regarding work contributed to the stress experienced by CPMs, or whether workplace-generated stressors had an impact on their personal lives and relationships

Several of these gap points can be seen to be reflected in the Will and Clare relationship. Certainly, the first bullet point above has been the major factor in Will's workload which, in turn, has been a major contributor to the stress he experiences. It is probably fair to say the contractual deadline/s on his key project/s contribute to him experiencing stressors in his life quite differently from people in construction organisations who are not impacted by contractual deadlines, and people from across business at large. This aligns with the second bullet point above. I have already dedicated a section in this chapter to the locus-of-control matter, but it is appropriate for reasons that will become apparent in the following chapters, that I leave further discussion of this point to a later chapter, along with the third bullet point above, which deals with industry culture impacts on the effects of stress.

We have a reasonable sense of what Will and Clare are personally experiencing, but as yet, we do not understand why each of them continue with avoidance behaviours which might well contribute to lack of resolution of the problems they are facing. The following chapters will provide an answer to that question.

Summary of Chapter

In this chapter, I reviewed literature pertaining to the definition and nature of stress and its effects, with the goal of understanding how stress develops and affects human beings. I examined literature regarding stress effects across business at large and identified useful information relating to stress impacts on CPMs. I investigated burnout with focus on how it impacts CPMs and studied the impact of stress on international economies and the Australian economy. Finally, I defined a knowledge gap.

In the literature I found no conclusive research that provided a firm basis for assuming the objectives of this study had previously been fulfilled. This identified lack of important knowledge justified the pursuit of the research objectives stipulated in Chapter 1.

In project management phases parlance, I have now reached the point of more clearly understanding the knowledge gap and confirmed the approach by which I intend to address it. In psychotherapy phases terms, I have a better understanding of Will and Clare's issue and would feel confident progressing to an intervention strategy that both addressed the elements of the issue that I currently understood, while continuing to gain deeper insights into the structure of the problem and its drivers as I progressed. Of course, a psychotherapist could not do this in the case of Will and Clare, because neither has seen the value in actually deciding to consult a mental health professional. Accordingly, we will continue to review and assess their situation in the context of this study, in the following chapters.

It is now time to move on to find answers to the knowledge gap identified, and Chapter 3 pursues that objective via an analysis of quantitative data collected.

References

1. Cohen, S, Janicki-Deverts, D & Miller, G 2007, 'Psychological stress and disease', *The Journal of the American Medical Association*, vol. 298, no. 14, pp. 1685–1687.
2. Cox, T, Griffiths, A & Houdmont, J 2006, *Defining a case of work-related stress. Research Report 449*, United Kingdom, HSE Books, viewed 17th August 2016, http://www.hse.gov.uk/research/rrpdf/rr449.pdf.
3. APSC 2017, *As one—working together: promoting mental health and well-being at work*. Australian Public Service Commission, Canberra, viewed 11th October 2017, www.comcare.gov.au/static/mental_health/files/assets/common/downloads/As%20One%20Working%20Together.pdf.
4. Noblet, A & La Montagne, A 2006, 'The role of workplace health promotion in addressing job stress', *Health Promotion International*, vol. 21, no. 4, pp. 346–353.
5. Lynch, C, Sundaram, R, Maisog, J, Sweeney, A & Buck-Louis, G 2014, 'Preconception stress increases the risk of infertility: results form a couple-based perspective cohort study—the LIFE study', *Human Reproduction*, vol. 29, no. 5, pp. 319–332.
6. Van der Molen, H & Hoonakker, P 2000, 'Work stress in the construction industry: causes and measures', *Proceedings of the Human Factors and Ergonomics annual meeting*, vol. 5, pp. 651–657.
7. Lingard, H, 2003, 'The impact of individual and job characteristics on 'burnout' among civil engineers in Australia and the implications for employee turnover', *Construction management and Economics*, vol. 21, no. 1, pp. 69–80.
8. Lingard, H & Francis, V 2006, 'Does a supportive work environment moderate the relationship between work-family conflict and burnout among construction professionals?' *Construction Management and Economics*, vol. 24, no. 2, pp. 185–196.

9. Shaw, P, Johnson, M & Shaw, R 1988, Counselling needs: emotional and relationship problems in couples awaiting IVF. *Journal of Psychosomatic Obstetrics and Gynecology*, vol. 9, pp. 171–180.
10. Edelmann, R, Connolly, K & Bartlett H 1994, 'Coping strategies and psychological adjustment of couples presenting for IVF', *Journal of Psychosomatic Research*, vol. 38, pp. 355–364, in 11
11. Eugster, A & Vingerhoets, A 1999, 'Psychological aspects of in vitro fertilization: a review', *Social Science & Medicine*, vol. 48, no. 5, pp. 575–589.
12. Lord, S & Robertson, N 2005, 'The role of patient appraisal and coping in predicting distress in IVF', *Journal of Reproductive and Infant Psychology*, vol. 23, no. 4, pp. 319–332.
13. Patching, A. 2016, 'A qualitative analysis of women who have undergone a multi-stage psychotherapy and hypnotherapy intervention to manage psychological stress while undergoing in-vitro fertilisation: what were their experiences and outcomes?' *International Journal of Counseling Psychotherapy and Psychiatry: Theory, Research and Clinical Practice*. Available from: http://ijpcp.com/journal02/J02a05.asp.
14. Keegel, T, Ostrey, A & La Montagne, A 2009, 'Job strain exposures versus stress-related workers' compensation claims in Victoria, Australia; developing a public health response to job stress', *Journal of Public Health Policy*, vol. 30, no. 1, pp. 17–39.
15. Rosch, P n.d., 'Reminiscences of Hans Selye and the birth of 'stress'', viewed 28th March 2017, https://www.stress.org/hans-selye-birth-of-stress/.
16. Selye, H 1936, *Textbook of Endocrinology*, University of Montreal, Montreal.
17. Selye, H 1950, 'Stress and the General Adaption Syndrome', *British Medical Journal*, viewed 28th March 2017, https://www.ncbi.nlm.nih.gov/pmc/articles/PMC2038162/pdf/brmedj03603-0003.pdf.
18. Yeung, A, Ivkovic, A & Friccione, G 2016, *The science of stress*, Ivy Press, Brighton UK.
19. Selye, H 1956, *The Stress of Life*, McGraw-Hill, New York.
20. Cannon, W 1915, *Bodily changes in pain, hunger, fear and rage*. D. Appleton and Company, New York, NY.
21. Flynn, G & Patching, A 2006, *Imprints for Success*, Brisbane, Revray Publishing.
22. Selye, H 1951, 'The general adaption syndrome', *Annual Review of Medicine*, vol. 2, pp. 327–342, https://doi.org/10.1146/annurev.me.02.020151.001551.

23. Leiter, M 1993, in Schaufeli, W, Maslach, C & Marek, T (eds.) 1993, *Professional burnout—recent developments in theory and research* Taylor and Francis, Philadelphia, PA.
24. Williams, P 2005, 'Design/construction consultant offers tips to prevent occupational burnout', *Daily Commercial News and Construction Record*, vol. 78, no. 22, p. 7.
25. Waite, A 2012, 'Battling workplace burnout', *OT Practice*, vol. 17, no. 17, pp. 9–12.
26. Lingard, H & Sublet, A 2010, 'The impact of job and organisational demands on marital or relationship satisfaction and conflict among Australian civil engineers', *Construction Management and Economics*, vol. 20, no. 6, pp. 507–521.
27. Patching, A & Best, R 2014, 'An investigation into psychological detection and management in organisations operating in project an construction management', *Procedia—Social and Behavioural Sciences*, vol. 119, pp. 682–691.
28. Pocock, B & Wilson, L (research assistant) 2001, *The effects of long hours on family and community life: A survey of existing literature*, Report for the Queensland Department of Industrial Relations, Queensland Government, Brisbane.
29. Alexander, M & Baxter, J 2005, 'Impacts of stress on family life among partnered parents of young children', *Family Matters*, viewed 7th April 2017, https://aifs.gov.au/sites/default/files/ma%281%29.pdf.
30. Baxter, J & Alexander, M 2008, 'Mothers' work-to-family-strain in single and couple parent families: the role of job characteristics and supports', *Australian Journal of Social Issues*, vol. 43, no. 2, pp. 195–214.
31. Teasdale, E 2006, 'Workplace stress', *Psychiatry*, vol. 5, no. 7, pp. 251–254.
32. Nakao, M 2010, 'Work related stress and psychosomatic medicine', *BioPsycho Social Medicine*, vol. 4, no. 4.
33. Arthur, A 2000, 'Employee Assistance Programmes: the emperor's new clothes of stress management', *British Journal of Guidance and Counselling*, vol. 28, no. 4, pp. 549–559, viewed 2nd August 2016, https://www-tandfonline-com.ezproxy.bond.edu.au/doi/pdf/10.1080/03069880020004749?needAccess=true.
34. World Health Organization 1946, Preamble to the Constitution of the World Health Organization as adopted by the International Health Conference, New York, 19–22 June 1946, signed on 22 July 1946 by

the representative of 61 states, Official records of the World Health Organization, no. 2, p. 100 (in 32).
35. Burton, J, Hoobler, J & Scheuer, M 2012, 'Supervisor workplace stress and abusive supervision: the buffering effect of exercise', *Journal of Business Psychology*, vol. 27, no. 3, pp. 271–279.
36. Otto, K & Schmidt, S 2007, 'Dealing with stress in the workplace: compensatory effects of belief in a just world' *European Psychologist*, vol. 12, no. 4, pp. 272–282.
37. Bhatara, M & Kumar, S, 2012, 'Corporate stress of managers', *Golden Research Thoughts*, vol. 2, no. 5, pp. 1–5.
38. American Psychological Association 2013, *Diagnostic and statistical manual of mental disorders* (5th ed.), American Psychiatric Press, Washington, DC.
39. American Psychological Association 2000, *Diagnostic and statistical manual of mental disorders* (4th ed. Text Revision), American Psychiatric Press, Washington, DC.
40. Bystritsky, A & Kronemyer, D 2014, in Kirsch, D & Woodbury-Farina, M (eds.) *Clinics review articles from psychiatric clinics in North America—stress in health and disease*. Elsevier, Philadelphia (p. 492).
41. Bystritsky, A & Kronemyer, D 2014, in Kirsch, D & Woodbury-Farina, M (eds.) *Clinics review articles from psychiatric clinics in North America—stress in health and disease*. Elsevier, Philadelphia (p. 493).
42. Jensen, E & Laurie, C 2016, *Doing Real Research*, Sage, London.
43. NIOSH 1999, *Stress at work*, National Institute of Health and Safety, Cincinatti (OH) Viewed 4th April 2017, https://www.cdc.gov/niosh/docs/99-101/default.html.
44. Selye, H 1975, *Homeostasis and Heterostasis*, Springer, New York.
45. Colligan, T & Higgins, E 2008, 'Workplace stress', *Workplace Behavioural Health*, vol. 21, no. 2, pp. 89–97.
46. Hanson, P 1986, *The Joy of Stress*, Pan Books, London.
47. Cooper, C & Baglioni, A 1988, 'A structural model approach towards the development of a theory of the link between stress and mental health', *The British Journal of Medical Psychology*, vol. 61, no. 1, pp. 87–102.
48. Mohsin, S & Wahab, A 2013, 'Stress management and steps of managing stress', *Asia Pacific Journal of Management and Entrepreneurship Research*, vol. 2, no. 1, pp. 164–172.
49. Steimer, T 2002, 'The biology of fear and anxiety-related behaviours', *Dialogues in Clinical Neuroscience*, vol. 4, no. 3, pp. 231–249, viewed

28th January 2018, https://www.ncbi.nlm.nih.gov/pmc/articles/PMC3181681/.
50. Harvard Health Publishing 2015, 'Race and ethnicity: clues to your heart disease risk?' viewed 30th January 2018, https://www.health.harvard.edu/heart-health/race-and-ethnicity-clues-to-your-heart-disease-risk.
51. ACSC 2007, *Compendium of workers' compensation statistics Australia 2004–05*, Safe Work Australia, Canberra, viewed 4th April 2017, https://safeworkaustralia.gov.au/system/files/documents/1702/compendiumofworkerscompensationstatistics_2004_2005_pdf_archivepdf.pdf.
52. Taylor, C 2014, 'Workstress on the increase in Australia', viewed 11th April 2017, www.hcamag.com/hr-news/workplace-stress-on-the-increase-in-australia-194165.aspx.
53. Siegel, D 2010, *Mindsight: the new science of personal transformation.* Random House USA Inc., New York.
54. Clark, H n.d., 'Adrenal fatigue—From chronic stress to complete burnout', viewed 13th October 2017, https://www.vibrantagain.com/adrenal-fatigue-from-chronic-stress-to-complete-burnout/.
55. Melchoir, M, Caspi, A, Milne, B, Danese, A, Poulton, R & Moffit, T 2007, 'Workstress precipitates depression and anxiety in young working men and women', *Psychological Medicine*, vol. 37, pp. 1119–1129.
56. Sapolsky, R 2010, *Stress and Your Body*. The Great Courses: Chantilly, VA.
57. Porter, E 1973, *Relationship awareness theory—manual of administration and interpretation.* Personal Strengths Publishing, Carlsbad, USA.
58. Baruch, Y 2009, 'Stress and careers: the role of workplace factors on health', in Cooper, C, Quick, J & Schabracq, M (eds.) *International handbook of work and health psychology*, Wiley, West Sussex.
59. Bedeian, A 1995, 'Workplace envy', *Organisational Dynamics*, vol. 23, no. 4, pp. 49–56.
60. Lingard, H & Francis, V 2009, *Managing work-life balance in construction*, Spon Press, Milton Park.
61. Sang, K, Dainty, A & Ison, S 2004, 'The impact of structure and culture of the construction industry on employee well-being: directions for future research', in Khosrowshahi, F (ed.) *20th Annual ARCOM Conference*, 2004, Association of Researchers in Construction Management, vol. 1, pp. 495–503.
62. Yip, B & Rowlinson, S 2006, 'Coping strategies among construction professionals: cognitive and behavioural effects to manage job stressors', *Journal of Education in the Built Environment*, vol. 1, no. 2, pp. 70–79,

viewed 13th October 2017, www.tandfonline.com/doi/pdf/https://doi.org/10.11120/jebe.2006.01020070www.tandfonline.com/doi/pdf/10.11120/jebe.2006.01020070.
63. Loosemore, M & Waters, T 2004, 'Gender differences in occupational stress in the construction industry', *Journal of Management in Engineering*, vol. 20, no. 3, pp. 126–132.
64. Blau, P 1964, *Exchange and power in social life*, New York, Wiley
65. Siegrist, J 2012, *Effort—reward imbalance at work—theory, measurement and evidence*. Department of Medical Sociology, University of Duesseldorf, Duesseldorf, viewed 30th January 2018, http://www.uniklinik-duesseldorf.de/fileadmin/Datenpool/einrichtungen/institut_fuer_medizinische_soziologie_id54/ERI/ERI-Website.pdf.
66. Coffey, M, Dugdill, L & Tattersall, A 2009, 'Designating a stress management intervention in social services', *International Journal of Workplace Health Management*, vol. 2, no. 2, pp. 98–114.
67. Miles, C & Hardman, E 1998, 'State dependent memory produced by aerobic exercise' *Ergonomics*, vol. 41, no. 1, viewed 14th October 2017, www.tandfonline.com/doi/abs/10.1080/001401398187297.
68. Lang, A, Craske, M, Brown, M & Ghanelan, A 2001, 'State dependent memory', *Cognition and Emotion*, vol. 15, no. 5, viewed 14th October 2017, www.tandfonline.com/doi/abs/10.1080/02699930125811.
69. Aronson, D 2009, 'Cortisol—its role in stress, inflammation and indications for diet therapy', *Today's Dietician*, vol. 11, no. 11, p. 38.
70. Cohen, S, Janicki-Deverts, D, Doyle, W, Miller, G, Frank, E, Robin, B & Turner, R 2012, 'Chronic stress, glucocorticoid receptor resistance inflammation and disease risk', *Proceedings of the National Academy of Science of the USA*, 109. 5995–5999, viewed 2nd April 2017, https://www.ncbi.nlm.nih.gov/pmc/articles/PMC3341031/.
71. Shonkoff, J, Boyce, W & McEwen, B 2009, 'Neuroscience, molecular biology and the childhood roots of health disparities: building a new framework for health promotion and disease prevention', JAMA, vol. 301, no. 21, pp. 2252–2259, viewed 14th October 2017, https://jamanetwork.com/journals/jama/fullarticle/184019.
72. A.D.A.M. 2017, 'Stress and anxiety', *New York Times Health Guide* (article edited by Simon, H. Harvard Medical School).
73. Brown, F & Fee, E 2002, 'Walter Bradford Cannon—Pioneer physiologist of human emotions', *The American Journal of Public Health*, vol. 92, no. 10, pp. 1594–1595, viewed 28th January 2018, https://www.ncbi.nlm.nih.gov/pmc/articles/PMC1447286/.

74. HGI 2012, '7–11 Breathing: how does deep breathing make you feel more relaxed? Human Givens Institute: United Kingdom', viewed 14th October 2017, blog.humangivens.com/2012/10/How-does-deep-breathing-make-you-feel.html.
75. Tyrell, M n.d., *Seven eleven breathing*, Audio programme, Uncommon Knowledge, viewed 28th July 2011, https://www.hypnosisdownloads.com/relaxation-techniques/breathing.
76. Beyond Blue n.d., 'Men in the workplace', viewed 15th May 2018, https://www.beyondblue.org.au/who-does-it-affect/men/what-causes-anxiety-and-depression-in-men/men-in-the-workplace.
77. Steptoe, A & Whitehead, D 2005, 'Depression, stress and coronary heart disease—the need for more complex models', *British Medical Journal*, vol. 91, no. 4, pp. 419–420, viewed 28th March 2017, https://www.ncbi.nlm.nih.gov/pmc/articles/PMC1768812/.
78. Lane, D, Caroll, D & Ring, C 2001, 'Mortality and quality of life 12 months after myocardial infarction; effects of depression and anxiety', *Psychosomatic Medicine*, vol. 63, pp. 221–230.
79. Lane, D, Caroll, D & Lip, G 2005, 'Depression, indirect clinical markers of carcial disease severity and mortality following myocardial infarction', *Heart*, vol. 91, pp. 531–532, viewed 28th March 2017, https://www.ncbi.nlm.nih.gov/pmc/articles/PMC1768854/.
80. Lane, D, Caroll, D & Lip, G 2003, 'Anxiety, depression and prognosis after myocardial infarction: is there a causal association?' *Journal of the American College of Cardiologists*, vol. 42, pp. 1808–1810, viewed 28th March 2017, https://ncbi.nlm.nih.gov/pubmed/14642692.
81. National Cancer Institute 2012, *Psychological Stress and Cancer*, viewed 14th October 2017, https://www.cancer.gov/about-cancer/coping/feelings/stress-fact-sheet.
82. Alhaug, C & McLaughlin (2006) 'Just coping: Australian female project managers' perceptions of stress', in Charlesworth, S, Douglas, K, Fastenau, M, & Cartwright, S (eds.) *Women and work 2005: current RMIT University research*. Melbourne, RMIT Publishing 2006:143–153.
83. Richmond, A & Skitmore, M 2006, 'Stress and coping: a study of project managers in large ICT organisations', *Project Management Journal*, vol. 37, no. 5, pp. 5–16.
84. Ericson-Lidman, E & Strandberg, G 2007, 'Burnout: co-workers' perceptions of signs preceding workmates' burnout', *Journal of Advanced Nursing*, vol. 60, no. 2, pp. 199–208.

85. Eugene, A & Masiuk, J 2015, 'The neuroprotective aspects of sleep', *Medtube Science*, vol. 3, no. 1, pp. 35–40, viewed 7th March 2018, https://www.ncbi.nlm.nih.gov/pmc/articles/PMC4651462.
86. ASA n.d., *Stages of sleep*, viewed 28th March 2017, https://www.sleepassociation.org/patients-general-public/what-is-sleep/.
87. HGI n.d., '7–11 Breathing: how does deep breathing make you feel more relaxed? Human Givens Institute: United Kingdom', blog.humangivens.com/2012/10/How-does-deep-breathing-make-you-feel.html
88. Elliot, R & Tyrell, M 2003, *The depression learning path*, Uncommon Knowledge Limited, East Sussex UK, viewed 22nd February 2017, www.uncommon-knowledge.co.uk/training_workshops.html.
89. Elliot, R & Tyrell, M n.d., *The uncommon knowledge depression programme*. Uncommon Knowledge, UK.
90. Moore, H 2004, '10 Proven antidotes for workplace burnout', *Vibrant Life*, vol. 20, no. 2, pp. 12–15.
91. ENR 2010, 'Blog research on burnout', viewed 22nd January 2017, https://www.enr.com/blogs/13-critical-path/post/15368-burnout-tell-us-if-construction-s-culture-of-self-sacrifice-is-killing-you.
92. CDCP 2013, 'Sleep and chronic disease', Centre for Disease Control and Prevention, viewed 28th March 2017, https://www.cdc.gov/sleep/about_sleep/chronic_disease.html.
93. Bianchi, M (ed.) 2014, Sleep deprivation and disease: effects on the body, brain and 'behaviour. Springer, New York.
94. Andrews, W, Twigg, E, Minami, T & Johnson, G 2011, Piloting a practice research network: a 12-month evaluation of the Human Givens approach in primary care at a general medical practice, viewed 28th March 2017, https://www.ncbi.nlm.nih.gov/pubmed/22903882.
95. Andrews, W, Wislocki, A, Short, F, Chow, D & Minami, T 2013, 'A five-year evaluation of the Human Givens Therapy using a practice research network', *Mental health Review Journal*, vol. 18, no. 3, pp. 165–176.
96. Bonanno, G 2004, 'Loss, trauma and human resilience: have we underestimated the human capacity to thrive after aversive events?' *American Psychologist*, vol. 59, no. 1, pp. 20–28.
97. Maddi, S 2005, 'On hardiness and other pathways to resilience', *American Psychologist*, vol. 60, no. 3, pp. 261–262.
98. Southwick, S, Vythilingam, M & Charney, D 2005, 'The psychobiology of depression and resilience to stress: implications for prevention

and treatment', *Annual Review of Clinical Psychology*, vol. 1, pp. 255–291, viewed 28th March 2017, https://www.ncbi.nlm.nih.gov/pubmed/17716089.
99. Herman, J, Ostrander, M, Mueller, N & Figueiredo, H 2005, 'Limbic system mechanisms of stress regulation: hypothalamus-pituitary-adrenocortical axis', *Progress in Neuro-Psychopharmacology and Biological Psychiatry*, vol. 29, no. 8, pp. 1201–1213.
100. Beilby, J 2004, 'Definition of metabolic syndrome: report to the National Heart, Lung, and Blood Institute/American Heart Association conference on scientific issues related to definition', *Clinical Biochemistry Review*, vol. 25, no. 3, pp. 195–198, viewed 28th January 2018, https://www.ncbi.nlm.nih.gov/pmc/articles/PMC1880831/.
101. Kaur, J 2014, *A comprehensive review on metabolic syndrome*, Cardiology Research and Practice, viewed 30th March 2017, https://www.ncbi.nlm.nih.gov/pmc/articles/PMC3966331/.
102. Grundy, S, Brewer, H, Cleeman, J, Smith, S & Lenfant, C 2004, *Definition of metabolic syndrome*, Report of the National Heart, Lung and Blood Institute for the American Heart Association conference on scientific issues related to metabolic syndrome.
103. George, K, Alberti, M, Zimmet, P & Shaw, J 2005, 'The metabolic syndrome: a new worldwide definition', *The Lancet*, vol. 366, no. 9491, pp. 1059–1062.
104. NIH 2016, *How is metabolic syndrome diagnosed?* National Institute of Health—The National Heart, Lung and Blood Institute, Viewed 30th March 2017, https://www.nhlbi.nih.gov/health-topics/metabolic-syndrome.
105. 'Diabetes Australia n.d., Hyperglycaemia', viewed 14th October 2017, http://www.diabetesaustralia.com.au/hyperglycaemia.
106. Diabetes.co.uk n.d., 'Visceral fat and insulin resistance', viewed 14th October 2017, www.diabetes.co.uk/body/visceral-fat.html.
107. Mayo Clinic 2016, *Metabolic syndrome: symptoms and causes*, viewed 30th March 2017, www.mayoclinic.org/diseases-conditions/metabolic-syndrome/symptoms-causes/dxc-20197520.
108. Lingard, H & Francis, V 2004, 'The work-life experience of office and site based employees in the Australian Construction Industry', *Construction Management and Economics*, vol. 22, no. 9, pp. 991–1002.
109. Woo, J-M & Postolache, T 2008, 'The impact of work environment on mood disorders and suicide: evidence and implications', *International*

Journal of Disability and Human Development, viewed 31st March 2017, https://www.ncbi.nlm.nih.gov/pmc/articles/PMC2559945/.

110. Largo-Wight, E, Chen, W, Dodd, V & Weiler, R 2011, 'Healthy workplaces: the effects of nature contact at work on employee stress and health', *Public Health Report*, vol. 126 (suppl.1) pp. 124–130, viewed 13th October 2017, https://www.ncbi.nlm.nih.gov/pmc/articles/PMC3072911/.
111. Shea, T, Pettit, T & De Cieri, H 2011, *Work environment stress: the impact of the physical work environment on psychological health. A snapshot review*, Monash University—Business and Economics, Melbourne, viewed 31st March 2017, https://www.iscrr.com.au/workplace-health-and-safety/maintaining-mental-health-and-wellbeing/monitoring-mental-health-at-work.
112. Sparks, K, Faragher, B & Cooper, C 2001, 'Well-being and occupational health in the 21st century workplace', *Journal of Occupational and Organizational Psychology*, vol. 74, pp. 489–509.
113. Albertsen, K, Rugulies, R, Garde, A & Burr, H 2010, 'The effect of the work environment and performance-based self-esteem on cognitive stress symptoms among Danish knowledge workers', *Scandinavian Journal of Public Health*, vol. 38, no. 3, pp. 81–89.
114. Clarke, S & Cooper, C 2004, *Managing the risk of workplace stress*, New York, Routledge.
115. WorkCover Queensland 2017, *Mateship Matters regional Queensland tour. Workplace Health and Safety*, viewed 30th January 2018, https://www.worksafe.qld.gov.au/construction/articles/mateship-matters-regional-queensland-tour.
116. Gaillard, A 1993, 'Comparing the concepts of mental load and stress', *Ergonomics*, vol. 36, no. 9, pp. 991–1005.
117. NBC n.d., *Job stress can affect your children—report on the annual meeting of the American Psychoanalytical Association* 2007, television programme, NBC News, viewed 30th March 2017, www.nbcnews.com/id/16795195/ns/health-lifescience/t/job-stress-can-affect-your-children/#.WNylRBKGPx4.
118. Rao, T & India, V 2010, 'Work, family or personal life: why not all three?' *Indian Journal of Psychiatry*, vol. 52, no. 4, viewed 30th March 2017, https://www.ncbi.nlm.nih.gov/pmc/articles/PMC3025152/.
119. Schieman, S in Agrell, S 2010, 'How job stress affects home life', *The Seattle Times*, viewed 30th March 2017, www.seattletimes.com/life/lifestyle/how-job-stress-affects-home-life/.

120. Tsutsumi, R & Webster, N 2009, 'GnRH pulsatility, the pituitary response and reproductive dysfunction', *Endocrine Journal*, vol. 56, no. 6, pp. 729–737, viewed 22nd August 2016, https://www.ncbi.nlm.nih.gov/pubmed/19609045.
121. Brkovich, A & Fisher, W 1998, 'Psychological distress and infertility: 40 years of research', *Journal of Psychosomatic Obstetrics and Gynaecology*, vol. 19, no. 4, pp. 218–228, viewed 22nd August 2016, www.ncbi.nlm.nih.gov/pubmed/9929848.
122. Isles, R, interview by Patching, A 2014, 'Saliva based bio-markers for stress in infertility and other matters', unpublished interview, London, [on-line] available at https://alanpatching.wistia.com/projects/bygnvigi69.
123. Sapolsky, R 2003, 'Stress and plasticity in the limbic system', *Neurochemical Research*, vol. 28, no. 11, pp. 1735- 1742.
124. Ebbesen, S, Zachariae, R, Mehisen, M, Thomsen, D, Hojgaard, A, Ottosen, L, Petersen, T & Ingerslev, H 2009, 'Stressful life events are associated with a poor in-vitro fertilisation (IVF) outcome: a prospective study', *Human Reproduction*, vol. 24, no. 9, pp. 2173–2182, viewed 18th July 2014, humrep.oxfordjournals.org/content/24/9/2173.long
125. Lazarus, R & Folkman, S 1994, *Stress appraisal and coping*. Springer (re-issue), New York.
126. Chirumbolo, A & Areni, A 2010, 'Job insecurity influence on job performance and mental health: testing the moderating effect of the need for closure', *Economic and Industrial Democracy*, vol. 31, no. 2, pp. 195–214.
127. Dill, K 2014, 'Survey: 42% of employees have changed jobs due to stress', Forbes Magazine—Leadership, viewed 30th March 2017, https://www.forbes.com/sites/Kathryndill/2014/04/18/survey-42-of-employees-have-changed-jobs-due-to-stress/#626712023380.
128. Besser, D 2006, *The experience of women in construction management: a hermeneutic, phenomenological study*, University of Minnesota Press, Minnesota, USA.
129. Arditi, D, Gloch, P & Holmdahl, M 2013, 'Managerial competencies of female and male construction managers in the Swedish construction industry', *Construction Management and Economics*', vol. 31, no. 9, pp. 979–990.
130. Varvogli, L & Darviri, C 2011, 'Stress management techniques: evidenced-based procedures that reduce stress and promote health', *Health Science Journal*, vol. 5, no. 2, pp. 74–89.

131. Melia, J & Becerril, M 2007, 'Psychosocial sources of stress and burnout in the construction sector: a structural equation model', *Psicotherma*, vol. 19, no. 4, pp. 679–686.
132. AFOM 1999, *Workplace attendance and absenteeism*, Australasian Faculty of Occupational Medicine, Sydney, viewed 12th May 2018, https://www.racp.edu.au/docs/default-source/faculties-library/workplace-attendance-and-absenteeism.pdf?sfvrsn=4.
133. Hawgood J, Heller, T & De Leo D 2006, 'Investigation into Suicide in Queensland's Commercial Building Construction Industry, Brisbane, Australian Institute for Suicide Research and Prevention, Griffith University.
134. BERT 2008, 'About mates in construction. Building employees redundancy trust', viewed 3rd August 2016, http://www.bert.com.au/Media/Default/Forms/AboutMatesInConstruction.pdf.
135. Action Alliance n.d., *A construction industry blueprint: suicide prevention in the workplace.* National Action Alliance for Suicide Prevention Resources, viewed on 15th October 2017, https://theactionalliance.org/resource/construction-industry-blueprint-suicide-prevention-workplace.
136. APS 2013, *Stress and wellbeing in Australia Survey 2013.* Australian Psychological Society, viewed 2nd August 2016, https://search.informit.com.au/fullText;dn=667381261970680;res=IELAPA.
137. Kain, J & Jex, S 2010, 'Karasek's (1979) job demands-control model: A summary of current issues and recommendations for future research', in Perrewé, P & Ganster, D (eds.) 'New Developments in theoretical and conceptual approaches to job stress' *Research in Occupational Stress and Well-being*, vol. 8, pp. 237–268.
138. Burg-Brown, S 2013, 'Work-life balance', *Journal of Property Management*, vol. 78, no. 4, pp. 48–53.
139. Knez, I 2016, *Toward a model of work-related self: a narrative review*, Frontiers in Psychology—Organizational Psychology, viewed 30th March 2017, journal.frontiersin.org/article/10.3389/fpsyg.2016.00331/full.
140. Iwasaki, K, Takahashi, M & Nakata, A 2006, 'Health problems due to long working hours in Japan: working hours, workers compensation (Karoshi) and preventative measures', *Industrial Health*, vol. 44, no. 4, pp. 537–540.
141. Statista 2017, Percentage of employees feeling severely insecure and stressed in their working environment in Japan from 1997–2015, viewed 30th May 2018, https://www.statista.com/statistics/623230/japan-stress-at-work/.

142. Iacuone, D 2005, 'Real men are tough guys: hegemonic masculinity and safety in the construction industry', *The Journal of Men's Studies*, vol. 13, no. 2, pp. 247–266.
143. Bacon, C & Morgan, H 2015, 'From tough guys to tears: the construction industry embraces safety', viewed 15th October 2017, the hill.com/blogs/congress-blog/labor/241365-from-tough-guys-to-tears-the-construction-industry-embraces-safety
144. AI Group 2015, 'Construction outlook', *Australian Industry Group*, viewed 12th July 2017, https://www.aigroup.com.au/policy-and-research/economics/constructionoutlook/.
145. ABS 2016, *Employee earnings and hours, Australia, May 2016*, Australian Bureau of Statistics, Canberra, viewed 6th April 2017, http://www.abs.gov.au/ausstats/abs@.nsf/0/27641437D6780D1FCA2568A9001393DF?Opendocument.
146. Mates in Construction n.d., *Industry partnership program*, viewed 1st February 2018, http://matesinconstruction.org.au/get-involved/partnerships/.
147. AISRAP 2006, 'Suicide in Queensland's commercial building and construction industry', The Australian Institute for Suicide Research and Prevention, Brisbane, viewed 21st February 2014, https://matesinconstruction.org.au/wp-content/uploads/2016/03/2006-MIC_AISRAP-Report.pdf.
148. Arthur, A 2002, 'Mental health problems and British workers: a survey of mental health problems in employees who receive counseling from Employee Assistant Programmes', *Stress and Health*, vol. 18, no. 2, pp. 69–74, viewed 2nd August 2016, onlinelibrary.wiley.com/doi/10.1002/smi.930/abstract.
149. Daniels, S 1997, 'Employee assistance programmes', *Work Study* (now the *International Journal of Productivity and Performance*) vol. 46, no. 7, pp. 251–253.
150. Cooper, G & Cartwright, S 1997, 'An intervention strategy for workplace stress', *Journal of Psychosomatic Research*, vol. 43, no. 1, pp. 7–16, viewed 2nd August 2016, www.sciencedirect.com/science/article/pii/s0022399996003923.
151. Cook, M & Cripps, B 2005, *Psychological assessment in the workplace*, Wiley, New York.
152. APSC 2017, *As one—working together: promoting mental health and well-being at work.* Australian Public Service Commission: Canberra, viewed

11th October 2017, www.comcare.gov.au/static/mental_health/files/assets/common/downloads/As%20One%20Working%20Together.pdf.
153. Tetric, l, Slack, K, Da Silva, N, & Sinclair, R 'A comparison of the stress-strain process for business owners and non-owners: differences in job demands, emotional exhaustion, satisfaction and social support', *Journal of Occupational Health Psychology*, vol. 5, no. 4, pp. 464–476.
154. Prottas, D, & Thompson, C 2006, 'Stress, satisfaction, and the work-family interface: a comparison of self-employed business owners, independents, and organizational employees', *Journal of Occupational Health Psychology*, vol. 11, no. 4, pp. 366–378, viewed 2nd August 2016, https://doi.org/10.1037/1076-8998.11.4.366.
155. Gällstedt, M 2003, 'Working conditions in projects: perceptions of stress and motivation among project team members and project managers', *International Journal of Project Management*, vol. 21, no. 6.
156. Keller, R 2001, 'Cross functional project groups in research and new product development: diversity, communications, job stress and outcomes', *Academy of Management Journal*, vol. 44, no. 3, pp. 547–555, viewed 24th August 2016, http://amj.aom.org/content/44/3/547.short.
157. Djebarni, R 1996, 'The impact of stress in site management effectiveness', *Construction Management and Economics*, vol. 14, no. 4.
158. Ng, S, Skitmore, R, & Leung, T 2005, 'Manageability of stress among construction participants', *Engineering, Construction and Architectural Management*, vol. 12, no. 3, pp. 264–282.
159. Leung, M, Chan, Y-S, and Olomolaiye, P 2008. 'Impact of stress on the performance of construction project managers', *Journal of Construction, Engineering and Management*, vol. 134, no. 8, viewed 2nd August 2016, https://doi.org/10.1061/(ASCE)0733-9364(2008)134:8(644).
160. Antonovsky, A 2002, in Marks, D (ed.) 2002, Marvelling the mystery of health: how people manage stress and stay well. Sage, London.
161. Stansfeld, S & Candy, B 2006, 'Psycho-social work environment and mental health—a meta analytic review', *Scandinavian Journal of Work, Environment and Health*, vol. 32, no. 6, pp. 443–462.
162. EU-OSHA 2009, 'OSH in figures—stress at work-facts and figures', viewed 16th September 2017, https://osha.europa.eu/en/tools-and-publications/publications/osh-figures-stress-work-facts-and-figures/view.
163. Chong, J & Chong, D 2017, *Neuro-Semantic Programming (NSP)-Epiepistemology*. C-Jade Publications Inc., Toronto.
164. APS 2017, *Stress and wellbeing in Australia Survey 2015*. Australian Psychological Society, viewed 2nd December 2017, https://www.hea

dsup.org.au/docs/default-source/default-document-library/stress-and-wellbeing-in-australia-report.pdf?sfvrsn=7f08274d_4.
165. Harvey, S, Joyce, S, Modini, M, Christensen, H, Bryant, R, Mykletun, A & Mitchell, P 2012, 'Work and depression/anxiety disorders—a systematic review of reviews', viewed 2nd April 2017, https://www.beyondblue.org.au/docs/default-source/research-project-files/bw0204.pdf?sfvrsn=4.
166. Bowen, P, Edwards, P, Lingard, H & Cattell, K 2014, 'Workplace stress, stress effects and coping mechanisms in the construction industry', *Journal of Construction Engineering and Management*, vol. 140, no. 3.
167. Sutherland, V & Cooper, C 1994, 'Stress in the work environment', in Rose, J. (ed.) *Human Stress and the Environment.* Gordon and Breach Science Publishers, Yverden, Switzerland.
168. WorkCover Queensland 2016, *Alcohol and drug use in the construction industry*, viewed 15th October 2017, https://www.worksafe.qld.gov.au/forms-and-resources/podcasts/podcasts-list/construction-forum/presentation-10-drugs-and-alcohol-in-construction.
169. Medibank 2008, *The cost of workplace stress in Australia*, Medibank Private, Melbourne, viewed 27th March 2015, www.medibank.com.au/client/documents/pdfs/the-cost-of-workplace-stress.pdf.
170. Hilton, M, Whiteford, H, Sheridan, J, Cleary, C, Chant, D, Wang, P & Kessler, R 2008, 'The prevalence of psychological stress in employees and associated risk factors', *Journal of Occupational and Environmental Medicine*, vol. 50, no. 7, pp. 746–757.
171. AHRC 2010, *Workers with mental illness: A practical guide for managers.* Australian Human Rights Commission, Sydney, viewed on 2nd April 2017, https://www.humanrights.gov.au/sites/default/files/document/publication/workers_mental_illness_guide_0.pdf.
172. Reynolds, C 2015, 'Australia's sick note culture: why we're reaching breaking point', *News.com.au*, viewed 2nd April 2017, www.news.com.au/finance/work/at-work/australias-sick-note-culture-why-were-reaching-breaking-point/news-story/45374d9a591a1d7e89f6c8ef43a770f0.
173. Guthrie, R, Ciccarelli, M & Babic, A 2010, 'Work-related stress in Australia: The effects of legislative interventions and the cost of treatment', *International journal of Law and Psychiatry*, vol. 33, pp. 101–115, viewed 2nd April 2017, www.abc.net.au/cm/lb/6150194/data/mental-stress-claim-get-harder-data.pdf.

174. Hassard, J, Teoh, K, Cox, T, Dewe, P, Cosmar, M, Grundler, R, Fleming, D, Cosemans, B & Van den Broek, K 2014 *Calculating the cost of work-related stress and psychosocial risk*, European Agency for Safety and health at Work, Bilboa, Spain, viewed 2nd April 2017, https://osha.europa.eu/en/publications/literature_reviews/calculating-the-cost-of-work-related-stress-and-psychosocial-risks/view.
175. Davies, N & Teasdale, P 1994, The cost to the British economy of work-related accidents and work-related ill-health. Health and Safety Executive, London.
176. Levi, L & Lund-Jensen, P 1996, *A model for assessing the cost of stressors at national level* European Foundation for Living and Working Conditions, Dublin.
177. Matrix 2013, Economic analysis of workplace mental health promotion and mental disorder prevention programmes and of their potential contribution to European health, social and economic policy objectives, viewed 3rd April 2017, http://ec.europa.eu/health/mental_health/docs/matrix_economic_analysis_mh_promotion_en.pdf.
178. Bejean, S and Sultan-Taieb, H 2005, 'Modelling the economic burden of diseases imputable to stress at work', *European Journal of Health Economics*, vol. 50, pp. 26–46.
179. Trontin, C, Lassagne, M, Boini, S & Rinal, S 2007, *Le Cout du stress professionnel en France en 2007*, Institut National de Recherche et du Securite, Paris.
180. Booz and Company in EU-OSHA 2014, 'Calculating the Cost of Work-Related Stress and Psychological Risks', European Agency for Safety and Health at Work, viewed 6th April 2017, https://osha.europa.eu/en/publications/literature_reviews/calculating-the-cost-of-work-related-stress-and-psychosocial-risks/view.
181. UGT, *Costes Socio-Económicos de los Riesgos Psicosociales*, UGT-CEC, 2013 [on-line], available at: http://www.ugt.es/saludlaboral/observatorio/publicaciones/new2013/GuiaCostes.pdf.
182. EASHW 2014, *Calculating the cost of work related risks and psychosocial factors*, European Agency for Safety and Health at Work, viewed 19th October 2017, http://publications.europa.eu/resource/cellar/c8328fa1-519b-4f29-aa7b-fd80cffc18cb.0001.01/DOC_1.
183. Camero & Martinez 2006, in EU-OSHA 2014, 'Calculating the cost of work-related stress and psychological risks', European Agency for Safety and Health at Work, viewed 6th April 2017, https://osha.europa.eu/en/

publications/literature_reviews/calculating-the-cost-of-work-related-stress-and-psychosocial-risks/view.
184. Ramaciotti, D & Perriard, J 2003, Die kosten des stresses in der Schweiz, Staatssekretariat für Wirtschaft SECO, Bern, [on-line], http://www.seco.admin.ch/dokumentation/publikation/00008/00022/01511/index.html.
185. Magnusson, V in King, W 2006, 'Stressed out: tension—a silent killer for Sweden's economy', viewed 4th April 2017, https://sputniknews.com/europe/20160331103725 6422-sweden-economy-stress-welfare/.
186. HSE 2011/2012, *Annual statistics report for 2011–2012*, Health and Safety Executive, London, viewed 18th August 2016, http://www.hse.gov.uk/statistics/overall/hssh1112.pdf.
187. HSE 2013, *Stress and psychological disorders in Great Britain*, Health and Safety Executive, London, viewed 18th August 2016, http://www.hse.gov.uk/statistics/causdis/stress/stress.pdf.
188. 2017, *Work related stress, depression or anxiety*, Health and Safety Executive, London, viewed 22nd October 2018, http://www.hse.gov.uk/statistics/causdis/stress/.
189. HSE 2016, Work related stress, anxiety and depression statistics in Great Britain, viewed 5th April 2017, www.hse.gov.uk/statistics/causdis/stress/stress.pdf?pdf=stress.
190. Maxon, R 1999, 'Stress in the workplace: a costly epidemic', *FDU Magazine*, viewed 4th April 2017, www.fdu.edu/newspubs/magazine/99su/stress.html.
191. Withers, D, Liu, D & Agrawal, S 2013, *Depression costs US workplaces $23 billion in absenteeism*, Gallup, Washington, viewed 4th April 2017, https://news.gallup.com/poll/163619/depression-costs-workplaces-billion-absenteeism.aspx.
192. Blanding, M, 2015, 'Workplace stress responsible for up to $190 billion annual US healthcare costs', HBS Working Knowledge in Forbes, viewed 4th April 2017, https://www.forbes.com/sites/hbsworkingknowledge/2015/01/26/workplace-stress-responsible-for-up-to-190-billion-in-annual-u-s-healthcare-costs/#7262ad2a235a (page no longer available).
193. EKU on line in Smith, J 2016, 'Stress at work is costing employers $300 billion a year: here's why' East Kentucky University, viewed 4th April 2017, https://www.businessinsider.com.au/how-stress-at-work-is-costing-employers-300-billion-a-year-2016-6?r=US&IR=T.
194. NIOSH 2002, *Stress at work*, National Institute of Health and Safety, Cincinatti (OH) viewed 13th August 2016, http://www.cdc.gov/niosh/docs/99-101/pdfs/99-101.pdf.

195. Mitchell, R & Bates, P 2011, 'Measuring health-related productivity loss', *Population health Management*, vol. 14, no. 2, pp. 93–98 viewed 4th April 2017, https://www.ncbi.nlm.nih.gov/pmc/articles/PMC3128441/.
196. Brown, A 2013, 'Gallup's top 10 US well-being discoveries in 2013', viewed 5th April 2017, news.gallup.com/poll/166640/gallup-top-discoveries-2013.aspx
197. Safe Work Australia 2013, *The incidence of accepted workers' compensation claims for mental stress in Australia*, viewed 11th April 2017, https://www.safeworkaustralia.gov.au/system/files/documents/1702/the-incidence-accepted-wc-claims-mental-stress-australia.pdf.
198. KPMG-Econtech 2008, 'Australian national, state and industry outlook,' Canberra, ACT.
199. Safe Work Australia 2017, *Australian workers compensation statistics, 2014–2015*, viewed 16th October 2017, https://www.safeworkaustralia.gov.au/system/files/documents/1707/australian-workers-compensation-statistics-2014-15-revised_1.pdf.
200. LaMontagne, A, Keegel, T, Louis, A, Ostry, A & Landsbergis, P 2007, 'A systematic review of the job stress intervention literature 1990–2005', *International Journal of Occupational and Environmental Health*, vol. 13, no. 3, pp. 268–280.
201. Stern, J 1983, 'The relationship between unemployment, morbidity and mortality in Britain', *Population Studies; a Journal of Demography*, vol. 37, no. 1, pp. 61–74.
202. Lundin, A 2011, 'Unemployment and morbidity and mortality—epidemiological studies', PhD thesis, Karolinska Institutet, Stockholm, viewed 16th October 2017, https://openarchive.ki.se/xmlui/bitstream/handle/10616/40759/Spikblad_Lundin.pdf?sequence=2&isAllowed=y.
203. AIFS 2015, *Review of government initiatives for reconciling work and family Life. Research Report Number 34*, Australian Institute of Family Studies, Canberra, viewed 5th April 2017, https://aifs.gov.au/publications/review-government-initiatives-reconciling-work-and-family-life/5-working-hours-and-other-aspects-employment.
204. Lee et al. 2007, in AIFS 2015, *Review of government initiatives for reconciling work and family Life. Research Report Number 34*, Australian Institute of Family Studies, Canberra, viewed 5th April 2017, https://aifs.gov.au/publications/review-government-initiatives-reconciling-work-and-family-life/5-working-hours-and-other-aspects-employment.
205. Yomiuri Shimbun (newspaper) 2017, 'Average monthly overtime likely to be capped at 60 hours', *The Japan News, Tokyo edition* p. 3.

206. Google Technology in Burg-Brown, S 2013, 'Work-life balance', *Journal of Property Management*, vol. 78, no. 4, pp. 48–53.
207. Weinberg, A, Sutherland, V & Cooper, C, 2010, *Organisational stress management: a strategic approach*. Palgrave Macmillan Ltd., London.
208. ABS 2003, *Australian social trends 2003*. Australian Bureau of Statistics, Canberra, viewed 6th April 2017, http://www.abs.gov.au/AUSSTATS/abs@.nsf/46d1bc47ac9d0c7bca256c470025ff87/923EC292ABA4493 2CA2570EC00006EE7?opendocument.
209. CIOB 2006, 'Occupational stress in the construction industry'. *Chartered Institute of Building research report*, viewed 6th July 2016, https://policy.ciob.org/wp-content/uploads/2006/03/Occupational-Stress-in-the-Construction-Industry-March-2006.pdf.
210. See 118. Sparks, K, Faragher, B & Cooper, C 2001, 'Well-being and occupational health in the 21st century workplace', *Journal of Occupational and Organizational Psychology*, vol. 74, pp. 489–509.
211. Fox, M, Dwyer, D & Ganster, D 1993, 'Effects of stressful job demands and control on physiological and attitudinal outcomes in a hospital setting', *The Academy of Management Journal*, vol. 36, no. 2, pp. 289–318.
212. Parkes, K, Mendham, C & Von Rabenau 1994, 'Social support and the demand—discretion model of job stress: tests of additive and interactive effects in two samples', *Journal of Vocational Behaviour*, vol. 44, no. 1, pp. 91–113.
213. Haynes, N & Love, P 2004, 'Psychological adjustment and coping among construction project managers', *Construction Management and Economics*, vol. 22, no. 2, pp. 129–140.
214. Love, P & Edwards, D 2005, 'Taking the pulse of UK constructions managers' health: influence of job demands, job control and social support on psychological wellbeing', *Engineering, Construction and Architectural Management*, vol. 12, no. 1, pp. 88–101, viewed 6th April 2017, https://doi.org/10.1108/09699980510576916.
215. Leung, M, Chan, Y-S & Yu, J 2009, 'Integrated model for stressors and stresses of construction project managers in Hong Kong', *Journal of Construction, Engineering and Management*, vol. 135, no. 2, viewed 6th April 2017, ascelibrary.org/doi/abs/10.1061/(ASCE)0733-9364(2009)135:2(126).
216. Comcare n.d., 'Creating mentally healthy workplaces', viewed 11th October 2017, https://www.comcare.gov.au/promoting/Creating_mentally_healthy_workplaces.

217. Gonzalez, J 2010, 'Lack of construction jobs: stress could lead to burnout', The Idaho Business Review, Idaho, USA.
218. Smith, D, Bruyns, M & Evans, S 2009, 'A project manager's optimism and stress management and IT project success', *International Journal of Managing Projects in Business*, vol. 4, no. 1, pp. 10–27.
219. Christ, T 2007, 'A Recursive Approach to Mixed Methods Research in a Longitudinal Study of Postsecondary Education Disability Support Services', *Journal of Mixed Methods Research*, vol. 1, no. 3, pp. 226–241, viewed 19th December 2017, http://journals.sagepub.com/doi/10.1177/1558689807301101.
220. Maciocha, A, Surakka, J, & Nasman, O 2012, 'Work ability and social inclusion project: enhancing collective knowledge through leadership and stress management', *The European conference on intellectual capital. Kidmore End Academic Conferences International Limited*.
221. Limm, H, Gundel, H, Heinmuller, M, Martin-Mittag, B, Nater, U, Siegrist, J & Angerer, P 2011, 'Stress management interventions in the workplace improve stress reactivity: a randomized controlled trial', *Occupational and Environmental Medicine*, vol. 68, no. 2, pp. 126–133.
222. Senaratne, S& Rasagopalasingam, V 2017, The causes and effects of work stress in construction project managers: the case in Sri Lanka, International Journal of Construction Management, vol. 17, no. 1, pp. 65–75, https://doi.org/10.1080/15623599.2016.1167358.
223. Department of Health 2007, 'National survey of mental health and wellbeing', Australian Government Department of Health, viewed 5th April 2017, abs.gov.au/statistics/health/mental-health/national-survey-mental-health-and-wellbeing-summary-results/latest-release.
224. LaMontagne, A, & Keegel, T 2012, *Reducing stress in the workplace - an evidence review: full report*, Victorian Health Promotion Foundation, Melbourne, viewed 11th October 2017, www.vichealth.vic.gov.au/workplace/.
225. Aitkens, A 2011, 'Coping strategies of project managers in stressful situations', PhD thesis, Bond University, Gold Coast, QLD.
226. Spector, P 1982, 'Behavior in organizations as a function of employee's locus of control', *Psychological Bulletin*, vol. 91, no. 3, pp. 482–497.
227. Lefcourt, H 1991, 'Locus of control', in Robinson, J, Shaver, P & Wrightman, L (eds.), *Measures of personality and social psychology attitudes* (pp. 413–425), Academic Press Ltd. London, https://doi.org/10.1016/B978-0-12-590241-0.50013-7.

228. Brown, E. 2011, "Duh' science: why researchers spend so much time proving the obvious', *Los Angeles Times*, Los Angeles.
229. McLeod, J 2003, *Doing counselling research*, Sage, London.
230. Khodadadi, E, Hosseinzadeh, M, Azimzadeh, R, & Fooladi, M 2016, 'The relation of depression, anxiety and stress with personal characteristics of nurses in hospitals of Tabriz, Iran', *International Journal of Medical Research and Health Sciences*, vol. 5, pp. 140–148, viewed 3rd November, 2018, https://www.researchgate.net/publication/308969364_The_relation_of_depression_anxiety_and_stress_with_personal_characteristics_of_nurses_in_hospitals_of_Tabriz_Iran.
231. Isikhan, V, Comez, T, and Danis, M 2004, 'Job stress and coping strategies in health care professions working with cancer patients', *European Journal of Oncological Nursing*, vol. 8, no. 3, pp. 234–244.
232. Patterson, G 2003, Examining the effects of coping and social support on work and life stress among police officers, *Journal of Criminal Justice*, vol. 31, no. 3, pp. 215–226, viewed 15th August 2017, ncjrs.gov/App/Publications/abstract.aspx?ID=200350.
233. Bray, R, Camlin, C, Fairbank, J, Dunteman, G & Wheeless, S 2001, 'The effects of stress on job functioning of military men and women', *Armed Forces Soc.*, vol. 27, no. 3, pp. 397–417.
234. Kohler, A 1996, *Managerial stress—the construction industry's hidden enemy*, Transactions of AACE International. PM4-PM4.7.
235. Ghorbani, N, Krauss, S, Watson, P & LeBreton, D 2008, 'Relationship of perceived stress with depression: Complete mediation by perceived control and anxiety in Iran and the United States', *International Journal of Psychology*, vol. 43, no. 6, pp. 958–968, viewed 17th August 2017, https://www.tandfonline.com/doi/abs/10.1080/00207590701295264?src=recsys&journalCode=pijp20.
236. Portello, J & Long, B 2001, 'Appraisals and coping with workplace interpersonal stress: A model for women managers', *Journal of Counselling Psychology*, vol. 48, no. 2, pp. 144–156, viewed 27th August 2017, https://www.researchgate.net/publication/287538036_Appraisals_and_coping_with_workplace_interpersonal_stress_A_model_for_women_managers.
237. Sommerville, J & Langford, V 1994, 'Multivariate influences on the people side of projects: stress and conflict', *International Journal of Project Management*, vol. 12, no. 4, pp. 234–243.

238. Yip, B & Rowlinson, S 2009, 'Job burnout among construction engineers working within consultancy and contracting organisations' *Journal of Management in Engineering*, vol. 25, no. 3, pp. 122–130.
239. Karasek, R, Brisson, C, Kawakami, N, Houtman, I, Bongess, P, & Amick, B (abstract) 1998, 'The Job Content Questionnaire (JCQ): an instrument for internationally comparative assessments of psychosocial job characteristics', *Journal of Occupational Health Psychology*, vol. 3, no. 4, pp. 322–355.
240. Kowalski, R, Harmon, J, Yorks, L & Kowalski, D 2003, 'Reducing workplace stress and aggression: an action research project at the US Department of Veterans' Affairs', *HR Human Resource Planning*, vol. 26, no. 2, pp. 39–53.
241. Rick, J, Hillage, J, Honey, S & Perryman, S 1997, *Stress: big issue—but what are the problems?* Institute for Employment Studies, Brighton UK, viewed 29th January 2018, http://www.employment-studies.co.uk/system/files/resources/files/331.pdf.
242. McCormick, H 2005, 'Stress busting', *Contract Journal*, vol. 430, no. 6542, pp. 24–25.
243. Maslach, C, Schaufeli, W & Leiter, M 2001, 'Job Burnout', *Annual Review of Psychology*, vol. 52, pp. 397–422.
244. Densten, I 2001, 'Rethinking burnout', *Journal of Organizational Behaviour*, vol. 22, pp. 833–847.
245. Siegrist, J, Starke, D, Chandola, T, Godin, I, Marmot, M, Niedhammer, I & Peter R 2004, 'The measurement of effort-reward imbalance at work: European comparisons', *Journal of Social Science Medicine*, vol. 58, no. 8, pp. 1483–1499.
246. Kristensen, T, Borritz, M, Villadsen, E & Christensen, K 2005, 'The Copenhagen Burnout Inventory: a new tool for the assessment of burnout' (abstract), *Work & Stress*, vol. 19, no. 3, pp. 192–207, https://doi.org/10.1080/02678370500297720.
247. Leka, S & Jain, J 2010, *Health impacts of psychosocial factors at work: an overview*. World Health Organisation, Geneva, viewed 29th January 2018, http://apps.who.int/iris/bitstream/10665/44428/1/9789241500272_eng.pdf.
248. Saylu, A 2007, 'Foreigners and workplace stress', *Journal of Independent Employment Rights*, vol. 12, no. 4, pp. 313–327.
249. Bimonte, A 1994, 'Beating workplace stress', *Workplace Safety*, vol. 39, no. 5, p. 6.

250. Renshaw, in McCormick, H 2005, 'Stress busting', *Contract Journal*, vol. 430, no. 6542, pp. 24–25.
251. Vagg, P & Spielberger, C 1998, 'Occupational stress: measuring job pressure and organizational support in the workplace', *Journal of Occupational health Psychology*, vol. 3, no. 4, pp. 294–305.
252. Lambert, V, Lambert, C & Yamase, H 2003, 'Psychological hardiness, workplace stress, and related stress reduction strategies', *Nursing and Health Sciences*, vol. 5, no. 2, pp. 181–184.
253. Siegrist, J 1996, 'Adverse health effects of high effort—low reward conditions', *Journal of Occupational Health Psychology*, vol. 1, no. 1, pp. 27–41.
254. Bowen, P, Edwards, P & Lingard, H 2012, 'Workplace stress experienced by construction professionals in South Africa', *Journal of Construction Engineering and Management*, vol. 139, no. 4, pp. 393–403.
255. Rotter, J. (1990) Internal versus external control of reinforcement: a case history of a variable. *American Psychologist*, 45. 489–493 [online]. Available from: https://pdfs.semanticscholar.org/c92a/377531f46046b32d6cc8e18c3787caaea310.pdf [Accessed on 25th January 2018].
256. Zimbardo, P in Baer, D 2004, 'How your locus of control drives your success (and stress)', *Business Insider Australia*, viewed 25th January 2018, https://www.businessinsider.com.au/proactive-people-are-successful-and-less-stressed-2014-7?r=US&IR=T.
257. Khan, A, Saleem, M & Shahid, R 2012, 'Buffering role of locus of control among the college/university teachers of Bahawalpur', *The Pakistan Journal of Commercial Social Science*, vol. 6, no. 1, pp. 158–167, viewed 25th January 2018, https://pdfs.semanticscholar.org/797e/1e64da6b141bac5e1b1fd9259900ad0cee3e.pdf.
258. Ongolla, P, Aloka, P, & Raburu, P, 2016, 'Relation between locus of control and stress management among high school principals in Kenya', *International journal of Applied Psychology*, vol. 6, no. 5, pp. 150–155, viewed 25th January 2018, https://doi.org/10.5923/j.ijap.20160605.03.
259. Patching, A & Waitley, D 1996, *The futureproof corporation*, Singapore, Butterworth-Heinemann, Asia.
260. Gächter M, Savage, D & Torgler, B 2011, 'The relationship between stress, strain and social capital', *Policing*, vol. 34, no. 3, pp. 515–540.
261. Crawford, L 2005, 'Senior management's perception of project managers' competence', *International Journal of Project Management*, vol. 23, no. 11, pp. 4–16.

3

Understanding What the Data Told About the Problem

Introduction

In the first chapter, I explained the evolution of this work from the results of a pilot study and began relating the book's content with the phases of project management and of psychotherapy. In Chapter 2, I progressed the work, via a literature review, along parallels of the planning stage of project management, wherein the development of basic project concepts depends upon progressive and consistent development of project documents based on the continued collection of salient information, and of the phase of determining problem extent in a psychotherapy process. The second chapter provided a deeper understanding of stress, addressing the science behind it and the impacts it can have physiologically and psychologically, as well as the impacts on

In project management (PM) parlance—the IMPLEMENTATION phase, and for this work the first sub-phase, execution—or getting on with the delivery of the main work of the project.
In psychotherapy parlance—the GATHERING DETAILED DATA AND DETERMINING INTERVENTION STRATEGY session.

A. Patching, *Attitudes to Psychological Stress Among Construction Professionals*,
https://doi.org/10.1007/978-3-030-93776-8_3

world economies. Important stress-related concepts, including General Adaption Syndrome, heterostasis and locus of control were explained.

In this chapter, I explain the findings from analysis of quantitative data collected, in order to determine important information about the problem of stress, its impacts on construction professionals, and the attitudes of those professionals to avoiding and managing it. Let us commence with a look at the stage at which we have arrived in our two parallel circumstances of project management processes and psychotherapy practice processes. You might be surprised at how these parallels take on greater importance in providing a framework within which to better understand the subject matter of this book as the work progresses.

In the implementation stage of project management, focus is on project delivery. This phase is broken into two sub-phases generally referred to as execution phase and monitoring and control phase. These terms are self-explanatory. In relation to the project of this research work, execution involves really developing an understanding of the problem being addressed—both its structure and its causes. The first of these is covered in this chapter while the second continues in the following chapter.

In the psychotherapy world, the third phase involves commencing the intervention strategy, but continuing to gain a deeper understanding of a presenting problem and its drivers, in order to refine the strategy to ensure the optimum outcome. The parallels between this psychotherapeutic process stage and the progressive collection and analysis of data in research are strong. I will now address the analysis of quantitative data collected.

To test the research hypotheses, I conducted descriptive and inferential statistics using the Statistical Package for the Social Sciences software (SPSS). Prior to running any statistical analyses, I checked assumptions to ensure that the data was suited for the use of multivariate analyses of variance (MANOVA). All analyses used an alpha level of 0.05, which was achieved unless otherwise stated. Given the exploratory nature of the research, I structured survey questions into sub-categories in order to obtain data relevant to each sub-component of the major hypotheses. I then analysed data in relation to these sections individually and computed no composite scores. Where percentages are relevant in tables within this chapter, I presented them in parentheses.

In the full study, inferential and descriptive statistics were conducted for the two independent variables, role of participant (RP) and organisation size (OS). However, to respect the word count limit for this book, I will present full details regarding RP-related findings, but only more important findings regarding OS.

Data Diagnostics

I checked the dataset for missing values. Initially 750 individuals responded to the questionnaire. Considering the G*power [1, 2] calculation indicated 385 participants would provide power of 0.95, I removed from the dataset respondents who did not answer all compulsory questions. The final number of participants was 489. For the optional items, the percentage of missing value did not exceed 20 percent, which I considered acceptable in research that involves a component of a social nature [3]. I checked the assumption of normality via visual inspection of the histograms and using skewness and kurtosis values. Data was negatively skewed at times. However, given the nature of the variables, I concluded that was to be expected. Additionally, MANOVA was found to be robust to slight violation of normality [4]. I identified univariate outliers with Box and Whisker's plots and identified multivariate outliers using Mahalanobis distance. I computed analysis with and without these extreme cases. Results showed that these outliers were not significantly affecting the data, and as such I decided to retain them. The assumption of linearity was met as shown with cigar shape scatterplots. I checked the absence of multi-colinearity and singularity using Pearson's correlation, and found it to be met. The dataset violated the balanced design assumption for OS χ (2, N = 489) = 133.04, $p < .001$ and for RP, χ (2, N = 489) = 74.98, $p < .001$. Details are provided later herein. Consequently, results had to be interpreted with caution. I found the assumption of homogeneity of variance to be met, unless otherwise specified in the text.

Description of the Participants Sample

Detailed Constitution of Final Participant Sample

There was a total of 489 participants. In statistical analyses I used two key independent variables (IV):

Organisation Size = OS
Role of Participant = RP

OS was established to align with the Australian Bureau of Statistics:

- A Small Organisation (SO) constituted 1–19 employees
  - 84 participants (17.18 percent)
- A Medium Organisation (MO) constituted 20–199 employees
  - 124 participants (25.36 percent)
- A Large Organisation (LO) constituted 200 or more employees
  - 281 participants (57.46 percent).

RP was one of three:

- Construction Project Management Professional, referred to herein as CPM
  - 253 participants (51.74 percent)
- Construction Administration Personnel and any other direct supporter of CPMs, referred to herein as AP
  - 124 participants (25.36 percent)
- Business Person employed in any business other than construction-related, referred to herein as BP
  - 112 participants (22.9 percent).

I initially found it difficult to source the desired number of CPMs due to their heavy work commitments. Accordingly, I engaged Qualtrics, a well-respected participants-sourcing service, to assist. The numbers targeted by Qualtrics were 70, 90 and 90 for CPMs, APs and BPs, respectively. The total number of CPMs who completed all compulsory questions of the online survey was 253.

There were 281 participants from LOs and 124 MO participants, because of different approaches to sourcing. While the main LO approached directly emailed all relevant employees and encouraged involvement in the research, the MO that was approached directly preferred to provide a randomly selected list of 20 potential participants, eight of whom completed the survey. Eight additional people from that MO provided data via semi-structured interviews. Other MO participants were subsequently sourced via Qualtrics.

Age of Participants

For interest, Table 3.1 presents the number and age of participants computed against RP.

The majority of CPMs (60.47 percent) were aged 31–50, compared with 39.52 and 44.64 percent, respectively, for APs and BPs.

Table 3.1 Participants' ages and roles

Age range	Role type					
	CPM		AP		BP	
	n =	%	*n* =	%	*n* =	%
Under 21	0	0	5	4.03	1	0.90
21–30	50	19.76	31	25.00	21	18.75
31–40	86	33.99	34	27.42	28	25.00
41–50	67	26.48	15	12.10	22	19.64
51–60	40	15.81	30	24.19	29	25.88
61–70	10	3.96	9	7.26	10	8.93
70+	0	0.00	0	0.00	1	0.90
	253	100	124	100	112	100

Participants' Gender Within Role Types

In line with expectations, CPMs were predominantly male—208 (82.22 percent) compared with 43 (34.67 percent) and 69 (61.61 percent) in AP and BP roles, respectively. There were 45 females (17.78 percent) in CPM roles and 81 (65.33 percent) and 43 (38.39 percent) in AP and BP roles, respectively. The higher percentage of females in AP roles might in part be explained by that category including secretarial and general administration staff. However, it also included, inter alia, accountants, financial controllers, lawyers and marketing and public relations professionals. These observations were supported by a significant chi-squared, χ (2, $N = 489$) = 84.09, $p < .001$. The next matter addressed is participants' education.

Participants' Level of Education

Table 3.2 presents an overview of participants' level of education.

Only 5.53 percent of CPMs lacked tertiary qualifications, compared with 16.13 percent of APs and 17.86 percent of BPs. Few participants held master's degrees, probably reflecting relative seniority of respondents, because employment in many professions requiring a master's degree is a relatively recent phenomenon. Some 46.64 percent of CPMs

Table 3.2 Participants' level of education

Education level	RP					
	CPM		AP		BP	
	n =	%	*n* =	%	*n* =	%
Secondary/High School	14	5.53	20	16.13	20	17.86
Certificate/Diploma	93	36.76	56	45.16	36	32.14
Undergraduate degree	75	29.64	28	22.58	27	24.11
Post Graduate Certificate	20	7.91	4	3.23	4	3.57
Post graduate Diploma	23	9.09	12	9.67	9	8.04
Master's Degree	26	10.28	4	3.23	16	14.28
Ph.D.	2	0.79	0	0.00	0	0.00
	253	100	124	100	112	100

held undergraduate degrees, post-graduate certificates or diplomas—substantially higher than the corresponding percentages for other role categories. The differences were statistically significant, χ (12, $N = 489$) $= 33.74$, $p = .001$.

Participants' Income Levels

Only 9.49 percent of CPMs earned less than \$75,000, compared with 53.23 percent of APs and 44.64 percent of BPs. CPMs who earned over \$100,000 totalled 73.91 percent compared with 26.61 percent of APs and 22.32 percent of BPs. Remarkably, 37.15 percent of CPMs earned over \$150,000 compared with just 8.06 percent of APs and 6.25 percent of BPs. This was interesting, and possibly reflected high demand for experienced construction professionals. It is noteworthy APs and BPs generally held higher education qualifications than CPMs, as addressed earlier. Differences in income levels within different OSs were statistically significant, χ (8, $N = 489$) $= 145.50$, $p < .001$.

Interestingly, 57.14 percent of participants from SOs earned under \$75,000, compared with 31.45 and 18.86 percent for MOs and LOs, respectively. Many SOs worked on smaller, simpler and lower priced buildings and did not need to pay for higher qualified and more experienced personnel. However, LOs generally constructed far more complex larger buildings requiring the skills of highly qualified and experienced CPMs who commanded high salaries for their talents and the long hours they worked to manage the pressures arising from multiple quarters, described in the next chapter.

Some 62.99 percent of participants from LOs earned over \$100,000, and most were CPMs. Just 17.86 employed by SOs and 42.74 percent employed by MOs earned over \$100,000. In other words, the highest paid participants worked for LOs as CPMs.

Let us now define more information about Will and Clare. We know both are well-qualified professionals, and we can now accept that both are on well-above-average salaries for the work they do. Being a very experienced CPM in a crushingly competitive market, Will is earning very well. About a year ago, when the pressure of work was becoming overwhelming, he approached his management to discuss resignation. Their response was to immediately offer 'something we've been considering for some time, given your sterling efforts'. The offer was an increase from $185 k to $225 k per annum, plus a substantial bonus for future projects completed on time and within budget. Importantly, management told Will this was a stepping stone to senior management in the organisation. He discussed the offer with Clare. It certainly ticked the box on confirming management's appreciation of Will's efforts, and Will and Clare saw that as a good thing, and long overdue. The potential for promotion to management also appealed, and even after tax, that increase offered better options for the kids' education, and opened the possibility of a great family holiday every couple of years.

All this looked very good to Will and Clare. However, like so many in similar circumstances before them, the attraction of what the additional cashflow might mean for the family strongly overshadowed any deep and critical thinking about the fact that neither they nor Will's manager had addressed the reason he had approached management in the first place. He was heading for either health or relationship troubles, or both, and neither of these issues had been addressed in any useful depth. Had the immediate appeal of financial benefit overshadowed the critical importance of dealing with the stress effects of workload and work pressures, and impacts of these on family life? I will return to this later in this chapter.

Participants' Personal Attitudes to Stress

All participants responded to a compulsory question regarding attitudes to stress and its management in the workplace. For the following analysis of quantitative data, I have commenced each section by providing in full the statements I presented to participants in relation to that section. In addition, I have either presented a summary definition of each abbreviation immediately after discussing inferential statistics and before addressing the relevant descriptive statistics, or used full descriptions of terms, to facilitate the reader's experience. Here now are the statements I presented in regard to participants' personal attitudes to stress:

1. Generally speaking, stress is caused more by Non-Work Factors than by work factors (NWF)
2. For me, stress is more significantly caused by Work Factors (WF)
3. The Work I do is Stressful (WS)
4. Regardless of whether stress is caused by work-related or non-work-related issues, it can have a significant Effect on Performance at Work (EPW).

I collected responses using a five-level Likert type scale, with the options being strongly disagree, somewhat disagree, neither agree nor disagree, somewhat agree and strongly agree.

I next addressed participants' responses to questions regarding sources of stress. The differences were statistically significant between role categories, χ (8, $N = 489$) = 70.46, $p < .001$, and additional details are provided in the following sections.

Statistics Regarding Personal Attitudes to Stress (to Test Hypothesis 1)

I used a MANOVA to investigate whether OS and RP had an effect on participants' personal attitudes towards stress. The assumption of homogeneity of variance was met except for WF ($p = .020$) and WS ($p < .001$). Consequently, a more stringent alpha level (0.01) was used to read these results. At a multivariate level, the interaction between RP type and OS did not yield a significant result, $F(16,1457) = 0.68$, $p = .82$. However, there was a significant effect of OS on participants' responses $F(8,954) = 3.02$, $p = .002$; $\eta^2 = 0.03$, power = 0.96. There was also a significant effect of RP type on participants' responses $F(8,954) = 4.11$, $p < .001$, $\eta^2 = 0.03$, power = 0.99.

Follow-up univariate results showed that the effect of OS was significant on variables NWF $F(2,480) = 5.06$, $p = .007$ and WS, $F(2,480) = 6.38$, $p = .002$. However, there was no significant effect of OS on responses to variables WF $F(2,480) = 2.92$, $p = .055$ and EPW $F(2,480) = 2.74$, $p = .060$, but they were close to significance. The effect of RP type was found on WF, $F(2,480) = 5.62$, $p = .004$, and

Table 3.3 Descriptive statistics regarding first hypothesis

Item	Org. size	n =	NWF		WF		WS		EPW	
			Mean	SD	Mean	SD	Mean	SD	Mean	SD
CPM	SO	18	2.83	1.10	3.50	1.30	3.72	1.18	4.00	0.97
	MO	51	2.82	1.11	3.90	0.92	4.08	1.04	4.39	0.78
	LO	184	2.48	1.01	3.87	1.04	4.08	0.82	4.27	0.88
AP	SO	31	3.13	1.02	3.10	1.30	3.16	1.04	3.84	1.13
	MO	34	3.09	1.08	3.38	1.07	3.12	1.15	4.18	0.90
	LO	39	2.78	1.15	3.59	1.15	3.68	1.12	4.29	0.87
BP	SO	35	2.86	1.00	3.29	1.13	3.11	1.08	4.00	0.80
	MO	39	3.26	0.88	3.18	1.07	3.28	1.08	4.03	0.93
	LO	38	2.79	0.96	3.47	1.18	3.55	0.89	4.13	1.02
Total	SO	84	2.95	1.03	3.26	1.25	3.26	1.10	3.94	0.96
	MO	124	3.03	1.06	3.53	1.06	3.56	1.16	4.22	0.87
	LO	281	2.58	1.04	3.76	1.09	3.93	0.93	4.26	0.90

WS $F(2,480) = 16.04$, $p < .001$, but RP was not significant on NWF $F(2,480) = 2.58$, $p = .077$ and EPW, $F(2,480) = 1.04$, $p = .355$. Refer to Table 3.3 for the descriptive statistics.

Descriptive Statistics Relating to the First Hypothesis

For ease of reference, in the descriptive statistics presented below, the abbreviations have the following overview meanings for participants:

1. NWF—stress is caused more by Non-Work Factors than by work factors
2. WF—stress is more significantly caused by Work Factors
3. WS—the Work I do is Stressful
4. EPW—stress can have a significant Effect on Performance at Work.

Table 3.3 presents the data relating to the first hypothesis.

There was a higher level of agreement with stress being caused by non-work factors than by work factors among APs and BPs than among CPMs in SOs, albeit the difference was marginal for BPs, and within

MOs and LOs there was a higher level of agreement by APs and BPs than among CPMs. There was more agreement with NWF by participants from SOs and MOs than from LOs, as anticipated.

The means for all OSs indicate there was a higher level of agreement with the proposition stress was caused significantly by work factors from CPMs than among APs and BPs. Despite the fact there was a higher level of agreement with WF among all participants from MOs than from SOs, and that a similar condition existed between participants from LOs and MOs, the inferential statistics show those differences are not statistically significant.

There was a higher level of agreement with the proposition the work participants do is stressful from CPMs than from APs and BPs. Participants from LOs expressed stronger agreement with WS than did those from MOs, and those from MOs were more strongly in agreement with WS than were participants from SOs.

There was higher agreement that stress can impact performance at work among CPMs from SOs than there was among APs from SOs, but an equal level of agreement between CPMs and BPs from SOs. Across MOs, CPMs showed a higher agreement with EPW than their AP and BP counterparts. However, across LOs, CPMs showed marginally lower agreement with EPW than did APs, while both CPMs and APs showed higher agreement than their BP counterparts. As indicated by the inferential statistics at the start of this section, these CPM differences were not found to be statistically significant.

Stress Management Training Within the Workplace

I posed the following statements to participants regarding stress management training within their workplace environments:

1. Our business trains Leaders and Managers to be able to Identify Stress effects/symptoms in employees (LMIS)
2. Our business trains All Personnel to be able to Identify Stress effects/symptoms in fellow employees (APIS)

3. An Employee Assistance Programme focussed on dealing with stress effects that employees report (i.e. after they have manifested) is Sufficient for a business like ours (EAPS).

Henceforth, I refer to the above propositions (1–4) as LMIS, APIS and EAPS, respectively. Response options included yes, no or unsure. Participants who provided a yes response were asked to rate the effectiveness of the strategy by responding to the statement, 'The programme is effective' with options including strongly disagree, disagree, neither agree nor disagree, agree and strongly agree.

Statistics Regarding Stress Management Training (to Test Hypothesis 2)

I used a second MANOVA to investigate whether OS and RP had an effect on attitude to stress management training in the workplace. The assumption of homogeneity of variance was found to be violated for LMIS ($p = .020$), APIS ($p < .001$) and EAPS ($p < .001$). Consequently, a more stringent Alpha level of 0.01 was used to interpret the result of these variables. At a multivariate level, the interaction between RP type and OS did not yield a significant result, $F(16,1457) = 0.79$, $p = .702$. There was no significant effect of RP type $F(8,954) = 0.83$, $p = .577$. However, there was a significant effect of OS $F(8,954) = 3.25$, $p = .002$, $\eta^2 = 0.03$, *power* $= 0.57$. Follow-up univariate analyses showed that this effect was not significant for LMIS $F(2,480) = 3.78$, $p = .023$, but it was significant for the other dependent variables,

$$\text{APIS} \quad F(2,480) = 7.68, p = .001$$

$$\text{EAPS} \quad F(2,480) = 8.96, p < .001$$

Descriptive Statistics Regarding Second Hypothesis

For ease of reference the overview meaning of abbreviated terms for variables is presented below:

1. LMIS—Business Leaders/Managers are trained to Identify Stress effects/symptoms
2. APIS—All Personnel are trained to Identify Stress effects/symptoms
3. EAPS—An Employee Assistance Programme is sufficient for a business like ours.

Table 3.4 presents an overview of data from the different RP categories and OS in relation to statements LMIS, APIS, EAPS and BPCS.

For all participant categories the distribution of results was tighter for SOs than for MOs and LOs. There was a similar spread of results for CPM and BP participants from MOs and LOs but a wider distribution for APs from MOs and LOs. The detailed data from role types is presented in Table 3.5.

Across all participant categories there were substantially more reports of no training of leaders and managers regarding identifying signs of

Table 3.4 Descriptive statistics regarding second hypothesis

Item	Org. size	$n =$	LMIS		APIS		EAPS	
			Mean	SD	Mean	SD	Mean	SD
CPM	SO	18	1.56	0.51	1.67	0.49	1.78	0.43
	MO	51	1.88	0.74	1.94	0.61	1.84	0.76
	LO	184	2.10	0.71	2.07	0.62	2.16	0.74
AP	SO	31	1.94	0.36	2.03	0.18	2.06	0.25
	MO	34	1.76	0.74	1.76	0.70	1.82	0.80
	LO	39	2.14	0.86	2.07	0.74	2.00	0.89
BP	SO	35	2.00	0.49	2.03	0.45	2.06	0.48
	MO	39	1.85	0.67	1.97	0.63	1.90	0.79
	LO	38	1.97	0.72	1.76	0.59	1.89	0.65
Total	SO	84	1.88	0.48	1.95	0.41	2.00	0.41
	MO	124	1.84	0.71	1.90	0.64	1.85	0.77
	LO	281	2.09	0.74	2.03	0.65	2.09	0.77

Table 3.5 Data regarding second hypothesis within role types and organisation size

P	R	RP						OS						Total
		CPM		AP		BP		SO		MO		LO		
		n =	%	*n* =	%	*n* =	%	*n* =	%	*n* =	%	*n* =	%	
LMIS	Y	63	24.90	35	28.23	26	23.22	15	17.86	43	34.68	66	23.49	124
	N	123	48.62	56	45.16	67	59.82	64	76.19	58	46.77	124	44.13	246
	U	67	26.48	33	26.61	19	16.96	5	5.95	23	18.55	91	32.38	119
Total		253	100	124	100	112	100	84	100	124	100	281	100	489
APIS	Y	46	18.18	27	21.77	23	20.54	9	10.71	32	25.81	55	19.57	96
	N	157	62.06	73	58.87	75	66.96	70	83.33	72	58.06	163	58.01	305
	U	50	19.76	24	19.36	14	12.50	5	5.96	20	16.13	63	22.42	88
Total		253	100	124	100	112	100	84	100	124	100	281	100	489
EAPS	Y	61	24.11	37	29.84	27	24.11	7	8.33	47	37.90	71	25.27	125
	N	113	44.66	54	43.55	64	57.14	70	83.33	48	38.71	113	40.21	231
	U	79	31.23	33	26.61	21	18.75	7	8.34	29	23.39	97	34.52	133
Total		253	100	124	100	112	100	84	100	124	100	281	100	489

P = Proposition; R = Response (Y = Yes; N = No; U = Unsure); all others defined previously stress than of training. The percentages for CPMs and APs reporting this were similar, and notably higher than for BPs. The unsure figures across all categories were curiously high, and the high percentage of BPs who were certain their organisations did not train managers in respect of LMIS was unexpected. However, the inferential statistics presented earlier did confirm a statistically significant effect of OS in regard to this variable.

I anticipated that the results for SOs would be lower than for MOs and LOs, but was surprised a relatively high proportion of LOs did not have the training in place. The descriptive statistics for LMIS were confirmed by the inferential statistics with a statistically significant effect of role type on LMIS.

Analysis next determined participants' perceptions of effectiveness of LMIS-related training. Given the level of 'unsure' responses previously reported, it is unsurprising that approximately 45 percent across all participants' role types selected 'not applicable' as their response to this question. CPMs' responses indicated 24.51 percent strongly agreed or agreed the training for leaders and managers in identifying signs of stress was effective, compared with 14.23 percent who disagreed or strongly disagreed, with 15.41 taking the 'neither agree nor disagree' position. The corresponding figures for APs and BPs were 23, 11 and 22 percent and 21.43, 31.25 and 20.54 percent, respectively.

The high percentages of all RP types' 'not applicable' responses were of concern but were consistent with the high number of reports of organisations that either did not have the subject programme, or if they did, might not have promoted it to employees.

Results were skewed towards CPMs regarding their programme as effective. Some 14.23 percent either strongly disagreed or disagreed the programme was effective while 24.51 percent agreed or strongly agreed. Responses from APs and BPs were also strongly skewed towards a positive attitude to programme effectiveness.

While just 24.9, 28.23 and 23.22 percent of CPMs, APs and BPs, respectively responded positively regarding LMIS, 54.15, 56.45 and 55.36 percent, respectively, offered an opinion regarding programme effectiveness. I concluded some participants considered not having a programme was effective for their organisation. As this curious aspect of response applied for several questions, the conclusion regarding this proposed reason for it is not repeated for future incidences.

Some 17.86 percent of SO participants agreed or strongly agreed their programme was effective compared with 10.71 percent who disagreed or strongly disagreed. The corresponding figures from MOs were 12.90 percent for the more negative attitudes as compared with 39.51 percent for the more positive.

For LOs, the results were more evenly distributed and 14.26 percent disagreed or strongly disagreed their programme was effective while 18.15 percent agreed or strongly agreed. These results were aligned with the findings of inferential statistics that organisation size was of statistical significance in relation to LMIS.

Descriptive Statistics Regarding APIS (All Personnel Being Trained to Identify Stress Effects/Symptoms)

Table 3.5 includes an overview of data from the different role categories and organisation sizes in relation to statement APIS.

The means revealed CPMs from LOs agreed with all personnel being trained to identify stress symptoms more than those from MOs, who in turn, agreed with it more than those from SOs. The pattern was somewhat different for APs, more of whom from LOs agreed with APIS than those from SOs and MOs (marginal in the case of SOs). These participants differed from CPMs in that more from SOs agreed with APIS than from MOs. The pattern differed again for BPs, with more from SOs agreeing with APIS than from MOs and, in turn, more from MOs agreeing than from LOs. These figures aligned with the inferential statistics presented earlier, which proved that organisation size but not role type had a statistical significance in respect of APIS.

For all participant categories, standard deviation results indicated the distribution was wider for MOs and LOs than for SOs.

Across all participant categories staff not being trained to identify stress symptoms was more common than staff being trained. The percentage of CPMs and APs who reported being unsure was similar, and substantially higher than for BPs. Inferential statistics presented earlier showed the effect of RP type to not be significant in relation to all personnel being trained to identify stress symptoms. However, OS was found to be significant, and data relating to that are presented next.

I anticipated the results for SOs would indicate a lower level of this type of training than existed in MOs and LOs. Contrary to my expectations, the data indicated a higher level of training of staff than anticipated within SOs, while there was a relatively high proportion of LOs and MOs that did not have staff training in place. Following is a brief review of perceptions of the effectiveness of all staff being trained to identify stress symptoms held by participants.

The high percentages of all RP types who provided 'not applicable' responses (between 46.75 and 48.25 percent) were of concern, but were consistent with both the 'unsure' responses to earlier questions and the high number of semi-structured interview reports organisations either did not have an APIS related programme, or had not publicised its existence.

Among CPMs, 17.79 percent either strongly disagreed or disagreed the programme was effective compared with 15.81 percent who agreed or strongly agreed. The AP and BP responses were far more strongly skewed towards a positive attitude. Again, it was OS and not RP type that was statistically significant in relation to APIS, and so those data are reviewed next.

A high percentage of 'non applicable' responses again prevailed across OS (69.05, 37.90 and 45.55 percent for SOs, MOs and LOs, respectively). From SOs 10.72 percent reported agreement or strong agreement their programme was effective compared with 8.33 percent who disagreed or strongly disagreed. Corresponding results were 29.84 and 15.31 percent for MOs and 13.16 and 18.16 percent for LOs. It was now important to determine whether participants believed an EAP was all that was required to address stress in their workplace.

Descriptive Statistics Regarding Whether Participants Believed an Employee Assistance Programme Was Sufficient for Their Organisation—(EAPS)

Table 3.5 presents the overview of data from the different RP types and OSs in relation to the statement that an employee assistance programme was all that was necessary for their organisation. The means revealed that CPMs from LOs agreed that an EAP was all that was required more than those from MOs, who in turn, agreed with it more than those from SOs. The pattern differed for APs, more of whom from SOs agreed that an EAP was all that was required than those from LOs and MOs, but APs differed from CPMs in that more from SOs agreed with EAPS than from MOs. The pattern differed again for BPs, as more from LOs agreed with EAPS than from MOs and, in turn, more from SOs agreed than from MOs. For all participant categories the distribution of results was wider for MOs and LOs than for SOs.

Across all RP categories there was substantially more disagreement regarding EAPS than there was agreement. Specifically, 44.66 percent of CPMs disagreed regarding EAPS, while 24.11 percent agreed. The APs and BPs were of similar opinion as CPMs. The data from different organisation sizes is presented in Table 3.5.

Ten times the number of SOs confirmed they did not agree than did agree with EAPS. Those from MOs presented a balanced opinion (37.90 percent agreed and 38.71 percent disagreed). The percentage from LOs who disagreed regarding an EAP being all that was required to deal with stress was 1.59 times larger than the percentage who agreed. I did not anticipate MOs would differ so much from SOs and LOs on this question. Analysis next determined perceived effectiveness of programmes across RPs.

There was again a high percentage of 'not applicable' responses across all RP types (43.04, 40.33 and 44.64 percent from CPMs, APs and BPs, respectively). Possible reasons include some participants having difficulty arriving at a definite opinion regarding an EAP being all that was required in organisations to deal with impacts of stress. For CPMs from organisations with an EAP, the results were very slightly skewed towards the programme being regarded as effective –17.78 percent either strongly disagreed or disagreed an EAP alone was effective compared with 18.28 percent who agreed or strongly agreed it was. The responses from APs were more strongly skewed towards a positive attitude to the programme effectiveness, with the corresponding figures being 26.61 and 9.67 percent, respectively. BPs were also positively skewed (16.07 and 12.5 percent).

Responses to this question were interesting. Analysis revealed while participants who had experienced the value of an EAP supported their existence, the strong overall opinion was an EAP alone, that dealt with stress effects after they manifested, was not sufficient for the modern work environment. I will now address perceived EAP effectiveness based on OS.

A high percentage of 'non applicable' responses again prevailed across OSs (60.05, 37.26 and 39.50 percent for SOs, MOs and LOs, respectively). Responses from SOs were evenly distributed with 9.52 percent disagreeing or strongly disagreeing with EAPS and 9.53 percent agreeing or strongly agreeing with it. Responses from MOs were strongly skewed towards the positive. For LOs, the results were again more evenly distributed. Inferential statistics presented earlier in this chapter confirmed that OS had a statistically significant effect on the EAPS dependent variable.

Participants' Personal Attitudes Towards Stress Management

A question was included in the online survey aimed at determining participants' personal attitudes to stress management and the training of organisational leaders and employees in stress management techniques. The question sought responses on a 5-level Likert type response scale. The possible responses were strongly disagree, somewhat disagree, neither agree nor disagree, somewhat agree and strongly agree.

The statements put to participants were:

1. Stress should be a matter for Individuals to deal with, and Not Employers (INNE)
2. A stress management approach should Include Training of All Leaders in identification of symptoms of stress in self and employees (ITAL)
3. A stress management approach should Include Training of All Employees in identification of symptoms of stress in self and work mates (ITAE)
4. A stress management approach should Include Training of Leaders in Stress Management and/or avoidance techniques (TLSM).

Henceforth herein, the above dependent variables were referred to as INNE, ITAL, ITAE and TLSM, respectively.

Effect of Organisation Size and Participants' Role Type on Attitude to Training Staff in Stress Avoidance and Management (to Test Hypothesis 3)

A third MANOVA was run to investigate whether OS and RP type had an effect on participants' personal attitudes to stress management and training of personnel in stress avoidance and/or management techniques. The assumption of homogeneity of variance was found to be met for all variables.

At the multivariate level, no significant interaction effect was found $F(16,1457) = 1.22$, $p = .241$. There was a significant effect of OS on personal attitudes to stress management and training $F(8,954) = 3.09$, $p = .002$, $\eta^2 = 0.03$, *power* = 0.97. There was also a significant effect of RP type on personal attitudes to stress management and training $F(8,954) = 2.10$, $p = .033$, $\eta^2 = 0.02$, *power* = 0.85.

Follow-up univariates showed that there was a significant effect of OS was on all four dependent variables:

INNE $F(2{,}480) = 4.48, p = .012$
ITAL $F(2{,}480) = 3.60, p = .028$
ITAE $F(2{,}480) = 5.36, p = .005$
TLSM $F(2{,}480) = 8.64, p < .001$

Similarly, there was a significant effect of RP type on all four dependent variables:

INNE $F(2{,}480) = 4.75, p = .009$
ITAL $F(2{,}480) = 8.06, p < .001$
ITAE $F(2{,}480) = 5.50, p = .004$
TLSM $F(2{,}480) = 7.12, p = .001$

Table 3.6 presents an overview of the means of the participants' responses within RP type and OSs. For ease of reference, overview definitions of abbreviations for the dependent variables are:

Table 3.6 Data regarding third hypothesis within role types and organisation size

Item	Org. size	*n* =	INNE		ITAL		ITAE		TLSM	
			Mean	SD	Mean	SD	Mean	SD	Mean	SD
CPM	SO	18	3.00	1.14	3.89	1.02	3.33	1.24	3.50	0.59
	MO	51	2.45	1.29	4.24	0.65	3.98	0.95	4.25	0.79
	LO	184	2.23	1.14	4.32	0.86	4.16	0.98	4.33	0.87
AP	SO	31	2.61	1.02	3.90	0.79	3.87	0.76	3.94	0.77
	MO	34	3.06	1.23	3.76	1.18	3.71	1.14	3.76	1.18
	LO	39	2.51	1.04	4.10	1.89	4.10	0.82	4.14	0.84
BP	SO	35	2.69	0.96	3.66	0.84	3.49	1.07	3.57	0.95
	MO	39	2.67	1.20	4.10	0.91	3.82	1.02	4.08	0.81
	LO	38	2.45	1.03	4.00	1.04	3.74	1.08	4.05	0.99
Total	SO	84	2.73	1.02	3.80	0.86	3.60	1.02	3.69	0.99
	MO	124	2.69	1.26	4.06	0.92	3.85	1.03	4.06	0.91
	LO	281	2.32	1.11	4.23	0.89	4.09	0.97	4.25	0.87

1. INNE—Stress should be a matter for individuals to deal with, and not employers
2. ITAL—All leaders should be trained in stress identification
3. ITAE—All Employees should be trained in stress identification
4. TLSM—All leaders should be trained in stress management and/or avoidance.

The CPMs from SOs agreed stress was a matter for employees to deal with and not employers more than those from MOs, who in turn, agreed with it more than those from LOs. The pattern was different for APs. The highest percentage of APs who agreed with INNE were from MOs, with participants from SOs being less in agreement than those from MOs, but more in agreement than those from LOs. The pattern from BPs saw participants from MOs and SOs with almost identical means that were both higher than the mean for participants from LOs.

For all RPs the standard deviation results indicated a broadly similar distribution across all OSs.

For all RPs, the results were strongly skewed towards disagreement and strong disagreement with the INNE proposition. The percentages of participants who either strongly disagreed or disagreed with the proposition were 67.59, 54.83 and 51.79 for CPM, AP and BP categories, respectively. These compared with 19.76, 28.23 and 21.42 percent, respectively, for those categories who either agreed or strongly agreed.

Put another way, the percentage of participants who believed employers should be doing something about the avoidance and/or management of stress was 3.42, 1.94 and 2.42 times the percentage who held a contrary opinion for CPMs, APs and BPs, respectively.

From an OS perspective, there was strong support for the alternate proposition that employers, and not individuals, should be responsible for dealing with stress in the workplace. Table 3.6 presents an overview of the proposition ITAL—A stress management approach should include training of leaders in identification of symptoms of stress in self and employees.

The means revealed CPMs from LOs agreed with the ITAL proposition marginally more than those from MOs, who in turn, agreed with it more than those from SOs. The pattern differed for APs, among whom the highest percentage who agreed with ITAL were from LOs. Participants from SOs were less in agreement than those from LOs, but more in agreement than those from MOs. BPs from MOs had the highest support for training of leaders in stress identification, and participants from LOs and SOs followed in that order. For all participant categories the standard deviations indicated a relatively broad distribution of results across all OSs. The detailed data from RPs is presented in Table 3.6.

For all RPs, results were strongly skewed towards agreement and strong agreement with leaders being trained in stress symptom recognition. The percentages of participants who either strongly disagreed or disagreed with the proposition were just 5.54, 7.26 and 6.26 for CPM, AP and BP, respectively. These compared with 89.72, 81.45 and 75.00 percent, respectively, who either agreed or strongly agreed with the proposition.

Put another way, the percentage of participants who considered that employers should be training leaders in stress symptom recognition was 26.23, 11.22 and 11.98 times the percentage who held the contrary opinion for CPM, AP and BP, respectively.

For all OSs, the results were strongly skewed towards agreement and strong agreement with ITAL. The percentage of participants who supported leaders being trained in stress symptoms recognition was 10.17, 17.16 and 13.79 times the percentage who did not for SOs, MOs and LOs, respectively. I shall now address analysis for the statement ITAE.

The means revealed CPMs from LOs agreed with all employees being trained in stress symptoms recognition marginally more than those from MOs, who in turn, agreed with it more than those from SOs. The pattern was different for APs among whom the highest percentage who agreed were from LOs. Participants from SOs were less in agreement than those from LOs but more in agreement than those from MOs. The BPs from MOs showed the highest support for the statement and participants from LOs and SOs followed in that order. The inferential statistics presented earlier indicated that both RP type and OS had a significant effect on the results for this variable. For CPMs and APs the standard deviations indicated a relatively broad distribution of results across all OSs, while BPs were relatively consistent across all OSs.

For all RPs, results were strongly skewed towards agreement and strong agreement with all employees being trained in stress identification. The percentages of participants who either strongly disagreed or disagreed with the proposition were just 8.70, 6.45 and 16.07 for CPM, AP and BP roles, respectively. These compared with 81.42, 79.84 and 66.97 percent, respectively, for those categories who either agreed or strongly agreed with the proposition.

Put another way, the percentage of participants who supported all staff being trained in stress identification was 9.36, 12.38 and 4.17 times the percentage who held the contrary opinion for CPMs, APs and BPs, respectively. I will now address data analysis for ITAE across OSs.

All OS results were strongly skewed towards agreement and strong agreement with ITAE. The percentage of participants who supported all staff being trained in stress identification was 4.67, 6.99 and 10.27 times the percentage who held the contrary opinion for SOs, MOs and LOs, respectively. Data regarding TLSM (training leaders in stress avoidance and management) are also presented in 3.06, and I will now address that.

CPMs from LOs agreed with TLSM marginally more than those from MOs, who in turn, agreed with it notably more than those from SOs. The highest percentage of APs who agreed with the TLSM were from LOs. Participants from SOs were less in agreement than those from LOs but more in agreement than those from MOs. The BPs from MOs gave marginally higher support for TLSM than those from LOs and both categories were markedly higher in support for TLSM than were those from SOs. Inferential statistics proved both RP type and OS had a significant effect on the results for TLSM. For CPMs and APs, the standard deviations indicated a broad distribution of results across all OSs, while those for BPs were more consistent across all OSs.

For all RPs, the results were strongly skewed towards agreement and strong agreement with leaders being trained in stress avoidance and management techniques. The percentages of participants who either strongly disagreed or disagreed with the proposition were just 5.93, 6.45 and 6.25 for CPMs, APs and BPs, respectively. These compared with 88.93, 80.65 and 72.32 percent, respectively, who either agreed or strongly agreed with TLSM. In other words, the percentage of participants who supported leaders being trained in stress avoidance and management techniques was 15.00, 12.50 and 11.57 times the percentage who held the contrary opinion for CPMs, APs and BPs, respectively.

Across all OSs, the results were strongly skewed towards agreement and strong agreement with TLSM and the percentage of participants who supported leaders being trained in stress avoidance and management techniques was 7.13, 16.82 and 15.51 times the percentage who held the contrary opinion for SOs, MOs and LOs, respectively. Overall, participants from all RP categories and OSs were very much in favour of leaders being trained in stress avoidance and management techniques.

Stress Management/Intervention Strategies in the Work Environment

One set of propositions sought data regarding stress management and intervention strategies used in workplace environments. The specific propositions were:

1. Our business has an Employee Stress Avoidance Programme in place (i.e. rules and processes to prevent stress becoming an issue for employees) (ESAP)
2. Our business has an Employee Stress Management Programme in place (i.e. stress is maintained at reasonable levels using relaxation or mindfulness programmes, gymnasiums and corporate health check programmes, etc.) (ESMP)
3. Our business has an effective Confidential Employee Assistance Programme (or EAP) in place for those who experience effects of stress (i.e. confidential counselling service or the like, at the expense of the employer) (CEAP).

The above propositions are referred to as ESAP, ESMP and CEAP, respectively, herein. Responses were collected using a dichotomous (yes or no) response. In addition, participants who provided a 'yes' response were given the opportunity to rate the effectiveness of the management/intervention strategy by responding to the statement, 'The programme is effective'. The available response options were strongly disagree, disagree, neither agree nor disagree, agree and strongly agree.

So What Stress Avoidance and Stress Management Systems Do Organisations Have in Place? (To Test of Hypothesis 4)

A fourth MANOVA was run to investigate whether OS and RP type had an effect on participants' perception of the effectiveness of the programme in place. The assumption of homogeneity of variance was found to be violated for ESAP ($p = .001$), ESMP ($p < .001$), and CEAP ($p = .028$). Consequently, a more stringent Alpha level of 0.01 was used to interpret the results. At a multivariate level, the interaction between RP type and OS did not yield a significant result, $F(12,1264) = 1.00$, $p = .443$. There was no significant effect of RP type $F(6,956) = 0.77$, $p = .592$. However, there was a significant effect of OS $F(6,956) = 2.76$, $p = .011$, $\eta^2 = 0.02$, $power = 0.88$.

Follow-up univariates showed that OS had no significant effect on ESAP, $F(2,480) = 3.40$, $p = .034$ and on ESMP, $F(2,480) = 3.51$ $p = .031$. However, OS had a significant effect on CEAP, $F(2,480) = 7.34$, $p = .001$.

Descriptive Statistics for ESAP

The overall descriptive statistics summary for ESAP was presented in Table 3.7. For ease of reference the summary of abbreviations for dependent variables is:

Table 3.7 Summary of descriptive statistics for data relating to third hypothesis

Item	Org. size	$n =$	ESAP		ESMP		CEAP	
			Mean	SD	Mean	SD	Mean	SD
CPM	SO	18	4.56	1.79	4.50	1.72	1.67	0.49
	MO	51	4.49	1.58	4.49	1.61	1.57	0.70
	LO	184	4.60	1.69	4.55	1.68	1.76	0.88
AP	SO	31	5.39	1.33	5.45	1.21	2.06	0.36
	MO	34	4.29	1.55	4.38	1.46	1.74	0.62
	LO	39	4.24	1.51	4.31	1.53	1.78	0.89
BP	SO	35	4.89	1.49	4.97	1.47	2.00	0.42
	MO	39	4.28	1.49	4.49	1.59	1.85	0.81
	LO	38	4.55	1.78	4.39	1.85	1.50	0.69
Total	SO	84	5.00	1.52	5.05	1.46	1.95	0.44
	MO	124	4.32	1.53	4.46	1.56	1.70	0.72
	LO	281	4.52	1.67	4.48	1.67	1.73	0.86

1. ESAP—Our business has an Employee Stress Avoidance Programme in place
2. ESMP—Our business has an Employee Stress Management Programme in place
3. CEAP—Our business has an effective Confidential Employee Assistance Programme.

There was higher confirmation a stress avoidance programme existed across all RP types in SOs than in MOs and LOs, albeit the difference in attitude between OSs for CPMs was marginal. Differences in means for responses from CPMs and APs from MOs and LOs were also marginal, but that difference was more pronounced within responses from BPs. The inferential statistics confirmed role type was of no significance. Table 3.8 includes data analysis from the three role categories and three organisations sizes in relation to proposition ESAP.

More CPMs and APs responded affirmatively regarding ESAP than did BPs. When CPMs and APs were combined, 25.46 percent of all participants working within construction-related organisations had reported affirmatively regarding the existence of a stress avoidance programme in their organisation, compared with 21.43 percent of BPs (non-construction-related). That represented 18.81 percent more.

Table 3.8 Data regarding fourth hypothesis within role types and organisation size

	R	RP						OS						Total
		CPM		AP	BP			SO		MO		LO		
		n =	%	n =	%	n =	%	n =	%	n =	%	n =	%	
ESAP	Y	66	24.09	30	24.19	24	21.43	7	17.86	42	33.87	71	25.27	120
	N	112	44.27	65	52.42	73	65.18	72	76.19	69	55.65	109	38.79	250
	U	75	29.64	29	23.39	15	13.39	5	5.95	13	10.48	101	35.94	119
		253	100	124	100	112	100	84	100	124	100	281	100	489
ESMP	Y	63	24.90	32	25.81	17	15.18	5	5.95	34	27.42	73	25.98	112
	N	117	46.25	66	53.22	83	74.11	70	83.33	74	59.68	122	43.42	266
	U	73	28.85	26	20.97	12	10.71	9	10.72	16	12.90	86	30.60	111
		253	100	124	100	112	100	84	100	124	100	281	100	489
CEAP	Y	133	52.56	44	35.48	42	37.50	10	11.91	56	45.16	153	54.45	219
	N	60	23.72	56	45.16	53	47.32	68	80.95	49	39.52	52	18.50	169
	U	60	23.72	24	19.36	17	15.18	6	7.14	19	13.32	76	27.05	101
Total		253	100	124	100	112	100	84	100	124	100	281	100	489

P = Proposition; R = Response (Y = Yes; N = No; U = Unsure); all others defined previously

Interestingly, 44.27 percent of CPMs and 52.42 of APs were negative regarding the existence of a stress avoidance programme compared with 65.18 percent of BPs. That was possibly explained by the fact that 29.64 and 23.29 percent of CPMs and APs, respectively, were unsure regarding this matter, whereas only 13.39 percent of BPs were unsure. The responses from participants within OSs were also of interest and these were also presented in Table 3.8.

Only 8.33 percent of SOs confirmed existence of a stress avoidance programme at work, and this was understandable given the competitive market conditions at the time of the survey. Importantly, participants from SOs knew whether their organisation had such a programme. Only 5.95 percent of participants from SOs were unsure compared with 10.48 percent from MOs and a difficult-to-comprehend 35.94 percent from LOs. While only 38.79 percent of LO participants confirmed their organisation had a stress avoidance programme, compared with 55.65 percent from MOs and 85.72 percent from SOs, the data suggested the statistic was strongly influenced by the lack of certainty that prevailed among LO participants.

One important aspect of this online survey question related to each participant's perception of how effective any stress avoidance programme was. This question was intended for participants who confirmed such a programme existed in their organisations. Responses to this follow-on question were collected via a Likert scale. The statement provided was 'This programme is effective', and the possible responses were strongly disagree, disagree, neither agree nor disagree and strongly agree (and N/A for not applicable, intended for participants who answered the main question with 'no' or 'not sure'). I shall now address responses within RP types.

'Not applicable" responses were again very high at 52.58, 47.58 and 50.89 percent across CPMs, APs and BPs, respectively, presumably for the reasons presented earlier herein. The notable finding was there is no apparent alignment between responses to this question and those to the associated previous question. While only 26.09 percent of CPMs affirmed existence of a stress avoidance programme, 47.42 percent reported an opinion regarding the effectiveness of a programme in place. This seems incongruent, but is possibly explained by participants concluding having no avoidance programme as an acceptable situation for their organisation.

The participants' responses reflected a level of disappointment with whatever was in place. Only 3.16, 2.42 and 1.79 percent, respectively, of CPMs, APs and BPs reported strongly agreeing their organisation's stress avoidance programme was effective. Some 22.14, 25.00 and 23.21 percent, respectively, neither agreed nor disagreed that their programme was successful. Some 14.22, 20.16 and 15.18 percent, respectively, agreed or strongly agreed their stress avoidance programmes were effective. The CPM figure was explained in part by data from semi-structured interviews to the effect that both being located on construction sites and having to do the work of a CPM prevented them from effectively participating in stress avoidance or management schemes. I shall now summarise responses within OSs.

These figures demonstrated a similar outcome as the figures for RP types. Specifically, while 8.33, 33.87 and 25.27 percent of participants from SOs, MOs and LOs, respectively, affirmed existence of stress avoidance programmes, a total of 33.33, 62.10 and 48.04 percent, respectively, provided an opinion regarding programme effectiveness. The apparent misalignment in numbers was again possibly explained by participants believing it was effective for their workplace to not have a stress avoidance programme, ostensibly because they preferred to deal with stress personally.

It was perhaps coincidental that 33.83 percent of participants from MOs confirmed an existence of a stress avoidance programme and 33.06 percent of participants from MOs either agreed or strongly agreed that the programmes were effective. The comparison figures from SOs and LOs were 8.33 and 25.27 percent, respectively, confirmed an ESAP and 8.33 and 10.67 percent, respectively, agreed or strongly agreed the programmes were effective.

Descriptive Statistics Regarding Participants' Organisations Having an Employee Stress Management Programme in Place

The overall descriptive statistics summary for ESMP is presented in Table 3.8.

There was relative consistency of response across all RP types for MOs and LOs. APs' and BPs' mean scores were markedly higher for SOs than they were for MOs and LOs. Inferential statistics presented earlier proved RP type had no significant effect in relation to ESMP, but OS did.

It was expected there would be similar responses within RP types regarding existence of a stress management programme in their organisations. This was the case for CPMs (with percentages of 24.90 for ESMP compared with 26.09 for ESAP) and APs (with percentages of 25.81 for ESAP and 24.19 for ESMP). However, there was a notable difference in the figures for BPs, with 15.18 percent confirming their organisation had a stress management programme as compared with 21.43 percent who confirmed existence of a stress avoidance programme. However, the percentage of BPs who reported negatively regarding ESMP was 60.24 percent higher than that for CPMs and 39.25 percent higher than that for APs. The percentages of the various RP types who were uncertain regarding ESMP were not markedly different from that for participants who were unsure regarding ESAP. I shall now present key aspects of data analysis within OS.

A higher percentage of participants from SOs reported negatively concerning existence of a stress management programme (83.33 percent) than those from MOs (59.68 percent) and LOs (43.42 percent). However, contrary to expectations, participants from LOs were far more likely to have reported being unsure about ESMP (30.60 percent as compared with 10.72 and 12.90 percent for participants from SOs and MOs, respectively). I shall address data analysis regarding perceived effectiveness of ESMP within RP types.

'Not applicable' responses were again between 47.58 and 54.46 percent for reasons previously addressed. As was the case for the analysis of responses in relation to the existence of a stress avoidance programme

(ESAP), a substantially higher percentage of participants from all RP categories provided an opinion regarding the effectiveness of a stress management programme than confirmed its existence. I have presented possible reasons have previously.

Substantially more CPMs and APs agreed or strongly agreed their organisation's stress management programme was effective than disagreed or strongly disagreed (17.78 and 22.58 percent as compared with 11.86 and 8.07 percent, respectively) but the statistics were marginal in the case of participants from BPs (11.60 percent compared with 10.72 percent). I shall now overview analysis within OS.

While only 5.95, 2.42 and 25.98 percent of participants from SOs, MOs and LOs, respectively, reported their organisations had a stress management programme, a total of 33.33, 58.07 and 50.53 percent, respectively, provided an opinion regarding programme effectiveness, regarding which phenomenon I provided a possible explanation earlier in this chapter.

For MOs, 27.42 percent of participants confirmed existence of a stress management programme and 29.84 percent either agreed or strongly agreed it was effective. The comparison figures from SOs and LOs were that 5.95 and 25.98 percent of participants, respectively, reported a stress management programme existed and 10.71 and 14.24 percent, respectively, agreed or strongly agreed it was effective. In the following section I address the descriptive statistics for CEAP.

Descriptive Statistics Regarding Existence of a Confidential Employee Assistance Programme

The descriptive statistics summary regarding the existence of a confidential employee assistance programme is presented in Table 3.8.

The standard deviation data revealed higher consistency and less spread in the responses from SO participants across all RP types than from MOs and LOs. In addition, that data indicated the spread was less for all RP types and OSs for the responses to this question than to the others in this group. CPMs from SOs and MOs recorded means lower than their AP and BP counterparts. However, CPMs in LOs recorded a mean only marginally lower than their AP counterparts, and appreciably higher than that recorded by their BP counterparts. Table 3.8 also summarises the responses to this question within role types.

There was markedly less uncertainty across RP types regarding the existence of a confidential employee assistance programme within organisations than there was regarding the existence of either an avoidance or stress management programme. An employee assistance programme was substantially more preferred as a means of addressing workplace stress than either a stress avoidance or stress management programme, effectively pointing to a preference for dealing with stress after it had taken effect rather than take steps to avoid stress and/or manage it. Specifically, 52.56 percent of CPMs confirmed their organisations used EAPs as compared with 26.09 and 24.90 percent who confirmed use of stress avoidance or stress management programmes, respectively. The difference was somewhat less for APs participants, 35.48 percent of whom confirmed an EAP, as compared with 24.19 and 25.81 percent who confirmed stress avoidance and stress management programmes, respectively. Some 37.50 percent of BP participants confirmed an EAP compared with 21.43 and 15.18 percent who confirmed stress avoidance and stress management programmes, respectively. Table 3.8 also summarises responses to CEAP within OS.

There was less uncertainty across organisations of different sizes regarding EAPs than regarding stress avoidance and stress management programmes. Importantly, an EAP was the most preferred approach to addressing workplace stress within LO and MO, notably more so than for SO. Specifically, 54.45 percent from LOs and 45.16 percent from MOs confirmed an EAP existed compared with 25.27 and 33.87 percent, respectively, who confirmed existence of a stress avoidance programme and 25.98 and 27.42 percent, respectively, who confirmed their organisation had a stress management programme. The difference was much less for SOs. Some 11.91 percent of them confirmed their organisation had an EAP, compared with 8.33 and 5.95 percent who confirmed existence of a stress avoidance or stress management programme, respectively. I shall now present summaries of responses regarding perceived effectiveness of existing EAPs within RP types.

More participants made comment on the effectiveness of their organisation's EAP (via their Likert scale responses) than confirmed existence of that EAP. I provided presumed reasons for this discrepancy previously.

Some 10.67 percent of CPMs either strongly disagreed or disagreed their EAP was effective compared with 27.27 percent who agreed or strongly agreed. The corresponding figures for APs were 4.03 and 25.00 percent, respectively, and for BPs were 7.15 and 21.43 percent, respectively.

These figures demonstrated a similar outcome as those for RP types. Specifically, while 11.91, 45.16 and 54.45 percent of participants from SOs, MOs and LOs, respectively, confirmed existence of an EAP, a total of 36.90, 58.07 and 63.34 percent, respectively, provided an opinion regarding programme effectiveness. The apparent misalignment in numbers was explained previously. The percentages of participants who strongly disagreed or disagreed regarding EAP effectiveness were 4.76, 12.10 and 7.12 for SOs, MOs and LOs, respectively, while the corresponding percentages of participants who agreed or strongly agreed that EAP was effective were 13.09, 29.84 and 24.90, respectively.

Absenteeism Due to Stress Related Issues or Illness

A question of the online survey sought responses via a five-level Likert scale to the statement, 'Our business experiences significant absenteeism due to stress related issues/illnesses'. The five response options on the scale were strongly agree, somewhat agree, neither agree nor disagree, somewhat agree and strongly agree. The variable was labelled ABSN for the purposes of this analysis and later discussion.

Descriptive Statistics Regarding Absenteeism Due to Stress

Table 3.9 summarises the means and standard deviations in relation to responses received.

The mean response from SOs was higher than that from MOs and LOs across all RP types. The mean response from MOs was higher than that from LOs for CPMs, but this was not the case for APs. The pattern for BPs was similar to that for CPMs. The standard deviations recorded indicated there was also a tighter spread of responses from CPMs than from APs and BPs.

Table 3.9 Descriptive statistics summary regarding absenteeism due to stress

Item	Role type	Org. size	Mean	Std. dev	$N =$
ABSN	CPM	SO	3.44	1.10	18
		MO	3.14	0.98	51
		LO	3.04	1.02	184
	AP	SO	3.90	0.98	31
		MO	2.85	1.21	34
		LO	2.92	1.02	59
	BP	SO	3.86	1.12	35
		MO	3.26	1.16	39
		LO	2.61	1.03	38
	Total	SO	3.79	1.07	84
		MO	3.10	1.11	124
		LO	2.95	1.03	281

Table 3.10 Attitudes to absenteeism due to stress within role types

Response	Role types						
	CPM		AP		BP		Total
	$n =$	%	$n =$	%	$n =$	%	
Strongly disagree	10	3.95	10	8.06	10	8.93	30
Disagree	65	25.69	27	21.78	21	18.75	113
Agree/Disagree	96	37.95	38	30.65	35	31.25	169
Agree	57	22.53	33	26.61	26	23.21	116
Strongly agree	25	9.88	16	12.90	20	17.86	61
Not applicable	0	0.00	0	0.00	0	0.00	0
	253	100.00	124	100.00	112	100.00	489

The nature of inferential statistics differed from those conducted for previous questions in that correlations were analysed between responses to this and other questions. The inferential statistics are presented later in this section. Table 3.10 summarises the responses based on RP types.

To achieve maximum value from the table, I analysed the data in light of the qualitative data collected (and reported in the next chapter). It was difficult to be confident in the figures for CPMs because many sufferers who needed to take time off were unlikely to nominate stress as the reason for fear of appearing weak in a strong person's industry. Accordingly, the relatively high percentages for the 'neither agree not disagree' option of the Likert scale are understandable. That same reasoning somewhat explains the combined percentage for agree and strongly agree options from APs (39.51 percent) and from BPs (41.07 percent) were 21.91 and 26.72 percent, respectively, being higher than for CPMs (32.41 percent). Table 3.11 summarises attitudes to absenteeism from an OS perspective.

Table 3.11 demonstrates one of the most disparate spreads of percentages from the entire study. There is a strong pattern of decreasing agreement with the statement (regarding stress causing absenteeism) with increasing OS. Specifically, 61.90 percent of SO participants either agreed or strongly agreed, while the corresponding percentages for MO and LO participants were 37.90 and 27.76, respectively. The relatively high percentage of participants from SOs who agreed or strongly agreed with the statement contradicted qualitative findings to the effect that

Table 3.11 Attitudes to absenteeism due to stress within organisation sizes

Response	Organisation size						
	SO		MO		LO		Total
	n =	%	*n* =	%	*n* =	%	
Strongly disagree	2	2.38	9	7.26	19	6.76	30
Disagree	8	9.53	30	24.19	75	26.69	113
Agree/Disagree	22	26.19	38	30.65	109	38.79	169
Agree	26	30.95	34	27.42	56	19.93	116
Strongly agree	26	30.95	13	10.48	22	7.83	61
Not applicable	0	0.00	0	0.00	0	0.00	0
	84	100.00	124	100.00	281	100.00	489

CPMs were unlikely to admit stress was the reason for absenteeism because of the risk of being seen as weak in an industry with a reputation for toughness. If this were true, it stood to reason that it would be more likely to be so in SOs where information was likely to quickly spread. On the other hand, some qualitative data indicated that in SOs there was more likely to be a supportive, family-like atmosphere wherein people were more likely to trust co-workers with confidential personal information.

Considering this latter insight, it is interesting to note that, while only 11.91 percent of SO participants either disagreed or strongly disagreed with the statement regarding absenteeism, the corresponding figures for their MO and LO counterparts were 31.45 and 33.45 percent, respectively. In other words, MO and LO participants responded in line with expectations, while those from SOs did not. Beyond the explanation provided in the previous paragraph, nothing more was found from the data analysis.

Inferential Statistics Regarding Absenteeism

A Pearson's correlation was computed to investigate the relationship between stress experienced by workers and the perception of absenteeism in organisations. The results showed the variables are significantly negatively correlated such that participants whose work was reported to be very stressful reported a lower perception of absenteeism. In other words, the more a participant reported considering his or her work to be stressful, the greater the likelihood that Pearson's correlation would indicate the participant would report a lower perception of absenteeism in his or her organisation. The correlation figures computed were as follows. The correlation between the variable 'For me, stress is more significantly caused by work factors' and perception of absenteeism was found to be small, negative and significant ($r = -0.17$, $p < .001$). The correlation between the variable 'The work I do is stressful' and perception of absenteeism was found to be small, negative and significant ($r = -0.21$, $p < .001$).

Personal Experience of Stress-Related Issues

The next section of the online survey sought data concerning participants' personal experience of stress-related issues. These were follow-up questions that sought additional information regarding previous major survey questions. Responses were recorded using a visual sliding scale with possible ratings between 0 and 100, the latter being the maximum. However, the first question in the section sought a response on a five-level Likert scale to the statement, 'Over the last month, I have felt stressed more consistently than I'd like'. The label allocated to this variable was PSPM.

Inferential Statistics Relating to PSPM

An ANOVA was conducted to test the effect of RP type and OS on experience of stress over the month previous to completing the online survey. A significant difference between RP types was found, $F(2,468) = 3.75$, $p = .024$, and there was also a significant difference of OS, $F(2,468) = 3.15$, $p = .044$, albeit this latter difference was marginal. There was no significant interaction between RP type and OS on level of consistency of feeling stressed over the month previous to completing the online survey, $F(4,468) = 0.89$, $p = .472$.

Descriptive Statistics Relating to PSPM

Table 3.12 summarises the descriptive statistics for the question regarding experience of stress over the previous month.

The means supported the effect of RP type identified in the inferential statistics above. They also supported the comment the effect of OS was marginal. The standard deviations indicated a similar spread of responses from BPs across OSs, whereas the response spread from APs was far broader across OSs. For CPMs, the standard deviations indicated a similar spread of responses for MOs and LOs, with that for SOs being a broader spread more in line with that for BPs.

Table 3.12 Descriptive statistics regarding participants' experience of stress over past month

Item	Role type	Org. size	Mean	Std. dev	$N =$
PSPM	CPM	SO	3.72	1.27	18
		MO	3.55	1.08	51
		LO	3.68	1.09	176
	AP	SO	3.20	1.45	30
		MO	3.29	1.27	34
		LO	3.66	1.10	56
	BP	SO	3.29	1.23	35
		MO	2.92	1.22	39
		LO	3.46	1.26	37
	Total	SO	3.35	1.32	83
		MO	3.28	1.20	124
		LO	3.64	1.11	269

Table 3.13 Level of agreement regarding experience of stress over past month

Response	Frequency ($n =$)	Percentage of respondents ($n =$ 477)	Percentage of all participants ($N =$ 489)
Strongly disagree	30	6.3	6.1
Somewhat disagree	81	17.0	16.5
Neither agree nor disagree	90	18.8	18.4
Somewhat agree	174	36.5	35.6
Strongly agree	102	21.4	20.9
Did not respond	12	Not applicable	2.5
	489	100	100

Table 3.13 presents the data overview for responses to the Likert scale-based PSPM question. The data for all respondents to this non-compulsory question ($n = 477$) are presented in a single table because, while this information is of some interest from the perspective of background information, the level of stress reported is more important for detailed analysis and is thus presented in the next section.

Some 57.9 percent of respondents indicated they either somewhat agreed ($n = 174$, 36.5 percent) or strongly agreed ($n = 102$, 21.4 percent) they had a person experience of stress over the previous month and 23.3 percent either somewhat disagreed or strongly disagreed. The high level of agreement that stress over the previous month was higher than participants would have liked was anticipated and so the online survey included follow-on questions, the responses to which assisted more detailed analysis of this phenomenon.

Additional Statistics Regarding Stress Levels Experienced Over the Month Prior to Completing the Survey

As well as understanding the level of agreement expressed with the statement introduced earlier, it was important to ascertain participants' perception of their stress levels experienced over the month prior to completing the online survey. This information was collected via a drag and drop pointer over a visual sliding scale within the survey which rated no stress as zero at one end of a continuum and full stress at 100 at the other.

An ANOVA was conducted to test the effects of RP type on different levels of stress experienced, and the results confirmed the findings of the descriptive statistics (presented below) that there was a significant difference between RP types of stress experienced over the month previous to completing the online survey $F(2{,}473) = 4.73$, $p = .009$. Table 3.14 presents an overview of the information obtained from analysis of the data received in response to the sliding scale question.

Table 3.14 Levels of stress experienced over the past month

Percentage stress level	Role type CPM percentage	AP percentage	BP percentage
50	32.7	41.7	36.9
70	59.6	68.3	73.0
80	82.9	82.5	90.1
90	93.9	95.8	96.4

Note Figures in Table 3.14 are percentages of participants who responded. E.g. 32.7 percent of CPMs reported they experienced stress at up to a 50 percent level, meaning that the percentage who experienced it above that level was 67.3

On the same basis, this data revealed that 40.40 percent of CPMs rated stress at 70 percent or higher as compared with 31.70 percent of APs and 27.0 percent of BPs. In other words, the number of CPMs who experienced stress at a 70 percent level was 27.4 percent higher than APs and 49.6 percent higher than BPs.

There was markedly less difference between the percentages of CPMs (17.1 percent) and APs (17.5 percent) who experienced stress effects at a level of 80 percent or higher, but the percentage of BPs who experienced stress at that level was just 9.9 percent. Experience of stress at a level of 90 percent or higher was reported by 6.1 percent of CPMs, 4.2 percent of APs, and 3.6 percent of BPs. CPMs experienced this level 45.2 percent and 69.4 percent more than APs and BPs, respectively.

Participants' Management of Stress (to Test Hypothesis 5)

One important finding from the qualitative data analysis (Chapter 4) was, even if employers encouraged involvement in stress avoidance and/or management activities, and provided the workplace facilities for these, there was a general reticence to use available facilities among CPMs. A key reason was their pressure of work was so high they had no time available. This was especially the case for participants with families.

The online survey contained three questions designed to gain insight into what actions, if any, participants adopted to avoid or manage stress. One question was optional and dichotomous, and sought a yes or no response regarding whether the participant took medication for stress-related illness. A second question sought information regarding whether the participant used meditation, progressive muscle relaxation, mindfulness or other similar well-respected techniques for managing stress and/or helping to avoid its impact. The third question was an extension of the second and presented a list of 20 stress management activities and asked participants to tick a box aligned with each to indicate any of the techniques they personally used. The list of stress management activities was similar to that used by the Australian Psychological Society (APS) in its regular surveys from which the APS produces its report,

'Stress and Wellbeing in Australia'. By adopting this question, it would be possible to compare responses from participants with those from the broader Australian community in later studies beyond the scope of this work.

For each positive response regarding a stress management technique employed, there was opportunity to also provide an opinion regarding the level of effectiveness of that technique via a five-level Likert scale with response options similar to those presented earlier herein. This analysis addressed responses to each of those questions.

Participants' Approach to Dealing with Stress—Medication

Because the question regarding medication use was dichotomous and sought a simple yes or no response, a non-parametric test was used to investigate any effect of OS and RP type on responses given. A Kruskal Wallis test was run to determine whether participants within the three RP types or from different OSs differed on use of medication to control stress. There was no significant difference across RP types (i.e. participants from any RP type were not more likely to take medication to control stress than participants from the RP types in which they were not employed) χ^2 (2, n = 476) = 1.05, p = .593). There was no significant difference across OSs either χ^2 (2, n = 476) = 0.86, p = .650. Table 3.15 summarises participants' responses to the dichotomous question regarding taking medication for stress-related illness.

Table 3.15 Stress management medication use within role types

Question	Role type					
Medication?	CPM		AP		BP	
Yes	32	13.06 (12.65)	18	15.00 (14.52)	19	17.86 (17.86)
No	213	86.94 (84.19)	102	85.00 (82.26)	92	82.14 (82.14)
Totals	245	100	120	100	111	100

Left column under each role type is number of participants, and right column is percentage of that participant type. The numbers in parentheses are percentages of the entire participant base within that category

Some 97.34 percent of all participants answered this non-compulsory question—96.84 percent of CPMs, 96.77 percent of APs and 99.11 percent of BPs. Unexpectedly, CPMs reported the lowest use of medication, but no further analysis of this question was intended for this work.

Participants' Rating of Effectiveness of Medication

The question regarding participants' perception of effectiveness of their medication was non-compulsory. Of 253 CPMs, 153 or 60.47 percent responded. Of 124 APs, 106 or 85.48 percent responded, and of 112 BPs, responses totalled 106 or 94.64 percent.

These statistics suggest the possibility of confusion among participants regarding the intent of the question, which was to determine the effectiveness of a medication regime in the perception of those who used it. Only 15.81 percent of CPMs, 17.74 percent of APs and 17.86 percent of BPs confirmed they took medication for stress, yet the percentage who rated medication effectiveness was substantially higher across all participant categories. I concluded participants reported their approach to dealing with stress was effective (or not) regardless of whether it involved taking medication. It is reasonable to accept this as realistic on the balance of probabilities, and in consideration of several factors, including:

- All final sample participants completed all compulsory questions
- 34.76 percent of participants who completed all compulsory questions came from an organisation whose management very actively encouraged participation in the study
- 55.2 percent of participants were sourced by a professional and highly respected service, which applied rigorous participation and identification and response review practices and quality assurance protocols.
- The remaining participants were sourced either from respected professional institutions, from people who had expressed interest in being

Table 3.16 Ratings of effectiveness of stress medication withing role types

Percentage stress level	Role type		
	CPM percentage	AP percentage	BP percentage
50	59.5	56.6	61.3
70	79.7	77.4	83

part of the research sample after hearing about the research at professional conferences, or registered interest via a very tightly targeted Facebook advertising campaign.

I further concluded the problem arose from a less-than-ideal construction of the survey question. The question was worded, 'Using the sliding scale below, how effective would you rate the management to be?' I should have used the introductory words, 'If you answered "yes" to the previous question…'. Having established a high probability that responses to this question were well intended, it remained only to report the descriptive analysis findings, which are summarised in Table 3.16.

Some 79.7 percent of CPMs considered their approach to be up to 70 percent effective and this meant that 20.3 (100 – 79.7) considered it to be more than 70 percent effective. The corresponding percentage of APs and BPs, respectively, were 22.6 percent and 17.0. Those percentages appeared to be quite low, given the extent to which participants reported being affected by stress.

Inferential Statistics—Participants' Approach to Dealing with Stress—Lifestyle Approaches

The question concerning the use of well-recognised techniques for avoiding and/or managing stress was also dichotomous, and sought a yes or no answer, but provided opportunity to name any technique used. A further opportunity was provided to select from a list of well-recognised relaxation activities. The purpose was to affirm or reject the proposition the participant used lifestyle approaches to stress avoidance and/or management such as yoga, exercise, meditation, progressive muscle relaxation or mindfulness. I conducted differential statistics regarding the question, using a non-parametric Kruskal Wallis test to determine whether participants from across the RP types or from different OSs differed on use of active non-medication-based techniques for managing stress. There was no significant difference across RP types (i.e. no participants from any RP type were more significantly likely to use active non-medication based techniques for managing stress than participants from the RP types in which they were not employed) $\chi^2(2, n = 476) = 0.62, p = .733$. There was no significant difference across OSs either $\chi^2(2, n = 476) = 0.15, p = .930$. Table 3.17 summarises the responses to the question.

This question was not compulsory. Nevertheless, 97.3 percent of the participants responded.

In light of qualitative data that emphasised the extent to which CPMs were overworked and lacked spare time, it is interesting that responses from CPMs indicated almost equal numbers for those who used stress management techniques and those who did not. Also, 47.5 percent of APs used some form of stress avoidance or management techniques, as did 45.95 percent of BPs. I considered it important to analyse participants' ratings of the effectiveness of the stress avoidance or management techniques they employed.

Table 3.17 Participants use of stress management techniques

Question	Role type					
Management techniques?	CPM		AP		BP	
Yes	123	50.20 (48.62)	57	47.50 (45.97)	51	45.95 (45.54)
No	122	49.80 (48.22)	63	52.50 (50.81)	60	54.05 (53.57)
Totals	245	100	120	100	111	100

Left column under each role type is number of participants, and right column is percentage of that participant type. The numbers in parentheses are percentages of the entire participant base within that category

Participants' Rating of Stress Management Techniques Employed

Table 3.18 summarises the responses to the question regarding the perceived effectiveness of general stress avoidance and management techniques used by participants. The rating was obtained using a visual slider within the online survey, as previously described.

CPMs from LOs reported a mean 61.45 effectiveness of their preferred stress management approach. The corresponding means for MOs and SOs were 55.97 and 59.94, respectively. BPs recorded means of 58.00, 60.12 and 51.00 for LOs, MOs and SOs, respectively. The corresponding means for BPs were 57.34, 58.70 and 52.11, respectively.

Given the high levels of workplace stress reported by CPMs, it is interesting to note CPMs from SOs and LOs responded to their stressful work environment by employing stress avoidance and management techniques that worked for them better than did the techniques chosen by APs and BPs, respectively. For participants in MOs, both APs and BPs rated their preferred stress management technique as more effective than CPMs rated theirs.

Table 3.18 Effectiveness of stress management within role types and organization size

Role type	Size	Mean	Std. dev	$N =$
CPM	SO	59.94	29.65	17
	MO	55.97	29.00	30
	LO	61.45	28.28	94
AP	SO	51.00	31.57	30
	MO	60.12	32.83	34
	LO	58.00	26.59	40
BP	SO	49.09	27.42	33
	MO	59.62	27.82	37
	LO	44.94	28.47	35
Total	SO	52.11	29.43	80
	MO	58.70	29.69	101
	LO	57.34	28.49	169
	Total	56.54	29.08	350

Sources of Stress for Participants

The online survey posed a single question. This was an extension of the earlier questions regarding sources of stress that were addressed earlier:

> Using the sliding scale below, at what level would you rate the stress you experience to be caused by work or non-work-related issues? (0= no stress, 100= maximum stress).

Participants were presented with two visuals, both of sliding scales with drag and drop pointers, and each slider notated with zero at the left of the scale and 100 at the right. There was a notation to the effect that, 'The total of both scales combined may exceed 100'. In other words, each measure was marked out of 100 rather than having 100 distributed across two measures. The sliding scales were labelled 'Work related' and 'Non work related'.

Inferential Statistics Relating to Causes of Stress

No linear relationship was reported by SPSS analysis between work-related stress and non-work-related stress. Accordingly, two separate ANOVAS were conducted, one related to work-related stress and the second to non-work-related stress.

Levene's test of equality found homogeneity of variance was met for the variable measuring non-work-related stress but was violated for the work-related stress variable ($p = .012$). A more stringent alpha of 0.01 was used to address this violation.

There was a significant difference in work-related stress between role types, $F(2,464) = 5.82$, $p = .003$. Post-hoc analysis revealed there was a significant difference between the role categories of professional and other. Specifically, CPMs reported higher levels of work-related stress than BPs. However, there was no significant difference reported between APs and BPs. Also, there was no significant difference in work-related stress attributable to OS, $F(2,464) = 1.93$, $p = .147$. In addition, there was no interaction between RP types and OS, $F(4{,}464) = 0.070$, $p = .595$.

There was no significant difference in non-work stress factors between RP types, $F(2{,}450) = 1.10$, $p = .303$. There was no significance between OSs in relation to non-work-related stress, $F(2{,}450) = 0.02$, $p = .984$. There was no significant interaction between RP types and OS, $F(4{,}450) = 1.27$, $p = .283$. Descriptive statistics were then conducted, with a focus on levels of stress that were reported by participants from the two sources.

Work-Related Causes of Stress

Work-related causes of stress were analysed first. Analysis was conducted with role types, with focus on participants who rated work-related stress at levels of 50, 70, 80 and 90 percent. Table 3.19 presents the percentages of participants, categorised within RP.

On the basis above, 73.10 percent of CPMs experienced work-related stress at the level of 50 percent or more, compared with 58.3 and 60.4 percent for AP and BP roles, respectively. In other words, the percentage of CPMs who experience work-related stress at the 50 percent level or above was 25.0 percent more than APs and 21.0 percent more than BPs.

The data indicated that 47.5 percent of CPMs experienced work-related stress at the 70 percent level or higher, compared with 37.3

Table 3.19 Participants' work-related stress levels

Role	50 percent	70 percent	80 percent	90 percent	$n =$	Percentage of category
CPMs	26.9	52.5	73.6	90.1	242 of 253	95.7
APs	41.7	61.7	81.7	91.7	120 of 124	96.8
BPs	39.6	56.8	1.2	86.5	111 of 112	99.1

Note Figures in the Table 3.19 are percentages of participants who responded. For example, 73.6 percent of CPMs reported they experienced stress at up to an 80 percent level, meaning that the percentage of respondents to this question who experienced stress above the 80 percent level was (100 – 73.6) = 26.40. Some 95.7 percent of CPMs ($n =$ 242) responded to this non-compulsory question compared with 96.8 percent ($n =$ 120) of APs and 99.1 percent of BPs (n = 111) percent of APs and 43.2 percent of BPs. In other words, the percentage of CPMs who experienced work-related stress at the 70 percent level or above was 27.35 percent more than APs and 9.95 percent more than BPs.

The percentages of participants from the different RP types who experienced stress at the 80 percent or above were 26.4, 18.3 and 28.8 for CPMs, APs and BPs, respectively. This meant the percentage of CPMs who experienced work-related stress at the level of 80 percent or above was 44.26 percent higher than APs, but 9.1 percent less than BPs.

The data indicated 9.9 percent of CPMs experienced stress at a level of 90 percent or more, as compared with 8.3 percent of APs and 13.5 percent of BPs. The percentage of CPMs who experienced work-related stress at the level of 90 percent or more was 19.27 percent higher than APs but 26.67 percent lower than BPs.

Descriptive Statistics—Non-Work-Related Causes of Stress

Table 3.20 presents the percentage of participants, within RP types, who rated non-work-related stress at levels of 50, 70, 80 and 90 percent.

These data indicate 26.7 percent (100 − 73.3) of CPMs experienced non-work-related stress at the level of 50 percent or more, compared with 44.0 percent and 40.5 percent for APs and BPs, respectively. In other words, the percentage of CPMs who experienced non-work-related stress at the 50 percent level or above was 39.32 percent lower than APs and 34.0 percent lower than BPs.

The data also shows 11.6 percent (100 − 88.4) of CPMs experienced non-work-related stress at the 70 percent level or higher, compared with

Table 3.20 Participants' non work-related stress levels

Role	50 percent	70 percent	80 percent	90 percent	$n =$	Percentage of category
CPM	73.3	88.4	95.3	98.3	232 of 253	91.7
AP	56.0	80.2	90.5	96.4	116 of 124	93.5
BP	59.5	80.2	91.9	96.4	111 of 112	99.1

19.8 percent of both APs and BPs, meaning the percentage of CPMs who experienced non-work-related stress at the 70 percent level or above was 41.41 percent less than each of APs and BPs. The percentages of participants from the different RP types who experienced non-work-related stress at the 80 percent level or above were 4.7, 9.5 and 8.1 for CPMs, APs and BPs, respectively. This meant the percentage of CPMs who experienced non-work-related stress at the level of 80 percent or above was 50.53 percent less than APs and 41.98 percent less than BPs.

Of CPMs, 1.7 percent experienced non-work-related stress at a level of 90 percent or more, as compared with 3.6 percent of each of APs and BPs. The percentage of CPMs who experienced non-work-related stress at the level of 90 percent or more was 52.78 percent less than both APs and BPs.

An early review of all data collected for this research revealed there was a strong body of qualitative opinion among participants that more often than not, home stress problems are not solely home stress problems. They are often likely to be work-related problems taken into the home environment where they escalate and their effects are exacerbated, before the problem is returned to the workplace, only to be further escalated before being again brought home in a stress increasing spiral. I now considered it important to evaluate how stress, regardless of source, affected performance at work.

Impact of Stress on Ability to Perform at Work

Having established CPMs experienced more stress from the work environment than APs and BPs, the question arises as to how, if at all, that might impact their performance at work.

One survey question invited use of a drag and drop slider to indicate the level each participant considered stress impacted his or her ability to perform at work (0 = no impact and 100 = severe impact). This question was not compulsory.

Inferential Statistics Regarding Impact of Stress on Ability to Perform at Work

To investigate the impact of OS and RP on participants' perception of the impact of stress on their ability to perform at work, I conducted a two-way ANOVA. No significant interaction effect was found $F(4,460) = 1.68$, $p = .152$. There was no significant effect of OS on stress impact $F(2,460) = 0.92$, $p = .399$. Similarly, there was no effect of RP on stress impact $F(2,460) = 2.12$, $p = .067$. However, the figures indicated that there was close to an effect of RP on perception of stress impact. This was reinforced by the analysis of the means and standard deviations from the descriptive statistics presented earlier.

I conducted a two-way ANOVA to investigate any difference of stress impact on performance at work between OSs and RP types. There was a significant difference between CPM and AP groups in relation to how much they think stress effects their ability to work, $F(1,352) = 4.30$, $p = .039$. Specifically, the CPM group rated the intensity of effect far higher than did those from the AP group. Neither OS nor the interaction had any significant effect on performance at work.

Descriptive Statistics Relating to Stress Impact on Ability to Perform at Work

Table 3.21 presents the number of participants who responded within both RP type and OS to the question asking them to rate the impact of stress on their ability to perform at work.

Some 95.91 percent of the full participant sample responded to this non-compulsory question and 94.47 percent ($n = 239$ of $n = 253$) of CPMs responded compared with 95.22 percent ($n = 119$ of $n = 124$) of APs and 99.11 percent ($n = 111$ of $n = 112$) of BPs. Percentage responses were relatively even across all OSs for BPs, but the means for BPs indicated a higher level of stress effect on performance at work for those who worked in MOs than those who worked in SOs and LOs.

Table 3.21 Impact of stress on ability to perform at work within role types

Role type	Organisation size	$n =$	Percent-age	Mean	Standard deviation
CPM	SO	18	7.53	54.72	26.09
	MO	51	21.34	53.84	24.36
	LO	170	71.13	45.91	26.12
	Total	239	100.00	48.27	25.92
AP	SO	30	25.21	36.00	28.53
	MO	34	28.57	49.35	24.49
	LO	55	46.22	47.16	28.54
	Total	119	100.00	44.97	27.72
BP	SO	35	31.53	42.03	23.82
	MO	39	35.14	49.79	28.66
	LO	37	33.33	46.33	24.27
	Total	111	100.00	46.59	25.62
Total	SO	83	17.70	42.60	26.69
	MO	124	26.44	49.79	25.89
	LO	262	55.86	46.33	26.31
	Total	469	100.00	46.59	26.32

The percentage column presented the percentage of the number who responded in each role category, and not of the total participant sample in that category

Percentage responses from CPMs and APs were skewed towards those working in LOs, as was expected, given the information above.

The means for APs from MOs and LOs were generally in line with those for BPs, and participants who worked in MOs expressed a slightly higher effect of stress on work performance than those from LOs. However, APs who worked in SOs indicated that stress had a substantially lower impact on their work ($M = 36.00$) than did participants from MOs ($M = 45.35$) and LOs ($M = 47.16$). The means for CPMs from SOs ($M = 54.72$) and MOs ($M = 53.84$) were substantially higher than for APs and BPs. The mean for CPMs from LOs (45.91) was similar to those for APs and BPs from MOs and LOs.

The noticeably higher mean for impact of stress on ability to perform at work for CPMs as compared with APs from SOs was explained by CPMs experiencing higher stress from the workplace than did participants from APs and BPs. The closer means between RP categories for MOs and LOs reflected the practical reality that even large workloads can be sufficiently shared in organisations with larger numbers of resources to a level that alleviated some effect of stress.

It was important to compare the results from CPMs and APs with those from BPs. I regarded a direct comparison of all categories the ideal approach for this comparison and made the decision to compare stress impacts at and above the levels of 60, 70, 80 and 90 percent across role types. Table 3.22 presents that comparison.

Interestingly, 23.8 percent of CPMs rated the impact of stress on their ability to perform at work at between 70 and 100 percent compared with 20.2 percent of APs participants and 18.9 percent of BPs. In contrast, the percentage of APs who experienced stress impact on ability to perform at between 90 and 100 percent was five percent—double that reported by CPMs (2.5 percent) and nearly triple that reported by BPs (1.8 percent). The analysis reveals more participants across all RP types from MOs experienced stress impacts on ability to perform at work at a rating of over 70 percent effect than from LOs and SOs. The percentage figures were 21.76, 25.80 and 16.87 percent for LOs, MOs and SOs, respectively.

From the perspective of project management process, we have now completed half of the project delivery—we understand the attitude of the participants to various aspects of avoidance and management of stress

Table 3.22 Comparison of level of perceived stress and ability to perform at work

Percentage affect	Role type CPM percentage	AP percentage	BP percentage
61–70	10.1	6.8	11.7
71–80	14.2	11.0	11.7
81–90	7.1	4.2	5.4
Above 90	2.5	5.0	1.8
Total 61–100 range	33.9	27.0	30.6

Notes
(i) All figures in role type columns are percentages of actual respondents to this question
(ii) The full sample of CPMs, APs and BPs comprised 253, 124 and 112 participants, respectively
(iii) The number of respondents to this non-compulsory question was 239, 119 and 111, respectively

within their workplaces, and we have a solid construct of the extent to which categories of participants experience stress compared with other participant categories. We now know CPMs experience stress primarily from work causes while APs and BPs sources of stress are primarily from non-work factors. It now remains for us to complete the project delivery by determining why CPMs experience stress primarily from their workplaces, and this is the objective of the next chapter.

Before moving on, let us take another look at the circumstances of Will and Clare in light of the findings of this statistical analysis. Neither of the couple has any doubt the main cause of Will's stress is work. However, Will's concern his long working hours and incessant difficult-to-achieve deadlines are beginning to have an effect on his relationship with his family members is adding additional stress. Despite becoming more aware of this as time passes and his stress increases, he does not raise it for discussion with Clare. He is at the point where work-generated stress is taken home and its impact in that environment exacerbates the problem. Meanwhile, the situation is very much the opposite for Clare, who you will recall is a non-construction professional. She is beginning to feel the stress from home-related factors including carrying the greater burden of responsibilities for the children, walking on eggshells around her obviously stressed husband, and feeling helpless about raising the matter for discussion for fear of increasing Will's already extremely high stress levels. Clare goes to work tired, often worn out, and work pressures, while currently nothing like Will's because of her well-structured working hours, are nonetheless adding to the stress she brings from home, with the result that she too is beginning to feel the negative impacts of stress, with increasing irritability and interrupted sleep being just two of her symptoms.

Will is well aware there is a stress management programme available in his organisation, but he does not take advantage of it, fearing the time spent would put him even more under pressure with his everyday work. When there was talk of stress avoidance training at work, Will was pleased it remained just talk. Where on earth would he or any of his CPM colleagues find time in their ridiculously busy schedules to attend such training? The training itself would be stress-inducing rather than stress-avoiding. Furthermore, Will's organisation recently announced availability of a confidential Employee Assistance Programme for all employees, and he considered using it, before concluding the 'confidential' aspect might be wishful thinking, and if anyone in management discovered he was seeing a counsellor, they might consider him weak, and he considered that might negatively impact his recently kindled promotion chances. After all, who would want a person who cannot stand the pressure of a job in senior management? Besides, he knew he was now on an excellent remuneration and rewards package, so surely he should be responsible for managing his own stress, regardless of where and why it arose. There was always medication, and he had considered seeing a doctor after realising the stress he was under was beginning to negatively impact his performance at work, but what if his employer found out he was taking it? In any case, it was the weaker people who took medication, wasn't it?

Clare was strongly of the opinion Will's managers should be doing something about the situation. She'd attended social events with Will's colleagues, and she had heard the discussion that revealed most of them were in the same situation as Will, and some of the female colleagues were really struggling with work and family responsibilities, but they all laughed the pressure off and proceeded to enjoy the day with a few drinks. But it was quickly becoming a few drinks too many as time passed.

The situation was precipitous, and both Will and Clare realised something needed to be done. Neither had any inkling what needed to be done, or how to go about doing anything anyway, because both were trying to avoid conflict that might escalate into serious stress impacts for both of them in the circumstances. Of course, it's usually best to determine what the problem is and what its causes are in some detail before attempting to solve it, and it is that objective to which I will now turn attention.

This quantitative data analysis identified the problem issues, especially for CPMs. It is appropriate to address what causes those issues, and the appropriate way to determine those was via qualitative data analysis. The next chapter presents the finding of that analysis.

References

1. Erdfelder, E, Faul, F & Buchner, A 1996, 'G* Power: A general power analysis program', *Behaviour Research Methods, Instruments and Computers*, vol. 28, pp. 1–11.
2. Faul, F, Erdfelder, E, Lang, A-G & Buchner, A 2007, 'G* Power 3: a flexible statical power analysis program for the social, behavioural and biomedical sciences', *Behaviour Research Methods*, vol. 39, pp. 175–191, viewed 5th February 2018, http://www.psycho.uni-duesseldorf.de/abteilungen/aap/gpower3//download-and-register/Dokumente/Gpower3-BRM-Paper.pdf.
3. Brand, A & Bradley, M 2016, 'The precision of effect size estimation from published psychological research: surveying confidence intervals', *Psychological Reports*, vol. 118, no. 1, pp. 154–170, viewed 27th June 2021, https://journals-sagepub-com.ezproxy.bond.edu.au/doi/pdf/10.1177/0033294115625265.
4. Tabachnick, B & Fidell, L 2013, *Using multivariate statistics*, New York, Pearson.

4

What Is Causing Stress Among Construction Project Managers?

Introduction

After explaining results of a pilot study and how they planted the seed for this work in Chapter 1, I provided the main findings from an extensive literature review in the second chapter in order to address the science behind psychological stress and the impacts it can have on the world's people and economies.

In Chapter 3, I explained the findings from analysis of quantitative data collected and found important information regarding its impacts on participants and about the different attitudes those participants held regarding stress, how to avoid it and how it should be managed in the workplace.

In this chapter, I investigate participants beliefs and lived experiences regarding the main causes of stress, especially in the workplace. I will

In project management (PM) parlance—the IMPLEMENTATION phase, part 2 (monitoring and controlling to determine and remedy problems).
IIn psychotherapy parlance—ADDRESSING CAUSES OF THE PROBLEM and MONITORING PROGRESS IN RESPONSE TO INTERVENTION session.

A. Patching, *Attitudes to Psychological Stress Among Construction Professionals*, https://doi.org/10.1007/978-3-030-93776-8_4

leave further development of the story of Will and Clare until later in this chapter.

From a project management process perspective, we are now at the stage of implementing the second stage of project execution, focusing on determining the reasons for existence of what we found in the previous chapter. From a psychotherapeutic process phases perspective, we are working at greater depth to determine causes of the presenting issues in order to prepare to gain substantial progress by helping Will and Clare both address their presenting issues and, to the extent possible, remove or ameliorate the underlying causes of those issues.

This chapter describes the findings from analysis of qualitative data and provides useful insights into the causes of stress for construction professionals in particular. In other words, qualitative methods determined the reasons for several significant findings from the quantitative analysis.

Participants had the option of completing the survey and then volunteering for a follow-up semi-structured interview, or to select the semi-structured interview without completing the survey. The majority opted for the former approach, and I randomly selected participants for semi-structured interviews.

Qualitative Data Analysis

I conducted this qualitative analysis using two sets of data collected using two separate methods. I collected primary data during 35 semi-structured interviews, and additional data via the online survey (there were 594 comments provided in response to five open questions within the online survey). Subsequent to the primary research, I conducted a follow-up confirmation study with 68 participants, 48 of whom answered all questions and 40 of whom were CPMs as defined for this study. and this confirmed the validity of qualitative analysis findings. A summary of confirmation study results is presented at the end of this chapter.

I found valuable qualitative data in transcripts of spoken interviews. That is not to diminish the value of responses to open questions in the online questionnaire. Alignment of data from the two sources was noteworthy. Importantly, the shorter answers serve as triangulation of responses from spoken interviews, and in turn, the collective qualitative data serve as solid triangulation of the quantitative data analysis. As an example of the alignment between shorter online responses and longer transcripts of interview recordings, one CPM revealed the following regarding the main causes of stress:

> *I've come to accept I have anxiety. That's who I am. I've also worked with people who've had anxiety and depression. I think it's been as a result of the industry, which tends to be very full on, with high paced, long hours and a huge workload. Everything is time and money driven. When you've got an employer and a client who are at you to save money and time at every turn, it can be quite stressful.*

By way of comparison, following were comments in response to a similar open question in the survey:

> *The volume and urgency of work determines how stressful work is, rather than the work itself.*

> *Keeping delivery times and costs down are the biggest causes of stress.*

Before proceeding with qualitative data analysis, it is of value to overview responses to online survey open questions. Table 4.1 presents that information.

Certain observations are possible even at this basic level of data review and analysis:

- There was inconsistency in CPMs' responses across OS. For all qualitative questions the number of responses from MOs was between 1.8 and 2.5 times than from SOs, while responses from LOs were between 2.72 and 3.73 times higher than those from MOs.
- In contrast, responses from APs varied little across OS. The highest response rate exceeded the lowest by a factor between 1.16 and 1.83 for this cohort of participants, and that was across a total number of responses of 158 as compared with 278 from CPMs.

Table 4.1 Schedule of responses to qualitative questions in the online survey

Qualitative questions	Total responses	Professional		Admin		Other		Comments > two lines
1. Please provide additional comments/personal experience regarding stress and its management in your workplace	169	S M L	8 18 61 87	S M L	13 12 14 39	S M L	10 18 15 43	29
2. Please provide additional comments/personal experience regarding stress intervention/avoidance programmes and absenteeism in your workplace	158	S M L	7 15 56 78	S M L	13 11 15 39	S M L	9 17 15 41	11
3. Please provide additional comments/personal experience regarding stress management training and programmes in your workplace	70	S M L	3 6 12 21	S M L	11 10 6 27	S M L	5 9 8 22	4
4. Please provide additional comments/personal experience regarding personal attitudes towards stress management	109	S M L	6 11 30 47	S M L	12 11 13 36	S M L	7 9 10 26	18

Qualitative questions	Total responses	Professional		Admin		Other		Comments > two lines
5. Please provide additional comments/personal experience regarding stress avoidance/stress management techniques	89	S	4	S	6	S	7	16
		M	10	M	6	M	8	
		L	31	L	5	L	11	
			87		17		26	
Totals	**594**	**278**		**158**		**158**		**78**
Percentage of total	**100**	**46.80**		**26.60**		**26.60**		

- Responses from BPs were closer to those from APs than were responses from CPMs, with the difference factor being within a range of 1.4 and 1.8 times (highest numbers of responses to lowest number of responses) across OS within responses to each of the five qualitative questions.

With that context described, I will now describe themes and categories identified within the qualitative data analysed.

Qualitative Analysis—Categories and Themes

I used a manual process to identify themes and categories within qualitative data. This provided opportunity for deeper immersion in the data and greater appreciation of it. Using a simple colour coding system to note similar items during reading and re-reading, I then identified themes by gathering and recording specific colour coded items within groups. I manually organised collections of inter-relating themes into the final categories used to report analyses results.

The final categories and themes are presented in Table 4.2. These differ from those identified by the initial thematic analysis and categorisation. As qualitative analysis progressed, I found no need to change categories, but good reason to both change the name of some themes and to combine others to achieve a more robust avenue of entry into the data and its meaning, after overlapping information became apparent. I initially allocated equal weight to tone of delivery and depth of emotional commitment of participants as to numbers of participants providing data relevant to particular themes. Later, I decided there were instances where to rate every piece of data at equal value without considering its importance to the participant would do the research significant disservice.

I articulated my final identification of themes and categories not only on the number of respondents who mentioned a particular point but also on apparent emotional commitment to points being made. These are scheduled in Table 4.2.

Table 4.2 Schedule of categories and themes that evolved from qualitative analysis

Category	Theme
1. Intense of major life experience	1. Loss or serious illness of a close friend or relative 2. Previous or current mental illness, breakdown, severe anxiety or depression 3. Divorce or other relationship breakdown
2. Specifically work/employer contributors to stress	1. Senior managers lacked understanding of CPMs' role and workload 2. Senior managers won work by drastically reducing margins and/or promised early delivery of projects which often necessitated working six day weeks and sometimes required catch up work on Sunday, thereby placing huge stress on CPMs 3. Management understaffed projects in terms of experienced CPMs and tended to overload the most experienced and best performing CPMs, making it difficult for them to have time off and exposing them to the risk of burnout 4. There was a high level of pressure on CPMs to satisfy clients, no matter what 5. Lack of communication between senior managers and CPMs resulted pricing and scheduling errors in tender submissions and in poor project planning which increased risk of significant negative consequences as the job progressed 6. Winning projects by submitting low-margin or no-margin tenders led to pressure on CPMs to increase profit despite the consequential problems of having to deal with lower quality subcontractors and the increased stress arising from that

(continued)

Table 4.2 (continued)

Category	Theme
3. Work–life balance issues	1. Pressure of work effects on primary family carer 2. Lack of quality time with family each day or each week 3. Lack of time for self after work and family commitments
4. Locus of control aspects of stress	1. Sense of a need to escape or get out of the industry but feeling it was not possible due to knowledge/competence limitations or salary level implications 2. Fear of losing one's job if one complained 3. Sense of inability to change a system that badly needed changing
5. Industry contributors to stress	1. Concern for aspects of safety that arose from a stressed and/or fatigued construction project management team 2. Union issues/pressures 3. Pressure from poor quality project contract documents as a consequence of clients putting fee reduction pressure on consultants 4. The cut-throat economic climate in some regions

To assist in comprehension of how stress affected people apart from leading to death by disease or suicide, following is a typical explanation from a CPM who worked for an LO:

> *I tell my doctor I was going to take two weeks off, and he said, "Mate, you need two months off (laughs)." He said, "You don't realise how much trouble you're in." He prescribed anxiety medication. It took two to three or four weeks, my brain went numb. I couldn't stand it. I had massive anxiety to the point of spending hours trying to get to sleep at night. But I'd sleep in the recovery position thinking I was going to die of a heart attack. That's pretty severe, I think. That was just two years ago. I was 38. It was the perfect storm scenario for me.*

All but three interviewees among participants from the construction MOs and LOs recognised stress was a major concern for their organisations, their co-workers and themselves. Even those who handled stress well recognised most people did not and the effect of stress on organisations was increasing.

Analysis of Categories and Themes

In this section I provide analysis of the qualitative data within the categories and themes presented in Table 4.2.

Category 1. Intense or Major Life Experience

This category title is self-explanatory.
Theme 1. Loss or serious illness of a close friend or relative

This stressor had an extremely high impact on all who experienced it. Eight of the 35 participants in semi-structured interviews reported it. All demonstrated affect as they narrated their experience and recalled their recovery. For most categories, I will present background information from data analysis before extracts from interview transcriptions. For this first category, I present data first to respect the power with which participants narrated their experiences, which are exemplified in the following interview transcripts from participants who experienced the loss or serious illness of a close friend or relative:

> *My wife was killed in a car accident, leaving me with three kids under the age of four, and I could not cope. I was angry. I was wild. I was really struggling. Then it struck me. I've got three small kids and I've got to look after the little buggers. They were driving me crazy and I'd lost the plot basically. And one day I thought – head on - I've got to do this. I can't keep on going like this because of the effect on the people around me. My employer was fantastic. I found that being at work and having that support made all the difference.*

One participant spoke with a tone indicating he felt for a workmate as he might for a family member:

> *We had a young bloke here, a subcontractor, who had twins born prematurely, and one died. The other has been in and out of hospital on numerous occasions. A huge stress on him and his family.*

Another participant offered the following narrative, which gave a strong sense he relived the experience as he spoke:

> *I had a mate commit suicide two years ago. He worked in construction and was stressed because of income. He lost his job … He jumped from the Story Bridge. He probably had other issues, like family issues that compounded the stress of work, and losing his job and not being able to meet bills made him go. But as with a lot of people who commit suicide, he seemed quite happy – I spoke with him a couple of weeks before, and it was all happy and gleeful…all happy one week and the next week he was off the bridge…It probably took me six months to get over that. But you can't let it keep you down; otherwise you end up unemployed, so back to stage one again. Facing bills – tra la la…*

Philosophical in tone, this speaks of resilience and recovery. However, there were many other instances where processing of event affects was not so openly explained, and possibly was repressed, a behaviour apparently typical of the tough-culture construction industry. One of the most passionately described incidences came from another participant:

We have another guy here and ... he's broken. He's a site project manager and he's broken. You can have family problems, but the addition of all the stress of the job has just broken him. He just wasn't up to it all and he had burnout. Well and truly he's burned out. There's nothing worse than seeing someone burn out. Fuck I feel sorry for them. It's terrible. He's flogged.

Qualitative data confirmed stress is experienced outside of work and within and from the workplace, but quantitative analysis confirmed for CPMs, the greatest source of stress is the workplace. Qualitative data from the online survey aligned with and reinforced that from semi-structured interviews:

You can't escape home stress at work, and at home you have work stress to deal with. I have a wife who lives on the edge of breakdown every day due to an illness that has not dissipated in over ten years. Managing that situation is hard enough, but couple it with going to work to manage tradies who don't think is the perfect storm.

When you see two colleagues have heart attacks within a year, you get to wonder if we are doing anything near sufficient to help contain the effects (of stress) on employees.

One participant revealed a hint of the construction industry's offbeat sense of humour:

Suck it up, sunshine, and make sure your loved ones are protected with your life insurance.

Maladaptive, certainly, and probably driven by ingrained industry toughness. Such attitudes are likely to prevail until change occurs in the culture that contributes to, sustains, and increases stress levels of CPMs.

That offbeat sense of humour often disguises deeply ingrained and worrisome problems. In the case of our couple Will and Clare, it was not death of a close friend or a loss in the usual sense of the word that was of concern. Rather, it was the fear of loss of the couple's relationship. Will realised his stress was escalating and must have been having an effect on his partner, despite her not making any comment to that effect, apart from the occasional hint that more family time might be good for him given the work pressure he faced. Clare was becoming stressed as well as she came to realise the pay increase and bonus Will had been given opened opportunity at the expense of having no resolution effect on the problems the couple was facing because of Will's work pressure. In much the same way as illness, and even the effects of looking after people who are ill, can have a substantial impact on relationships, the pressure of work was really having a substantial impact on Will and Clare's relationship.

Theme 2. Previous or current mental illness, breakdown, severe anxiety or depression

Even after recovery from stress-induced anxiety and depression, fear of relapse can be a powerful additional stress. Organisational stress avoidance and management programmes need to be directed more towards alleviation of stressors than towards remedial action after stress had taken its toll.

Twenty-three interview participants—approximately 65 percent—reported dealing with effects of mental illness, including anxiety and depression, in themselves or those they managed. The following interview extracts provide some understanding into their experience:

> *We had a training session recently with the people from Mates in Construction. I had to leave it early because I had to pull out a young guy who was getting a bit upset. The session had a negative affect on him because his brother had killed himself last year. He was getting upset – he shouldn't have been there, really. But how can you know?*

That well-read participant, knowledgeable about human behaviour, spoke with reflective tone and demeanour. He later explained he considered leaving construction because the suicide victim had been a construction worker, like his brother who was upset at the meeting.

Another CPM suffered a nervous breakdown when running his own business:

> *One personal experience was shitty and probably the worst of my life. I had a business partner not doing the right thing and I had a bit of a nervous*

breakdown because of the pressures of work and general stresses of life – which is a lot more complicated than it used to be. When all this shit happened to me I had to take 18 months off.

This participant now gets involved when colleagues are doing it tough. I considered it important to understand the depths from which he had recovered and why he had become that valuable resource. His explanation was powerful:

When it happened, it happened really bloody quickly. I was pretty bloody stressed and then it all fell apart. Without my wife I would have curled up in a ball. I used to think, 'why would people want to commit suicide? You only have one life.' Then it was like, 'I can now see why people would do that'.

Another CPM spoke with less emotion, but equal recognition of the need for managing his condition. The depth of his hurt is heart wrenching, but the joy that emerges as he explained what changed his life is uplifting:

I've had experience with both stress and mental problems because I suffer manic depression and can still have turns of that from time to time. I was 17 when they first diagnosed me with depression following a family breakup. Most people would see me as a perfectly normal person – but it was all a façade. I'm broken underneath – but not so much anymore, especially since my young one came along 18 months ago. I've definitely got a better reason to live than I've ever had.

These extracts leave no doubt about the depth and severity of stress, anxiety, depression and other mental disorders. One concern is the prevalence of these problems among CPMs might be greater than observers might realise and the following narrative extracts support that proposition:

Twice I've had forty-year old guys come into this office and cry their eyes out. I'd had no Mates in Construction training so I didn't know what to do with the first. The second time I was OK – I'd had the training. Those two guys now know they can call me whenever they want. I'm not sure ten years ago that would have happened.

I've suffered from anxiety and depression. It manifested after I started in the industry - I don't know if there's a link or not. It came down to weighing up a female's role and having a full-time career – deciding on whether to have a family and how this could be balanced with the industry. I've come to accept I have anxiety – that's just who I am.

One participant reflected how seeing others affected by stress can affect observers.

We have one bloke on our team who does struggle with the slightest things. It affects him to the point where you do worry about yourself a bit. It's just the industry.

Another indicated how CPMs push themselves, even under stress:

I was under massive stress and … I was having a heart attack. It ended up being a panic attack. If you told me I'd have panic attacks one day I'd have told you that you were a dead set moron. After a month it happened again…I saw a cardiologist who said I might have heart problems. Then I saw a naturopath who said, "mate, there's nothing wrong with you apart from you being fried beyond belief." I was burnt out.

This type of story was not restricted to CPMs from LOs. Five of eight CPMs interviewed from MOs offered similar narrations:

Make no mistake about it I'm under stress to the eyeballs. I'm concerned about continuing with my current workload from the perspective of getting anxiety or depression. I have management responsibilities and am also overloaded operationally – in managing delivery of the jobs we've won. Too much time on one creates massive pressure on the other. I don't have time to exercise and when the pressure's on, which is most of the time, I tend to work weekends rather than spend time with the family. That's pushing terrible additional pressure onto me. If I work on the problems the work stress goes away because I know I'm beginning to get on top of things. But I worked seven full weekends recently – yeah. 70-80-hour weeks. But while I'm reducing the mountain of work pressure by doing that, it's wearing me out and creating enormous guilt and stress about the family situation.

I spent several weeks in hospital because of stress-related problems. These things only happened when I was really worn down from overwork and pressure at work – just plain burnout... While I loved the job, the stress simply did get to me. Make no mistake; construction project management is very stressful.

One very experienced CPM provided a sense of the depths of desperation to which anxiety and depression can take people:

The people at work know about my depression because I had several lengthy periods off work in hospital when I was a participant in a psychiatric research study into the effects of TMS (Trans-cranial Magnetic Stimulation). They try to be supportive, but it's the construction environment, and the tough culture comes through very clearly. My current biggest stress is the concern that I will never get better. The anxiety and depression are worse than ever, and I worry they'll never go away. (Grins) I'll get buried reading a book on depression.

CPMs from SOs were also affected:

Running a small business in this country is made so hard by government regulation that every day is stressful. If you have not run your own business, you have no idea what it involves and how much it affects your health.

It's part of small business – huge amounts of stress for little or no reward.

CPMs were unlikely to admit when affected by stress for fear of appearing weak. Both qualitative and quantitative data indicated, even if people took time off for stress, they probably would not declare stress was the reason. Participants opined much absenteeism was due to stress but were not certain. The following comments are relevant:

Culture creates a perception that absenteeism is weak, so people turn up even if they are unwell. Stress is more likely to contribute to attrition than absenteeism.

The stress-related absenteeism within our business is more seen when the person is at the point of mental breakdown.

Two SO participants demonstrated that cultural influence:

Stress is a part of small business. If you cannot cope, go and work as a public servant.

If you run a business you have to get on with the tasks at hand. You cannot allow stress to interfere with your work. You just have to get on with it.

The attitude within construction organisations of not admitting stress being the reason for taking time off is notable for its consistency. This prompted investigation into whether the attitude was a function of the CPM role, or more related to industry culture. An effective way to analyse the responses to qualitative questions within the online survey from APs rather than CPMs. The following exemplify and summarise the findings:

I would not consider staying home in fear of having my employment terminated.

When I'm stressed either at work or at home, I still attend work. The pressure is always there to turn up to work each day.

I also reviewed responses from BPs to open questions within the online survey and the following responses were typical:

Stress would not often be claimed as the cause of sick days but does play a role in absenteeism.

Some employees have lost their jobs due to stress-related problems.

Clearly, stress had affect on APs and BPs as well as CPMs.

The above narrative extracts from people who had experienced anxiety, depression and burnout/breakdown might have opened the minds of our storyline characters, Will and Clare, and motivated them to openly discuss their issues, possibly with professional assistance given the extent to which the problems had quite rapidly developed. However, while they were both aware their relationship was approaching rough waters, neither really knew how to articulate precisely what the main contributing factors were. The blame game had begun. Neither openly blamed the other for their predicament, but each of them was quick to bring up issues that should have been addressed a long time previously whenever stress mounted to the point at which simple irritations triggered an outburst (in line with Selye's explanation of heterostasis, presented in Chapter 2). This was not a matter of each of them having had enough of the other. This was a sign of stress mounting for each of them until the point each at least was experiencing anxiety symptoms. With other factors also having an effect, any current anxiety had every possibility of deteriorating into depression, and perhaps even burnout in Will's case, if some remedial action was not urgently taken. Stress for Will now was not only from work factors, because the home situation was exacerbating the stress that began in the workplace. For Clare, this was a classic case of home stresses giving rise to anxiety that she took to work, where it too was often exacerbated.

It goes without saying these circumstances are hardly conducive to good mental health. In fact, they also posed a strong risk for the couple's (until now) quite resilient relationship. Stress does not only often contribute to relationship breakdown, it can be the consequence of relationship problems as the next theme will reveal. While stress is more likely to be work-related for CPMs, it was likely to begin a spiral affect often increasing stress levels both at work and externally. For sufferers, there appears to be no relief from their combined experience of stress. These circumstances tend to have negative effect on relationships, and I will now address that theme.

Theme 3. Divorce or relationship breakdown

Extracts from transcriptions provide insights into the experience of significant relationship breakdown stress in participants' lives. These include a compelling narrative of effects of an early-life relationship breakdown on a middle-aged CPM.

Relationship breakdown was not the core issue, but a consequence of the main issue—CPMs working extensively more than contractually defined hours. When personal relationship problems emerge in these circumstances, they become a major stress often taken to work and a spiral of stress-based health deterioration often follows. Accordingly, participants regarded relationship breakdown as much a cause of workplace stress as caused by workplace stress.

The way one participant managed work to minimise effects on relationship indicates how challenging this was to achieve:

> *I'm 64 and I can manage stress. I schedule time for other than work activities to stop me working 70 hours a week. Sometimes that causes me a little stress because I have to leave work to do something that isn't work. That's a good thing. The major components are sport or exercise and family stuff. That's what I schedule. If I haven't got that I spend more time at work - that soon causes indirect stress on me because I don't see the family. I don't see my wife, and that affects relationships.*

Few participants had this participant's insight. With the information he provided—it was important for CPMs to prioritise stress-balancing activities—I analysed data from participants for whom relationship breakdown either resulted from major stress in their lives, or caused it. Following is a relevant extract:

> *I was twelve when my family broke up and I had to look after my little sister. She was nine. The message came through that my mother would pick me up, which she did – and took me to a different house – so she just up and left (dad). She was out every night of the week doing, well, I don't wanna know what. So I was left to raise my little sister. I would have to get her up in the morning because my mother would still be hung-over in bed. So I'd get up in the morning, get her dressed, pack our lunch, and we'd go to primary school. Then I had to walk to the high school - six kilometres down the road. So that's left some lasting scars I feel to this day. Look, I deal with it, but I think all my mental health issues date back to that time. It's only in the last few years of getting psychiatric help that I've learned to be able to openly talk about it. You know, I was always ashamed of my mental health issues.*

The same participant offered the following insight from his experience of upper management in construction:

> *You just have to look at the number of divorces in the industry. A lot of people lose their marriages, and most of them are from upper management. It's the amount of time you're expected to be here. Everything is on your head.*

Another comment from this participant might reflect looking after his sister as a youth. The emotion in his voice was palpable:

> *I'm (often) still here at seven o'clock at night no matter what time I start. I don't get to see my daughter those days and that, to me, causes more grief than anything. If I don't see my daughter for a day, which rolls on to two days – even worse – if you get (long reflective pause).... It starts to really get me down.*

Often, it was not relationship breakdown that caused stress, but rather fear that working long hours could lead to divorce:

> *When I do a job now, it is almost a given that you are working six days per week, and for us, that means fifty-five to sixty hours per week. It's just not manageable. So then stress does not just come from work, you've got pressure from your family. "What the hell are you doing there?" So you're between a rock and a hard place. You either finish your career and do what you want to do, or end up single, which is the way a lot of people in the industry seem to be going.*

Work pressure led one recently divorced female CPM to start her own consulting business, which resulted in different problems:

> *Some men who knew I was now single saw an opportunity and would confuse work and private life, and hit on me. I understand that's natural and had no problem explaining that business is business. However, some of them didn't like that and took it as rejection, even though I didn't mean to insult anybody. They then took that out on me in business ways - delaying payments etc., and I found that very hurtful and stressful.*

Another CPM spoke with intense frustration when describing how long periods working on remote sites, prevented him from adequately addressing relationship issues. He frequently spent six to 12 weeks away, with two weeks at home between trips:

> *I want to address the relationship issue, but I'm so glad to get home after being away that you just don't want things to deteriorate into conflict really quickly. But I decided when I finish this job around Christmas, I'll address the issue. My fuse is getting shorter with the people at work. All I know is that, when the job finishes later this year, I am working out the issues one way or the other for my own sanity and to be fair to all the people who work with me. To be fair to my wife as well.*

That participant is now divorced. Some CPMs working on fly in—fly projects regard the dedicated work time balanced by relatively long periods at home as good for relationships, but the majority found the time away difficult to deal with:

> *The biggest problem for people in that type of construction management work … was the effect of fly in – fly out on relationships. Certainly the type of work I do, which is mainly fly in – fly out and overseas work, has taken a toll on my relationship.*

> *I did a lot of fly in – fly out work in construction for mining and found a lot of turnover in marriages. Working away from home is a big stress. I think the major issue in construction project management is you're dealing with more alpha males than any other industry. It's about 'chin up and carry on'. With bills and kids there's no real option other than what you know. I've contemplated changing industries myself, but you can't get paid the same amount. Once you've got a mortgage and kids and everything else, you've got to look after that, don't you?*

A former senior CPM who moved to other construction-related work offered an insightful opinion following a year away from construction management problems:

In construction this drive for performance perfection tends to take priority and that happened with nearly every construction person I know, and that's why we get so much burnout and relationship problems – because we move beyond that point where work becomes a balance for home stressors and work stressors catch up and get on top of you. It's a bad cycle, but one that's becoming commonplace.

No question concerning personal relationships was asked either in the survey or of interviewees. It is remarkable 15 CPMs volunteered personal narratives or observations of colleagues regarding workplace stress impacts on personal relationships, in response to a simple open question about impacts of workplace stress.

One CPM reported a relationship breakup that differed from most in that industry stress did not give rise to the relationship matter but rather the breakup impacted him in a way that affected others with whom he worked. The relationship breakup occurred when the participant was ten, and he discovered the extent to which he had been affected in his late thirties. Colleagues and staff often experienced the consequences of the breakup scars in the form of angry outbursts and other reactive behaviour, which nobody at the time comprehended. Part of this participant's narrative completed the scenario:

My life and my personality changed when I hired a counsellor to run a conference on Emotional Intelligence. The staff volunteered me for a demonstration. I declined, but they persisted, and the instructor detected more than larrikinism in their persistence. He ignored my resistance and calmly stated that the staff might learn so much more from a demonstration in which I was involved. I again refused. He stated that emotionally intelligent organisations must be emotionally intelligent from the top down. A fellow director volunteered and the instructor gave a demonstration that was incredible. I called the instructor the following week - to have a shot at him actually. He said something like, "Why would someone in your position pass up on such a great opportunity to show your real self to your colleagues?" It knocked me for six. To cut a long story short, I had a series of personal sessions with him about a few issues from life and work, and he observed that I didn't trust anyone who worked for me. I disagreed but when I talked with my colleagues, they all agreed with him. A few sessions later, he had me in tears – I don't remember

> *crying since I was a young boy before that day. I'd mentioned that I'd not seen my mother in thirty years and had no compulsion whatever to do so. He asked me to tell him about the last time I spoke to her, and I was overwhelmed when the memory came to me. Each fortnight, she'd drop me at the local barber, go grocery shopping and pick me up after. One day when I was ten, she dropped me off, but my auntie picked me up, telling me my mum had some problems she had to attend to. I had not seen her since that day. That therapist's words are still crystal clear. "Do you still really believe you have no trust issues?" A few sessions later, I was a changed man, and I caught up with mum and now have a good relationship with her. I had no idea of the problems she was facing at the time. My management style changed completely after that.*

Most important is the manner in which the participant's management style, and to an extent, aspects of his personality at work, seem to have been strongly formed from a life experience that had been so painful for him that he had effectively repressed it. His story raises a question regarding what factors impact people's behaviour at work in a way that could give rise to stress for themselves and others, and to what effect this stress impacts on home life and vice versa, and that question provides an opportunity to check back on Will and Clare.

Imagine if Will and Clare could have read the narrative extracts presented above. If only they could realise how commonplace are work stresses being taken home to add to stress of family members and, in turn, home stresses being taken to work and exacerbating pressures there. If only they could get some clarity regarding how destructive to family relationships this pattern can be. If only they could understand the impact of limited time with their children, not only on the children but also on each of them. Perhaps most importantly, if only they could learn from the insight of the first narrative extract presented above in relation to this theme—things do not change automatically, people have to make them change, usually by setting priorities as well as objectives, and almost always by conducting both home and work life within clearly defined boundaries.

A good place for Will to prepare to establish such boundaries might be to ask himself questions to gain deeper understanding of the causes of the pressures he experiences at and from work. The following themes and categories were addressed with the expectation that some answers to these questions might be found in the process, and a summary of the potential meaning for Will and Clare of the following themes is presented at the end of the category.

Category 2. Specifically Work/Employer Contributions to Stress

I began thematic analysis by recording the frequency of perceived causes of stress appearing in participants' narratives. On reviewing and re-reviewing this data in the usual process of qualitative analysis, I recognised that emphasis on, or intensity in describing various points were important factors in identifying themes. In other words, I gave at least equal rating to apparent importance of the theme to the participant, as perceived by phraseology, tone and intensity of presentation, as I gave to theme frequency of appearance throughout the data.

Theme 1. Senior managers lacking understanding of CPMs' role and workload

Fifteen of the 35 interview participants mentioned the theme topic in response to questions. The tone of responses ranged from cynicism—employees were little more than unimportant numbers in a game laser-focussed on profit. To a rarer and more positive view—managers are not always the problem and people tend to place significant pressure on themselves. The extent to which participants raised this issue, combined with the intensity of emotion with which comments were made contributed to this theme being one of the easiest to identify.

The data behind this theme highlighted the urgent need for systemic change within the industry, especially regarding how work was distributed or won. The following extracts from interviews with CPMs provide insight into feelings and attitudes regarding this theme:

> *It doesn't matter if it's \$200,000 or \$200,000,000...the workload is the same regardless of the value of the project. It's not just my company, it's tier one as well as tier two companies – and it's always the same at the upper management level. It's all price and time driven – everybody wants it done quicker*

and for a hell of a lot less money. That ends up falling on the construction (project) management people.

The (sub-contract) budget was $100,000 but we let the job for $60,000, not logically thinking that the bloke at $60,000 missed half the inventory he should've priced. But management don't care because the budget looks better, so they hand it to the site project management staff and we're expected to get the same profit and product we would from a $100,000 contractor, despite other prices within five grand of each other reflecting what the price should be.

Not all participants from LOs held negative attitudes towards their management, and more positive narratives provide insight into potential gateways to improvement for the industry:

There is that culture – that backup where you can talk to people. There's no separation between the construction worker and management. It's a culture of, 'you're all in, boys.' That's another positive. There's no separation.

A site (project) manager wants to maintain reputation so they keep on time and on budget. It can also come from office management putting pressure on to perform well. Pressure comes from both angles. My point is you can't discount the pressure people put on themselves.

Six people from MOs addressed senior office-based managers lacking understanding of the stress on CPMs. The following interview extract demonstrates the point:

The basis for salaries in the industry is that mythical 38-hour week, but we're all working a minimum of 55 hours. In one company I worked for there was immense pressure from the top that we filled out time sheets saying that we only work eight hours a day. You're working 10 or 11 hours a day, but you're made to put down eight. Management would pro rata overheads across the hours the satellite offices worked. Everybody in the satellite office felt they weren't being recognised for the big hours they were putting in. It didn't matter whether you wrote eight hours on your timesheet, or 80 hours, you were still getting paid the same. But that mental constraint – not being respected for the hours of work. Yeah....it caused a huge amount of stress. I simply don't think our directors have any sense of the level of stress they're causing.

For other MO participants, stress got down to not being appreciated for effort put in. The following comment was typical:

You get told, "get to the end of the job, and there's a bonus for you." But when the end of the job comes around, there's no money left. You've been working your clacker off, but you're left high and dry.

One participant was forced to leave her MO due to enormous pressure. I could sense the frustration in her account:

I always felt unsupported. At times I felt overwhelmed by what was expected of me. I realised that, in one sense, it was recognition of my ability to give me more work, but the management seemed to be more concerned about the profit being made and less concerned about the impact the extra work was having on me.

One comment from a CPM provides insight regarding rectifying this problem:

Realistic programmes and systems to reduce workloads on site would reduce stress considerably. Going home every day knowing you have not completed all the tasks and paperwork is stressful and takes away from job satisfaction.

Participants who had experienced mental health problems were generally motivated to help others who were struggling with the heavy workloads:

I consider myself reflecting in them and see that they are troubled, so I usually go and talk to them. It's important to me that they see they are not alone. That they know it can happen to anybody.

I'll talk to anybody about it. If I see other guys in the office who are potentially heading down the same line, I'll chat to them about it and let them know that I've blown up in the past, and I tell (them) at the rate some of the guys are going, they'll do the same.

CPMs felt motivated when management recognised additional effort and particular achievements. Regrettably, this was more the exception than the rule. The consequence was often CPMs who felt unsupported and unappreciated, sometimes thinking management were strictly profit-focused, regarded employees as expendable and replaceable, and did not understand the effort CPMs contributed:

> *I always felt unsupported. At times I felt overwhelmed by what was expected of me. I realise that in one sense it was a recognition of my ability – to give me more work – but management seemed to be more concerned about profit made and less concerned about the impact the extra work was having on me.*

Some comments in this theme demonstrated frustration, but the percentage of participants who commented, and the fact that they came from all OSs reinforced the importance of this topic to CPMs. The next theme's importance was equally strongly established by shorter and punchier extracts from participants' transcriptions.

Theme 2. Senior managers won work by drastically reducing margins and/or promised early delivery of projects which often necessitated working six-day weeks and sometimes required catch up work on Sunday, thereby placing huge stress on CPMs

At this point, I reflected on the extent to which themes overlapped with or strongly influenced (or were influenced by) themes from other categories. After discussion with the expert panel, I reduced the number of categories from six to five, with four themes subsumed into other themes, thus reducing excessive overlap.

Eleven interview participants referenced this theme. Nine participants who completed the online survey offered unsolicited comments, providing useful triangulation of qualitative data.

Some participants indicated profit reduction to ludicrously low levels and shortening of schedules to often-unachievable durations was commonplace throughout the industry. Contractors often offered reduced schedules and low margin or no margin prices before clients raised the issue, to attract favouritism and win more work. Experienced CPMs realised using reduced schedules to win work placed projects in an almost impossible-to-deliver situation before they began.

Contractors cannot responsibly take on that level of risk, especially if the project carries high liquidated damages (late completion costs), so they opt to work six-day weeks to manage risk, effectively pushing risk onto CPMs.

Another strategy to manage risk was to subcontract to lower-priced tradespeople who often were under-resourced or lacked competence to deliver. This necessitated CPMs managing incompetent subcontractors' resources to avoid flow-on effects impacting others. Project administration had to be done after hours, placing even more pressure on CPMs. Working a six-day week to achieve a tight schedule usually required CPMs to work evenings and Sundays to manage contract administration. The consistency of participants' reporting this removed weekly recovery and family time and caused substantial stress was too clear to ignore. The following interview extracts provide an insight into the problem and the frustration caused:

Some of my friends have suffered from stress and it's probably to do with programs – which are about driving to get delivery of the project. If management puts pressure on me, that ends up affecting the site managers and that affects the subcontractors and trades.

The programmes are not correct. They never are. They are always hoping for the best and not preparing for the worst. It doesn't matter how much you think you cover issues, there's going to be stuff that comes up on every job that's going to push the job back further... Whether you keep your job or lose your job really depends on how you perform.

Participants from MOs were equally forthright:

Programmes are ridiculous and unattainable in this day and age. We don't have the skill-set among the workers generally to maintain this type of programme.

I've got buckets of these jobs with terrible tender margins, which means you have to take atrocious contracts with atrocious subcontractors and try to convert to a decent product with a higher margin. It's just a massive stress. To try to take a two percent bucket of snot to eight or ten percent is a nightmare.

These comments were triangulated by responses to open questions of the online survey:

> *The industry is becoming more and more unrealistic, and expectations are that projects be completed in shorter time frames using less staff. I believe this to be the major factor in the additional stress.*

> *The nature of construction PM work is stressful due to finance and contract driven deadlines, and the PM is the person who constantly has to clean up problems caused by deadline pressures in particular.*

Senior managers often allocate riskier projects to more experienced and highly competent CPMs. In managing one risk using this approach, managers often exposed organisations to another, potentially more serious risk. This is addressed in the next theme, regarding which 10 of 35 CPMs (five from each of the LOs and MOs) provided data. Senior CPMs made it clear while time, cost and quality pressures were major stressors for CPMs, they were also symptoms of deeper industry culture problems. Those deeper issues had to be exposed.

Theme 3. Management understaffed projects in terms of experienced CPMs and tended to overload the most experienced and best performing CPMs, making it difficult for them to have time off and exposing them to the risk of burnout

In a perfect world, when managers of contracting organisations reduced time and cost to win work, it would be delivered on time and within budget by the requisite number of enthusiastic, not necessarily senior, and not overly-expensive CPMs. However, delivering complex construction projects is seldom perfect, and stress on CPMs has become an everyday reality. The data points to causal factors. Senior managers often needed to offer clients unrealistic prices, schedules and contractual conditions to win work. They were faced with a double-barrelled quandary if did win. On one hand the conditions offered did not allow for hiring new staff to deliver the work, and on the other the terms agreed were so demanding, the managers had little choice other than delegate supervision of less expensive junior CPMs on the new work to their most experienced and best performing CPMs, thereby increasing often already high levels of stress on the organisation's highest performing resources.

To make matters worse, managers who offered long working weeks and cut prices engaged cheaper subcontractors to increase profit levels. When they fell behind schedule, follow on subcontractors were affected. The usual intervention was, again, to appoint a senior CPM to take over the job or mentor the junior incumbent. Both options contribute to additional project costs and senior management rationalised a quickly-deteriorating project financial situation by spreading already stretched senior, competent and experienced CPMs across a number of troubled projects, further increasing stress that could burn out their best people. The data suggest some managers continue to do what simply will not work over the longer period, in the naïve hope things would change before they lost their best CPMs to health impacts or resignation.

Extracts from the interview transcriptions of CPMs from LOs and MOs provide insight into the severity of the impact on the senior professionals most affected:

> *You end up jumping from one job to another dealing with problems that need solving, and generally the problem is time or money, so the only thing you can do is put more time into it. So, for me, it's never ending you know.*

> *... and the resources available are not sufficiently competent. Three juniors are often not as good as one competent but severely overworked contract administrator.*

Customer service demands also required organisational management's attention and that is central to the next theme in this category.

Theme 4. There is high pressure on CPMs to satisfy clients, no matter what

Ten semi-structured participants from construction LOs and MOs provided data regarding senior management insisting on client focus. These CPMs understood the need for client service in business and that their management was driven by the idea, if they can impress a client with performance, quality and service, there would be an increased probability the client would want to directly negotiate future contracts with them. A negotiated contract typically involved higher profit than a tender win and the emphasis put into client focus and service was worth the effort if only the occasional project win was negotiated. This was especially so where the tendering climate was cut-throat, and lump-sum tendering margins were between zero and two percent.

There are well-recognised business principles about which the management of construction organisations often demonstrated scant understanding. Most comprehended a service provider delivering to the specified standard within agreed cost and schedule parameters on first effort, would realise at least the profit included in the price. Most also understood sub-standard work would require rectification at the supplier's cost, and too many errors on a low margin contract could cause the supplier to make a loss. Managers experienced in construction, but not in broader business, who respond after winning a low-margin bid by employing low-cost subcontractors to enhance profit, risk errors and require experienced CPMs to step in to manage quality standards, with significant stress the usual outcome. What some contractors appear to not understand is, in trying to satisfy all clients at all costs, rather than deliver precisely what is specified to precisely the quality standard defined in each contract at precisely the contract price, the additional costs involved in over servicing represents a direct cost against profit. Furthermore, when negotiating the next contract, the client expects a similar price and level of service (for a similar project) as for the previous project. The result can be a slow but inevitable demise of the business.

This background discussion covers sources of stress for CPMs from conflict between client service demands and a project's contractual provisions. The following extracts from interviews with CPMs are relevant:

> *We don't have a choice – if we don't work a six-day week, then the opposition will... The clients say, 'I want it now. I don't give a shit how many hours you work.' So the client sets himself up to make more money off the project and the poor builder's pushing it from the start, and then has to come back again for four months fixing up the defects that were caused by the tight time frame. You don't get a chance to finish things properly. The builder ends up saying, 'Let's take some short cuts here and we'll fix it later'. It's stress at all levels.*

So, increase productivity, in shorter time frames and smaller budgets - and we're expected to do it faster at a better quality every time we do it. There's just no logic to that thinking.

The next theme addresses ineffective communication and planning during and after the winning and internal distribution of projects.

Theme 5. Lack of communication between senior managers and CPMs resulted in pricing and scheduling errors in tender submissions and in poor project planning which increased risk of significant negative consequences as the job progressed

Participants were strongly of the opinion decisions regarding budget and schedule made during tender negotiations with the objective of winning work, were often made in the absence of communication regarding increase in stress on CPMs charged with delivering the project. Interestingly, participants did not specifically mention 'lack of communication' or 'failure to discuss' issues. However, from repeated reading of interview transcriptions I was left with little doubt these participants referred to lack of communication at a crucial stage of winning the project. The following interview extracts provided insight into the situation:

Head office people should not commit to changes in budgets or schedules without communicating with the people those decisions most effect – the people who have to deliver the bloody project.

If you don't design your build properly it doesn't take long for you to be up shit creek without a paddle, and that's exactly what happened on the job I'm working at the moment. (Senior management's) planning errors frustrate everybody. We were aiming at one point five percent profit on this job - that's ridiculous. You only need to be out by $1.50 on every hundred-dollar budget item and you're in trouble.

In the next theme I more deeply review the issues of having to deal with poor quality and incompetent subcontractors.

Theme 6. Winning projects by submitting low-margin or no-margin tenders led to pressure on CPMs to increase profit despite the consequential problems of having to deal with lower quality subcontractors and the increased stress arising from that

Seven participants from LOs and five from MOs offered input that illustrated the depth of participants' feeling regarding this theme. Following are examples of those comments:

> *The jobs are all about money and time, really all about money, they never give you enough time…If you get good subbies, you can get there, but there's not always enough money to get good subbies.*

> *The subbies don't care whether they're on schedule or not. They just don't care. You can't upset the subbies – they have so much work that, if you upset them, they will just leave.*

One participant presented a contrary view, based on being satisfied with the level of profit built into the price, regardless of how small it was, and not on chasing profit increase by employing low cost and incompetent subcontractors:

> *We like to form relationships and the dollar is always going to be part of that. There is a direct cost and an indirect cost and the indirect cost includes rectification of poor work (that comes from) the pressure of time frames, and unprofessional behaviour – that is considerable. Don't take the cheapest price, mate, because if the cheapest price is not a good performer, it completely ties up the supervisor – or I end up with all the rework. The temptation to win a job at low profit, and then go for a greater profit during the job is always there, and we're not exempt from that. But we're certainly not as involved in that type of behaviour as other contractors are.*

A succinct comment from a CPM summarised the core of this theme:

> *You're dealing with shit subcontractors trying to get a mint finish. That's the hardest thing.*

It is virtually certain, had Will been a participant for this research, his input would not have differed significantly from that of the participants whose narrative extracts were presented above. I expect he would have reported his management won work in tough times by bidding for it at low margin and even no margin prices, and then closing deals by offering shorter project delivery durations, thus getting the better of the competing tenderers. The approach was survival and profit driven, with little concern for the consequences. It is doubtful Will would have spoken the words he would have liked to—that the estimates of time and cost to complete the project were completed by office-based professionals with little if any input from site based CPMs, and to make any profit at all in some cases would necessitate employing sub-standard, sometimes even incompetent subcontractors, notorious for poor performance and often incompetent at project management, and that would necessitate putting a very experienced and probably already over-loaded CPM—someone like Will—on the project to ensure it was successfully completed at a profit, often by having to do the subcontractors' project management for them.

I would expect Will might also be flabbergasted at management's instruction that the clients on such projects be given everything they want, within very broad boundaries of reason. I can almost hear Will lamenting, 'They have to be kidding. Management want us to give these clients a project at a ridiculous price and then hope to have those clients negotiate their next project with us rather than tender, so we win more work – probably at ridiculous prices'.

Will could be forgiven for wondering if his circumstances could ever change, despite his partner Clare hoping for things to change sooner rather than later. Will had considered changing to another job, but now the family was well established in living to the means provided by his year-ago pay increase and bonus payment, he could not find a single job related to construction that paid anything like he would need to maintain the family's current lifestyle. Of course, Clare could consider working more hours, but even that might not make up the gap Will might need to accept between current remuneration and what might be on offer for positions with far less work pressure. And in any case,

Clare's level of stress with family and work responsibilities was not all that different from Will's in their current circumstances.

They simply needed to find a way to achieve a decent work–life balance, and they both knew it. They simply had little idea how.

I will now address work–life balance issues.

Category 3. Work–life Balance Issues

Most participants were impacted to some extent by this category's themes. Those who were single and somewhat immune to the impact of nuclear family related themes nonetheless felt the impact of dedicating more time to work than was contractually expected.

One theme had few contributing participants, albeit additional data collection and analysis (presented at the end of this chapter) confirmed its importance. The affected participants were family primary carers.

Theme 1. Pressure of work effects on the primary family carer

Despite signs of change the construction industry remains anchored to its culture and tradition and continues to attract many to whom its 'tough' image appeals, giving rise to problems, addressed in the final category of qualitative analysis. What was an almost male-only domain twenty years ago now attracts an increasing number of females, both in trades and professions. A female from one LO explained:

> *There are more men than women overall but there are more women in the office than on site. There are not as many of us on site, but you know the numbers are increasing on site, but not compared to your ladies in business and stuff like that.*

That statement has impact because construction head offices are not populated only with general administration staff but rather with a supporting professionals from a range of disciplines. The increase in the number of women working as CPMs over the past decade looks set to continue, with universities reporting the numbers of women and men undertaking construction management programmes as being approximately equal.

Younger newcomers bring modern values to workplaces, but comments from participants in this research implied more traditional values persist, including regarding family roles and responsibilities. Specifically, women were the primary family carers. Within this context, only three people offered comments that contributed to this first theme, and two were women. However, they provided input with a strength of emotion leaving no doubt it would have been a travesty not to recognise and analyse this theme. The following interview extracts exemplify this position:

> *Take me as a mum, trying to find time to do things to make sure my children are getting – you know, that I'm doing everything I need to do for my kids. To me, to make my household work I need to go to work, whereas my mum, she didn't. That's an additional stress in itself.*

> *And then there's the whole stress of like, 'okay, my kids are sick and I've got to pick them up and look after them. Because I'm only working X days (omission to preserve confidentiality) each week, I have to use up all my sick leave, so that when I get sick from being stressed out, I do not have the time available to take leave. There's a lot of stuff going on, and I think that the guys working full time... I hate to separate it into a male and female thing – it is definitely different from male to female, no matter what people might say.*

This participant agreed it was a role-based rather than gender-based issue. However, her point—that women are more likely to face this problem than men within the industry—appears correct. The following was another transcription extract that powerfully demonstrated the importance of the theme:

> *I found, coming back from having the baby, no team wanted to work with me. In their minds, they wanted five days work and I would be working less than that. It's the age-old worry that they needed full time help, and that "she's a mum, and she's gonna take time off for kids and we'll be over-worked." I was trying to argue that I'm a senior professional in my role and you are getting the first days each week, but in those days I'd do more than a junior professional could do in two weeks, because I don't need training, I don't need to be mentored, but they never saw me like that.*

While this theme dealt with family primary carers, others in family situations were strongly affected by the stresses of working long hours as CPMs, and that interfered with family responsibilities. The next theme concentrated on the effects of CPMs lacking quality time with their families.

Theme 2. Lack of quality time with family each day or each week

Ten interview participants, five from each of LOs and MOs, contributed comments leading to identification of this theme. Even participants with happy home lives expressed concern about work expanding beyond reasonable boundaries and impacting family time. The theme was almost universal, but its manifestation ranged from a focus on avoiding trouble with a partner to guilt arising from inability to dedicate appropriate quality time to family. It was not so much getting home later than desired causing most angst, but rather having to work at home after an already long day. A strong sense of conflict between work and family commitments emerged from comments relating to this theme:

> *Sometimes I'm sitting on the couch and my wife's talking to me, but (mentally) I'm on the job, you know, thinking about what I've got on, whatever it might be.*

> *That leads to guilt because the time that they're supposed to be spending with family, they're not really with family – having dinner thinking about the work they have to do after dinner – after the kids are off to bed and they're back to the emails…That's the kind of thing that's clearly a big stress in construction…It's very difficult to manage your family – work relationships.*

This theme was reinforced by ten qualitative comments from the online survey. The comments submitted served as triangulation of data already presented:

> *Family pressure can be relationship or financial, or both. When on FIFO these pressures often felt more "real". The extra dollars was offset by more pressure. It made me feel like I was not doing any role in my life well.*

...taking days off is very much frowned upon and yet they tell us that we can only work so many hours per week. Most professional level people need to take work home and not record doing it, which means that home life is affected negatively, and then we bring that stress to work and the vicious cycle continues. It is common in this profession and it is not conducive to work-life balance, or to a stress-free life.

The following comment provides valuable insight into the attitude the industry needs to adopt to effectively deal with CPMs' stress:

Our members are loyal to their careers and complete daily long hours on the job; we need to be vigilant and watch for signs that people are not breaking under the load from their work; in addition that they take time back and days off when available, to spend with their loved ones.

Even in rare instances where CPMs achieve work–family balance, lack of time for self often remains an issue.

Theme 3. Lack of time for self after work and family commitments

Perfect balance between work and family responsibilities is an ideal. However, achieving this at the expense of insufficient time for oneself could give rise to stress, and eventually impact work, family or both. A better ideal is a work–life balance including time for self.

Eleven participants from LOs and MOs raised lack of time for themselves:

Everyone's got mobile. Everyone's got email – everyone is always contactable. If you're not contactable, it's a problem. My dad comes from a construction and architecture background...He had time to think things through and answer questions properly. Sometimes you need to pick up the phone and have that conversation and get the right outcome. We're not teaching our young people how to do that.

I've been told to take time off – but I cannot get out from what I currently have to do. Unless there is someone to deal with my load I cannot relax and take time off. I need to prioritise but there is too much in the high priority list for me to relax and take the holiday they recommend.

This theme extended to lack of time to think about problems and solve them at work, without interruptions:

That expectation that, when you get an email, you should be able to respond to it straight away without proper consideration and evaluation. The foreman or supervisor doesn't even get the chance to sit down and think about a problem. They're expected to make quick decisions, and the more made without proper thought – the more problems or stress.

When people regularly worked 55–70 hours per week, the thought of regaining a full weekend was appealing, but also gave rise to concerns about weekend work other than not having sufficient time for self and/or family. Some CPMs questioned the practicality of it from a productivity perspective, while others emphasised its importance to workers trying to save some cash. Following are examples across the range:

You've got a handful of blokes who've been on the piss all night, so they can get hung over. They're all in weekend mode, so to get them wound up generally takes a lot longer than it does during the week. We should keep Saturdays up our sleeves as catch up time when necessary, we should not be working every Saturday. People need catch-up time, and rest.

...all people who work on these sites – myself included – are in debt to the eyeballs. They need the money from working on Saturdays, and if they don't see they get equal time during the week from additional hours, they'll push back against the weekend proposal.

If you work the weekend, you end up with other pressure at home. You feel bad about not being with family and you are thinking how my wife is pissed off because I've not spent any time with her. Whereas, on the two-day break, she loved it – she was great. She knew that I had at least one day a week for her. If you work six days a week you don't have one day a week for anyone – you're exhausted, so you wanna put on the TV or lock yourself in a room. It's the only opportunity you get to shut down.

Some CPMs openly criticised management being focused on profits at the expense of people, but others accepted management had little choice but to do what they were doing to win work, remain in business and keep people employed until market conditions improved. Some expressed appreciation for their employer, stating they would not want to work elsewhere. Gestures like site and office bar-b-ques, a family-like atmosphere with personnel photographs in the office and no social separation between management levels were appreciated and seen as motivating. The following insight from an experienced participant is an appropriate close for this theme:

> *They're looking at not working Saturdays – then you're looking at working ten hours a day during the week. If we are going to have deadlines, we need to make sure we have the support system in place for job health before the job starts - ready to go – for the people who aren't coping to be able to put the hand up and say, look, I need a hand. We need to be sure we don't go and blow up the site manager when things aren't going perfectly. You say to them, "try to make the next deadline". You work with the person and make sure they're being offered assistance instead of just blowing a gasket.*

Before progressing, let us spend a couple of minutes back with Will and Clare. Work–life balance is one of the things they would most like to achieve at the moment, yet it simply seems completely beyond their reach. Will has learned the hard way that increased salary tends to lead to higher expectations by management, and while that comes with the honour of your ability being respected, it hardly does anything to overcome the stress from work and its impacts on individuals and families. As the narrative extracts above indicated, construction-related professions are no longer a male-only domain, but while the industry professions remain majority-male, the situation I am describing with our storyline for Will, might well be the same for any number of Wilmas. In our story, I have previously addressed the matter of pressure and stress on Clare as primary carer for the family (which, again, would today be the same for any number of Clarences) and the narrative extracts above indicate her circumstances to be anything but only a story. Those extracts also demonstrate that Will's lack of quality time with family are commonplace among CPMs—not to mention lack of time for self being a long distant memory for our fictional Will and many of the real participants in this research. Some aspects of Will and Clare's lives simply appear to be out of control, and that is something I will now address by presenting one of the most important themes from individual CPMs' perspectives.

Category 4. Locus of Control Aspects of Stress

Psychologist Julian Rotter coined the term Locus of Control, referring to a person's perception of their ability to effect outcomes [1]. People with an internal locus of control have better coping ability dealing with stress than those with external locus of control [2, 3]. People operate from internal locus of control if they perceive personal strengths and abilities impact the outcome of actions, while people demonstrating an external locus of control perceived outcomes are dependent on luck, fate or even the actions of others [4].

After securing a job and earning promotion, many CPMs were delivering complex projects under increasingly unrealistic price and schedule parameters. They began to experience job stress, but any complaint was either met with silence, or attracted a remuneration increase, but the pressure remained, and often intensified. All too often, a pressured CPM experienced stress-induced anxiety or depression and began thinking about career options. However, their skillset was limited to construction or similar work, and the only possible way to maintain current salary level was to do similar work for a competing organisation. Established family-spending patterns usually ruled out accepting lower salary, and the decision was made to stay. There was seldom any attempt to reset to an internal locus of control. The more likely scenario was for the person to accept their life circumstances prevented change, intensifying a strong sense of being trapped—the classic indication of external locus-of-control thinking, and a factor that contributed to increase in stress. The first theme in this category addressed this concept.

Theme 1. Sense of a need to escape or get out of the industry but feeling it was not possible due to knowledge/competence limitations or salary level implications

Three CPMs from LOs, three from MOs, and one from an SO addressed this theme.

The common feeling expressed by CPMs, or detected in their words and tone of voice, was frustration. Some felt was they could keep their employers or their families happy, but they could not successfully do both. One senior CPM, divorced and with no children, articulated this as follows:

> *In construction you can earn very good money, if you're prepared to put in the hours. But if you decide to put in the hours to earn the money for a good lifestyle, you run the risk of your partner or family getting sick of you being away working. They want the money but they want you at home more – they want the best of both worlds. When that kicked in, my stress levels went through the roof.*

CPMs felt their skills were not transferable to other career paths at their construction salary levels. The core problem was not so much the transferability of skillset but rather the fact family had become accustomed to a revenue level, and a career change to reduce stress and improve health was regarded as subordinate in importance to maintaining current income level. The flickering light of career change possibility was quickly extinguished by the prospect of reduced salary, and the decision to dive headlong into further stress in the current job was almost automatic and perceived as unavoidable. Most CPMs appeared to think about this issue with external locus of control, and family preferences regarding place of residence, type of school, holiday location and the like were not to be questioned. At work, management demands were accepted without hesitation. These highly-trained, competent professionals, charged with everyday decision-making to solve complex problems costing hundreds of thousands, even millions of dollars, seemed to simply park the internal locus of control central to effective and successful execution of that duty, and become compliant with external locus-of-control dynamics when it came to managing aspects of their own lives. The following provide insight regarding this theme:

In regard to feeling trapped:

> *With bills and kids there's no real options other than what you know...I've contemplated changing industries before, but I can't get paid the same amount*

so, you know, once you've got a mortgage or kids and everything else. You've got to look after that, don't you?

In regard to considering career options:

I roll with it quite well and I can deal with most of the crap that happens during the day, but after a while you get to the point where you feel you've had enough. You know I'm 52. I'm thinking there's got to be a better way to earn a living.

In regard to getting to the limit of endurance:

If I had my time again I don't know what I'd do, but it wouldn't be construction.

It is appropriate to close analysis of this theme with an extract from a CPM who appeared to be operating very much from an internal locus of control:

A mate got sick of working for construction companies and found a job in maintenance for a shopping centre. He was getting burned out but now he's enjoying work again. After all the years in construction with one company, I feel I need a break. I've spoken with my team about it. A lot of young blokes coming through are going to need mentors because they don't really have the attitude we used to have. They need guidance. Happy to do that rather than keep working on the jobs.

An alternate way to address the issue was to do something about work environment. The next theme addressed this point.

Theme 2. Fear of losing one's job if one complains

Seven CPMs offered comments relating to this theme. It was concern over jobs contraction that largely drove a strong sense of fear:

I remember working in Sydney around the time of the GFC (Global Financial Crisis). Everyone was too scared to complain about working conditions and hours of work because everybody just wanted to keep their jobs. Want to keep good employees? Then you need to make sure they're not stressed out.

I worry about a downturn in building, and job redundancies.

One organisation openly communicated that employees who spoke up about issues would not suffer recriminations. Employees believed otherwise. Participants believed organisations would quickly replace them from a perceived abundant source of competent and readily available CPMs. Remarkably, this opinion was held by the same professionals who emphasised management continued to overload its best performers due to lack of availability of competent resources.

It made little sense to hold both points of view. Nonetheless, participants believed management might replace a complaining employee in a heartbeat, regardless of his or her value:

The culture is if you don't handle (the work) there'll always be someone else who will take your position. You're just a number. I'm old school. If you're responsible for a project you just don't take time off unless you absolutely have to, because you're needed.

For junior personnel, fear of pushing back against management about workload was driven more by fear of appearing weak:

The problem is that young people, in particular, are probably not going to take the opportunity (of complaining) because they're afraid something will get back to management. They're afraid they'll seem weak in what's supposed to be a strong profession, and they're afraid they'll lose their jobs because of that.

In summary, despite an ideal attitude by some organisations encouraging open feedback and promising no recriminations, many participants remained cynical. An AP summarised this as follows:

One of our company policies is that if you speak up you won't get fired. It's written in our induction manual. It's something we try and push, but you do have people that don't read it – or don't believe it.

Participants generally believed it was imprudent to challenge management:

Construction projects managers can't push back too hard against top management. They might be in control of the project, but they've also got to control themselves.

Theme 3. Sense of inability to change a system badly in need of change

CPMs were aware of key contributors to stress but believed things could not be changed. They criticised management for taking on too much work and distributing it in a manner significantly contributing to CPMs' stress. They also accepted their management had little choice but continue that practice in difficult economic times or risk demise. Importantly, they collectively recognised the majority of workplace stressors were industry systemic problems. They believed stress was part of industry culture, and there was no way out of that.

Stress avoidance and management for CPMs was primarily remedial rather than preventative and constituted band-aid therapy, particularly when CPMs had insufficient personal and family time, and so could not use any tools made available to them. This sense the construction industry would not change despite the need is demonstrated in the following:

…it's impossible to do what we do in the construction industry without feeling some element of stress... You've got constant pressure from your team leader to make money. You've got constant pressure from your project manager to make sure everything is on time. Some days it feels like it's coming at you from twenty different angles.

The real answer is cultural change at the top, and not just EAPs to fix problems that should never have happened in the first place, and probably wouldn't have, if only CPMs could get the ear of senior management on any issue other than profits.

Some participants laid the blame for the problem squarely at the feet of management:

What causes stress is we can't control the effect on us. Anyone who's been around construction long enough realises that if you're going to be taking the cheapest subcontractor and driving a profit out of a bad situation, you're going to have guys you have to lift up and carry over the line. It's part of your job description - you're expected to do it. But it's more the stuff that you don't expect, and it comes from the place you least expect – your own management. And you can't do anything about it.

Even when management try to resolve a problem they do so without speaking with the people managing the project and often make matters worse... it really causes additional stress. The industry forces them to keep making deals needing really tight programmes and then they think having a counselling service can manage all the problems that causes.

Others saw the problem as systemically entrenched:

What you're talking about is a good idea, but it will never come to fruition. You're talking about a whole culture change across industry.

The problem was perceived as deteriorating:

...we are a lot more stressed than we were ten years ago. The phone is dinging every ten minutes with emails, and that doesn't help. For me, probably the most stressful part of work is emails. These things that come through and you're expected to answer them, you know. It's the same amount of work. But if you have a particularly bad day, when you get twice as many emails, then all of a sudden, your time's gone. There's not someone looking over your shoulder saying, 'do this, do that.' It's just that you can feel that pressure constantly.

External locus of control was again evident in some responses, exemplified by the following:

I sometimes feel concerned and not able to feed back to management an opinion they might not want to hear because then you sound like a whinger who can't do the job properly. We feel at our level we can't do anything about it. Management are the ones causing the stress but (we) can't seem to get that acknowledged.

Will and Clare eventually sought the assistance of a qualified and experienced psychotherapist. They attended as a couple. Clare's revelations at an early session were along the lines Will had expected, and her words seemed to somewhat lift a burden from both of them. Will's words, however, shocked Clare. They painted a picture of a person who might look at the pinnacle of career success from the outside but felt trapped without any hope of escape mentally. He felt control for most of his life was in the hands of his management at work and the clients they served. There was very little of his life that he felt he had any control over. As explained in Chapter 2, locus of control issues can be major drivers of stress when the things one perceives one can control in life are substantially fewer than the things one perceives one can control. This was precisely the position in which Will found himself. He wanted to escape but felt imprisoned by his salary and benefits and did not want to walk away from remuneration which benefited him and his family in many ways. He often felt the desire to complain to his management but always opted for maintenance of the status quo for fear of losing his job. For a long time, he simply accepted that he worked in a system badly in need of change, but accepted that change was unlikely to be forthcoming any time soon. While the couple's therapy sessions could not change the causes of stress they faced, it would eventually balance their locus of control thinking and lower heterostatically-raised stress level to a point where various alternative solutions could be discussed without being rejected out of hand. At last, perhaps there was a light at the end of the tunnel, and perhaps it was not an oncoming train.

With participants generally expressing concern much of the problem concerning industry stress was caused by systemic factors, industry contributors to stress emerged as a separate theme.

Category 5. Industry Contributors to Stress

There was a noticeable strength of opinion offered by participants regarding themes in this category. I considered combining some themes, but each seemed to be sufficiently important to stand alone and be analysed separately. Participants generally believed with continuing stress came fatigue, which increased the probability of safety breaches on site. Participants raised this to the extent it emerged as a separate theme within this category.

Theme 1. Concern for aspects of safety arising from a stressed and/or fatigued construction project management team

Five semi-structured interview participants from MOs and LOs commented regarding this theme. The core concern was additional stress imposed on CPMs by the imperative to micro-manage poorly performing or incompetent subcontractors might lead to those CPMs missing quality or safety transgressions they otherwise would never have overlooked. This problem was worse when CPMs were required to cover two roles—site project manager and site safety manager, for example. The following succinctly provide insight into this point:

> *Extreme external stress can affect work performance...clouding judgement, and adding further stress.*

> *If you're stressed, you tend not to focus properly and therefore, mistakes can be made.*

> *Stress is involved in making bad choices and spur of the moment decisions.*

Participants, were sensitive about decreasing safety attentiveness being triggered when increasing stress and fatigue were at play. One participant who had worked in both a normal construction environment and construction for mining provided attention-getting insight into the intensity of these concerns:

> *My observation was that far more mistakes were made and far more injury was experienced at the end of rotating shifts than at the beginning. I remember quite a few over a period we were doing 11 days on and four off. That was heavy. There were a lot of injuries around that period. I suppose the main cause would've been fatigue, but in addition, towards the end of a shift, looking towards going home, your mind may be wandering – looking forward to not being there.*

Non-mining construction CPMs also saw the potential of stress effects to manifest as safety issue:

I believe a little bit of stress will start at home, and the pressure of work regarding productivity and safety issues – incidents and stuff like that – will amplify that stress into something much bigger. And as the days go by, more pressure gets put on for productivity. And then they have to make sure the site is safe – and they can't stop work, so the pressure is building and building.

Interestingly, this was another theme wherein the lack of control concern became more established as a consistent and core aspect of CPMs stress:

There's always stress when you're the project safety manager, trying to do the right thing. There's always someone looking down from the top. Obviously, I don't want anyone to get hurt or have an incident so I want to make sure everything is alright, but there's a lot of things I don't have control of, and that puts stress on me as well.

In any area where safety issues became a focus, the increased interest of unions was expected. I will now address that topic:

Theme 2. Union issues/pressures

Six interview participants from LOs raised union influence, but data revealed a balance of opinion with the positive aspects no better articulated than in the following interview extract:

The image out there is that construction is just a bunch of big unions bashing our souls. They're not; they're just human beings trying to make a living and have issues to deal with. Ninety percent of workers are solid blokes who want to turn up to work, and not make a big deal about anything. They want to look after the family. I mean you're going to get your (occasional) ratbag in industry; I don't care what industry it is. Our shop steward – he's a great bloke.

Despite things today reported as better than they were yesteryear, CPMs negatively impacted by union activity held clear memory of their experience and the stress it caused:

You get a subpoena to the Royal Commission because they do something stupid on my site, you tell the truth because everyone's going to say you're lying if you don't, and from then on you're the worst person in the world in the eyes of the union, and then there's nowhere you go that they won't attack it.

And then I started this new job and I had this union delegate on site telling everyone he's gonna rape me and stirring lots of shit. I know what the unions are like – they stop at your house, you know. No surprises when they're rattling on your door late at night – that sort of thing.

The next theme involves a different industry contributor to stress.

Theme 3. Pressure arising from poor quality contract documents as a consequence of clients putting fee reduction pressure on consultants

Five participants from LOs spoke with emotion that demanded recognition beyond what might be given based only on the comments made. Stress for CPMs resulted from effects of sub-standard documentation on pricing accuracy and contract administration. The root cause was seen as developers' reducing fees to ludicrously low levels and consultants providing a minimum level of service:

The developers are screwing down the consultants so much and they are responding by doing the minimum job feasible in production of documents. So you add poor documentation, and stress goes through the roof trying to manage it.

This action affected CPMs having to deal with its consequences:

The crappy design team, and all the rest of it – sure enough, I got the tightness in the chest. Got the anxiety and all that.

Some CPMs believed consultants needed to improve their performance:

I think consultants aren't very good at the job anymore. There are some good ones. But I think that consultants got used to builders pulling them out of the shit and when I come back to a fully documented project, it doesn't really lend itself to the standards and their own obligations, and that causes stress and arguments.

Perhaps consultants, like contractors, suffered the effects of economic circumstances. I address that as the last theme in this category.

Theme 4. The cut-throat economic climate in some regions

Fourteen CPMs offered comments contributing to this theme, 10 from LOs and four from MOs. The data again contained strategies for winning work and the consequential stress thereof. Participants saw management reducing budgets and schedules to win work as justified, even necessary, given economic circumstances.

When market sectors become saturated, smaller organisations facing difficulty winning work penetrate a larger segment and won work for two reasons. Firstly, their lower pricing appealed to developers not concerned by flow-on effects on an already-saturated market. Secondly, if the upwardly-mobile organisation is a subcontractor, contractors employ them because their low price provides opportunity to increase profit on projects won at low margin in a cutthroat economic environment. The outcome was increased stress for CPMs:

> *There are so many contractors in Southeast Queensland that something's got to happen. When I started there were fewer, and they weren't cut-throat towards each other. Some are getting work by cutting prices too far. And that's a lot of stress. Managers will cut time out of a job to win the job and it falls back on the site project managers to deliver in the highly risky short times they had to agree to win the work. It can be very stressful.*

CPMs were cynical regarding management's part in practices driven by a tough economic climate. The first extract exemplifies that cynicism, while the second takes a more level, but equally concerned approach:

> *Stress – well it all gets down to the almighty dollar, really. It starts with the owner who screws the principal contractor, and then it goes down the line with the principal contractor screwing the subbies, and so on. It's just one big price war – everyone trying to get a better job for a cheaper price.*

> *We were aiming at a 1.5% profit on this job. That was the target. It's absolutely ridiculous to be running on that sort of margin.*

The more desperate activities of both contractors and developers were also addressed by participants:

> *It's an industry – wide issue at the moment. My company are in a tough spot...smaller builders are willing to work much cheaper...trying to break into the bigger end.*

> *Developers are going with projects that should not be proceeding. Everyone's got to the point with margins being cut to shreds – it's at the point we can't go any lower. That's stressful for everybody.*

Some participants believed their organisations would earn as much by placing funds on fixed deposit, a strategy not supportive of maintaining market position until better economic circumstances returned. However, the suggestion provided insight into the depth of CPMs' frustration. The following extract was a case in point:

> *It's absurd. At the end of the day, management could probably take the money and put it in a managed account and make more than we do on some projects (laughs loudly).*

Pushed shorter schedules and lower costs had been a well-known characteristic of working with some developers for decades. One participant articulated reasons for this behaviour:

> *For a lot of developers, the job is bank funded, so the longer the project goes, the more impact the interest on the money they borrowed. So they react with the attitude, "quick, get it done faster, so we can get cash flow, and pay the bank back sooner." They pay less interest and make more profit.*

The data revealed contractors took steps not considered acceptable a decade ago to optimise chances of achieving short construction schedules:

> *... hours are restricted and you may not be able to work on Sundays or past 6pm in the evening. But the project manager says "we have to get the job done and I don't mind paying the six grand if we get fined for working longer hours*

because that six grand fine is nothing compared to the liquidated damages to be charged by the client if we don't finish the job on schedule".

These measures undoubtedly contributed to significantly increased stress for the professionals affected. It is not new practice for clients to sometimes request consultants and contractors to provide up-front work at no cost in return for being given the job or being paid for their effort when the project proceeded. That practice was now commonplace, despite economic circumstances preventing many projects proceeding, including some that should never have progressed beyond an initial financial feasibility study. Consultants were reticent to reject such requests, fearing their competition would say 'yes' to rare projects that proceeded.

When contractors became involved, concern projects might not proceed necessitated existing staff being allocated to the project—usually the more experienced, competent and already overloaded CPMs, and their stress was further increased:

(Government Projects) can almost be as bad as the situation with developers where they will have you working on a project as a consultant (doing) several iterations of testing, checking, running a lot of work with no payment unless this project goes ahead. And then they pull the pin at the last minute.

The effects of harsh economic circumstances were felt even in normal tendering practice, which was also stress-inducing. In saturated supply situations, contractors expected to win fewer tenders, and needed to carry the cost of losses, hoping those costs would be covered by profit from jobs won. This everyday reality was a major contributor to stress across management levels of the construction industry. The following interview extract offers further explanation:

Even in the normal tender situation for a \$50-\$60 million job, you're going to be spending a couple of hundred thousand on bidding. If you lose the job, you've got to catch that up on another one, so if you lose three or four jobs before you win one, you're behind the 8-ball before you start. Something's got to give.

One CPM articulated the problems engendered by a cutthroat economic environment, and identified the standard to which CPMs would like to return:

> *To win the job we might say that we can do it much faster than our opponents. So you've got to work a six-day week or you've got to work a 12-hour day. You've got to take shortcuts and rush things and that inevitably ends up with all these fires that you have to put out. You end up shooting from the hip and trying too many things on the run, instead of taking the time to put the forethought in and get it right the first time.*

The final theme addressed a most important driver of stress in the construction industry.

Theme 5. Industry culture—It is a tough industry, and this creates a fear that reporting the effects of stress will be seen as weakness

Ten CPMs in semi-structured interviews raised industry culture, and 11 online survey participants offered comments. This was a theme about which participants possessed thorough understanding and held strong opinions.

An outstanding finding was lack of trust generated by conflict between two diametrically opposed management attitudes. On the one hand, management tended to initiate and encourage involvement in stress avoidance and management programmes and increasing numbers of construction organisations establish Employee Assistant Programs (EAPs). On the other hand, management continued to put stress-inducing pressure on CPMs in particular, to deliver increasingly complex projects under increasingly difficult contractual conditions. Participants held doubts concerning EAPs:

> *People are being told it's confidential to talk to an EAP but they don't believe it, because the same people who are telling them about confidentiality are telling them to push - the drive to make treble profits is coming across as all-important. People align the thought that the bosses are on the one hand offering assistance for stress but, on the other hand, want this maximum performance. People suspect that if they show weakness in performance, they could lose their jobs.*

In context of the above, the following comments are not surprising:

People are too scared to take time off for stress. Our company experience is staff are very reluctant to use the EAP - they believe this will have a negative impact their career.

We try to encourage people to talk about it. You'd look like a wuss if you told management. That's the way it is.

While construction remains a predominantly male career, the number of female CPMs is increasing, with one interesting development. While men are slowly accepting change is necessary, women professionals appear to follow the example well-entrenched by industry men over decades. This proposition (from the data) was put to a female CPM, who replied:

I agree with you. Women have learnt to – not cope with that – but to be able to hide it so they don't look weak in the industry they're working in.

The same participant also had valuable input regarding a tendency for female CPMs to want to fit in:

I think it's definitely more stressful for some on-site guys. There's no balance between male and female really. Everyone is really rough, kind of, and they don't sit around talking about things females do (laughs). Does that make sense?

I regarded it important to complete this qualitative analysis by presenting some important pieces of the data. The first extract explained why the problem continued:

Our industry is not conducive to teaching professionals stress recognition, avoidance and management. We attract people who love the tough image of construction culture but then they get trapped into feeling weak if they report a stress-related problem. Many consultants experience this as well. We build great things, but the approach we use is not all that concerned with the impacts on people of getting things done. The nature of what we do and how we get it done causes stress but people do not have the skills to deal with that stress. Some industry leaders demonstrate exactly the opposite of what is required for a stress-reduced workplace. They work long hours with a drive to achieve budget and schedule at all costs and they seldom take time (for) themselves – and they expect their teams to follow suit. In that regard, it's a toxic industry to work in.

The final extract summarises the opinion of a participant who had experienced the worst of stress effects and came through the ordeal. On the one hand, he recognised the need for CPMs to be open about stress-related issues. On the other hand, he still expressed concern about discussing personal anxiety:

Men are changing and their roles are changing. Women have equal opportunities and our (men's) role in life is changing, and we open up far more than we used to are doing it. We still have the rufty-tufty tradie thing happening, of course (laughs). We are kinda harsh blokes. We've had to work hard to get what we want. I think being around a lot of other males in that situation puts you in a place where you don't really wanna open up. I mean the way I've spoken to you. I would never tell anyone else this. It's actually a skill opening up and talking to people. It really is.

Thankfully, Will's training and experience prepared him well to always prioritise maintaining safety on his projects and he had never had an experience of stress leading to safety breaches. He had also been blessed with a great group of union representatives on his projects and, unlike many CPMs, had suffered no union-related problems. However, he had certainly experienced the effects of documents produced by consultants whose fees had been driven down to unrealistic levels by unscrupulous developers seeking to maximise their own profits at the expense of pretty much everyone involved in delivering their projects. Usually, this problem had to be rectified by the builders faced with interpreting the poor-quality documents, and that usually meant the CPMs carried the stress of this often-burdensome problem. We have previously addressed Will's experience trying to drive a profit from projects won at low margin and no margin prices in a cut-throat economic climate.

Will broke down in a couples' therapy session when he admitted to himself that because of the tough image and culture of his chosen career industry, he never considered strongly objecting to the unreasonableness of his management. He had always convinced himself that management didn't really like driving their top performing CPMs to the point of breakdown, but had to do it to keep the company profitable and prevent many people losing their jobs. He now realised that would certainly be the case for some companies in some circumstances, but more importantly he realised that he, like hundreds of his colleagues in construction organisations across the country were, to a large extent, victims of the profit focus of their management. The problem, he now realised, could not be placed solely at the feet of management. CPMs had to accept the very things they avoided doing for fear of appearing weak might actually be seen to constitute a demonstration of weakness. Understandable weakness perhaps—one does not capriciously risk losing a job that builds a nice family lifestyle (even if building the lifestyle involved demolishing the person attempting to do the lifestyle building)—but when failing to act when necessary was a key factor in much overdue industry change being progressed, at some level that represents a weakness. In the case of the construction industry, that weakness, to a large extent, lies in a culture that is long overdue for systemic change.

I think now would be a good time to admit to a purposeful misleading of readers throughout this book until now. I have consistently referred to Will and Clare as our metaphoric couple. They actually are not a metaphor for the lives of the many professional CPMs of the construction industry, albeit I think their lives very much represent a parallel of several participants from the construction industry in particular. However, the couple *also* constitute a strong metaphor, not for participants but for the industry at large. I will discuss this in the next and final chapter.

Confirmation Study

At the commencement of this chapter, I referred to a supplementary study I undertook after I completed analysis of the primary quantitative and qualitative data collected. In some instances of the qualitative analysis, while I was satisfied a sometimes-low number of participants contributing to identification of a theme was adequately compensated by qualitative factors (e.g. intensity and tone of voice of the participant) I wanted to be certain the work was not open to criticism by a reader who might not agree with the formation of a theme based on just a few participants' responses. For this reason, and to prepare for the writing of journal articles following completion of this book, I completed a supplementary study to determine broader attitudes among CPMs regarding all the themes identified by my qualitative analysis.

Participants were sourced using a Facebook advertising campaign, and apart from demographic type information, the only questions put to participants were those relating to the causes of stress as defined in my primary qualitative study, as outlined in Table 4.2, and responses were sought using a five option Likert scale with possible responses being strongly disagree, somewhat disagree, neither agree not disagree, somewhat agree and strongly agree. Thirty five of the 48 respondents who answered all compulsory questions of the survey fitted this book's description of a CPM. Twenty-one were aged between 21 and 40, and 11 between 41 and 70. In response to some marketing bias towards female CPMs in seeking participants for the supplementary study, sixteen were males and 19 were females. Eleven received salaries less than $75,000 per year while 28 were remunerated with between $75,000 and over $250,000. Education level was noticeably higher than for the original research cohort, with 31 holding undergraduate degrees or higher, seven holding Diplomas and two being high school graduates.

Their responses are presented in Table 4.3.

This supplementary study strongly confirmed the themes identified within the qualitative data which summarised the most experienced causes of stress for CPMs. It was never the purpose of this study to be fully analysed for this book, but rather to address any doubts that

Table 4.3 Responses to supplementary research survey questionnaire (number in parentheses is the percentage of participants—$N = 40$)

Number	Proposition	Strongly agree	Somewhat agree	Neither agree not disagree	Somewhat disagree	Strongly disagree
1	Stress is primarily caused more by intense or major life experiences such as loss or serious illness of a friend or loved one, previous mental illness, anxiety or depression, or divorce (or relationship breakdown) than by work-related factors	9 (25.71)	12 (34.29)	7 (20.00)	5 (14.29)	2 (5.71)
2	Stress result from senior managers lacking understanding of my role and workload	10 (28.57)	14 (40.00)	7 (20.00)	4 (11.43)	0

Number	Proposition	Strongly agree	Somewhat agree	Neither agree not disagree	Somewhat disagree	Strongly disagree
3	Stress results from companies winning work by drastically reducing tender price margins	12 (34.29)	8 (22.86)	11 (31.43)	4 (11.43)	0
4	Stress is caused by managers understaffing projects and then, if problems arise, compensating by overloading experienced high-performing managers (CPMs), thus preventing time off and exposing them to burnout	16 (45.71)	14 (40.00)	2 (5.71)	3 (8.57)	0
5	Stress is caused by the requirement to satisfy clients, no matter what personal effort that might require	9 (25.71)	18 (51.43)	4 (11.43)	4 (11.43)	0

(continued)

Table 4.3 (continued)

Number	Proposition	Strongly agree	Somewhat agree	Neither agree not disagree	Somewhat disagree	Strongly disagree
6	Stress is caused by failure of managers to communicate (with CPMs) regarding price and schedule before tendering, increasing stress if the job was won, because *inter alia*, lower priced and often less-competent subcontractors needed to be appointed to achieve or maintain a profit margin, and these required far more supervision by already overworked (CPM) managers	15 (42.86)	12 (34.29)	7 (20.00)	0	1 (2.86)

Number	Proposition	Strongly agree	Somewhat agree	Neither agree not disagree	Somewhat disagree	Strongly disagree
7	Stress is caused by pressure of work effects on the primary family carer (such as lack of quality time with family each week or lack of time for self after work and family commitments)	12 (34.29)	15 (42.86)	4 (11.43)	4 (11.43)	0
8	Stress is caused by fear of losing one's job if one complains about stress causing problems at work	11 (31.43)	9 (25.71)	9 (25.71)	5 (14.29)	1 (2.86)
9	Stress is caused by inability to change an industry badly *in need of change*	11 (31.43)	15 (42.86)	6 (17.14)	3 (8.57)	0

(continued)

Table 4.3 (continued)

Number	Proposition	Strongly agree	Somewhat agree	Neither agree not disagree	Somewhat disagree	Strongly disagree
10	Stress is caused by aspects of safety that arise from already stressed and/or fatigued team members being less alert than the job requires	8 (22.86)	13 (37.14)	18 (51.43)	6 (17.14)	0
11	Stress is caused by union issues/pressures	6 (17.14)	6 (17.14)	15 (42.86)	6 (17.14)	2 (5.71)
12	Stress is caused by poor quality contract documents as a consequence of clients putting fee pressure on consultants	9 (25.71)	15 (42.86)	10 (28.57)	1 (2.86)	0
13	Stress is caused by cut-throat economic conditions in some regions	5 (14.29)	20 (57.14)	8 (22.86)	0	1 (2.86)

some readers might have had concerning the low numbers of participants who provided data in relation to some identified themes. It was encouraging to find that only 34.28 percent of CPMs strongly agreed or somewhat agreed unions were a cause of stress in the industry today. With all other propositions of the study receiving agreement or strong agreement from at least 57 percent of participants and over two thirds of participants strongly agreeing or somewhat agreeing with all but four of the propositions, the supplementary exercise stands as solid support for the qualitative findings from the original study.

In Conclusion

Having identified and compared attitudes to the avoidance and management of stress within construction industry and other workplaces using quantitative methods, and having identified likely causes of the stress that CPMs experience using qualitative methods (and confirmed those qualitative findings by a supplementary quantitative study, it is now time to review findings with a view to making useful recommendations for industry, and that is the purpose of Chapter 5.

References

1. Zimbardo, P in Baer, D 2004, 'How locus of control drives your success (and stress)', *Business Insider Australia,* viewed 25th January 2018, https://www.businessinsider.com.au/proactive-people-are-successful-and-less-stressed-2014-7?r=US&IR=T.
2. Khan, A, Saleem, M & Shahid, R 2012, "Buffering role of locus of control among the college/university teachers of Bahawalpur', *The Pakistan journal of Commercial Social Science,* vol. 6, no. 1, pp. 158–167, viewed 25th January 2018, https://pdfs.semanticscholar.org/797e/1e64da6b141bac5e1b1fd9259900ad0cee3e.pdf.
3. Ongolla, P & Raburu, P 2016, 'Relation between locus of control and stress management among high school principals in Kenya', *International Journal*

of Applied Psychology, vol.6, no. 5, pp. 150–155, viewed 25th January 2018, https://doi.org/10.5923/j.ijap.20160605.03.
4. Rotter, J 1990, 'Internal versus external control of reinforcement: a case history of a variable', *American Psychologist*, no. 45, pp. 489–493, viewed 25th January 2018, https://pdfs.semanticscholar.org/c92a/377531f46046b32d6cc8e18c3787caaea310.pdf.

5

Where to from Here for Construction Project Managers?

Introduction

A pilot study inspired this work was described in Chapter 1, and findings from an extensive literature review regarding the science behind and impacts of stress were presented in Chapters 2, 3, and 4 explained the findings from analysis of quantitative and qualitative data, respectively, taking me to the position where I had a solid comprehension of answers in relation to my research questions, and the main causes of stress, especially for CPMs.

The purpose of this chapter is to discuss the research findings, to draw conclusions regarding the extent to which study hypotheses were supported and to address implications of findings for the construction industry at large. I intend to do this by reporting the most important findings from the work but avoiding any unnecessary repetition of work described in detail in other chapters. I end this chapter with observations

In project management (PM) parlance—the CLOSEOUT phase (learning from experience and making necessary change)
In psychotherapy parlance—THE HOW TO AVOID RELAPSE session

A. Patching, *Attitudes to Psychological Stress Among Construction Professionals*,
https://doi.org/10.1007/978-3-030-93776-8_5

of recent developments and innovations in the construction industry that, with appropriate and energetic leadership present an opportunity for change, provided the key obstructions to possible change are sensibly addressed.

Before commencing that discussion, I think it appropriate to contextualise the importance of the study findings not only to CPMs, but also to all people working in stressful environments.

Contextualising the Importance of the Study

The importance of workplace mental health in Australia was emphasized in 2006 when the Australian Compensation and Safety Council identified mental disorders as one of eight occupational disease/disorder categories to be addressed over the life (2002–2012) of that national strategy [1]. The major cause of work-related mental disorders in Australia was mental stress [2].

Mental stress is not a diagnosable condition, but rather a state within a person that increased his or her capacity to develop clinically diagnosable health conditions [2]. As early as 1998, some identified stress in a manner that seemed prophetic for the construction industry—a reaction to excess work pressure and conflicts under poor management and with inadequate coping resources and little if any support [3]. It has been more simply expressed as an outer force that has command over inner feelings [4]. That definition lacks depth from a psychological perspective, but probably succinctly summarises the experience of sufferers of stress effects.

There were two strategies identified as effective for dealing with workplace stress. One is to address the symptoms after they develop, and the other is to identify and remove as many causal stressors as possible [4]. The second approach is better but often the less followed in construction organisations, within which this study revealed a preference for dealing with stress affects after they manifested. This seems to indicate either a lack of understanding of the problem or a lack of leadership in addressing with it. For balance, I recognise busy times often foster maintenance of the status quo, for reasons including:

- Management believing stress comes more from home than work and was for individuals to deal with rather than employers
- CPMs are time poor and often regard stress avoidance and/or management activities as increasing rather than reducing stress levels
- CPMs are likely to believe attending stress avoidance programmes might be seen as weakness. This was not unique to CPMs, although it might be argued they have raised it to an art form. Workplace culture across general business prevents people admitting to having a problem at work, such as bullying or harassment [5]
- Many CPMs are located on construction sites and it is difficult to conduct programmes for widely dispersed personnel. This was even more the case when CPMs worked under fly-in fly-out arrangements.

These explanations are understandable, but not acceptable. In 2006, Noblet and La Montagne [6] highlighted attending to manifested stress effects in individuals was reactive and, might even contravene health and safety legislation in several industrialised nations. From a practical perspective, it could be questioned if such an approach was ethically acceptable or delivered real benefits organisations [7]. The literature generally supported that position, but without denying the value of EAPs and counselling services as part of an effective mix for addressing the rapidly increasing problem of workplace stress. Ideally, a settings approach—one addressing both symptoms and sources of stress within a workplace, would be adopted [7].

Yip and Rowlinson [8] reported the nature of work caused potential for stress to be high but noted a positive consequence of this was practitioners developed greater expertise at handling it. However, a greater propensity to deal with stress did not equate to an immunity to its impacts. Site-based CPMs arguably experience more extreme stressors than office-based consultants [9]. However, it is likely there are possible contributors to stress beyond job demands. CPMs people often perform well at work, are success-oriented and may run an increased risk of overload and stress symptoms [10]. The previously referenced study confirmed a level of pride in work that explained in part the long hours professionals such as CPMs work. The work environments of many CPMs were simply described by Weinberg, Sutherland and Cooper [11].

Survival of the fittest becomes the name of the game and the pace and speed at which players can adapt to the continually changing environment is the fact that will determine survival.

With that background, it is now appropriate to revisit study questions and review what data analysis revealed.

Discussion of Data Analysis Findings in Relation to Whether CPMs Held Different Attitudes to the Main Causes of Stress Than Other Professionals

This section addresses the questions posed and the knowledge gap identified in Chapter 2 Each hypothesis is addressed in the order it was presented in Chapter 1.

Discussion Regarding CPMs' Attitudes to Causes of Stress

I hypothesised 'That CPMs would hold a different attitude towards the main causes of stress than would APs and BPs', used one group of survey questions to collect data in relation to this hypothesis, and presented analysis of that data in Chapter 3.

Salient Findings Regarding this Hypothesis

Descriptive statistics revealed APs' and BPs' stress was caused more by non-work factors while CPMs' stress was caused more by work factors and, importantly, CPMs also recorded markedly higher scores across all OSs than did APs and BPs in response to the proposition that stress was caused by work factors.

A major finding of this research was participants' role type was significant regarding work being the main cause of stress, and work being stressful. Specifically, while stress was caused by non-work factors significantly more than by work factors for APs and BPs, it was caused significantly more by work factors for CPMs.

While I found no significant effect of either OS or RP on stress effects on ability to perform at work, despite OS being close to significant, the CPM role type did have a significant effect on participants' responses regarding stress being caused from work factors, and CPMs' work being regarded as stressful. Qualitative data analysis supported CPMs believed their work was stressful, and perceived their stress was caused by work rather than non-work factors. CPMs also reported stress had the capacity to affect performance at work.

Both RP and OS had a significant effect on personal attitudes to stress. Within construction organisations, descriptive statistics regarding impact of stress on ability to perform at work revealed the means for CPMs across all OSs were higher than the corresponding means for APs.

I found a negative correlation between stress experienced by workers and perception of absenteeism. In other words, CPMs, who recorded a substantially higher mean across all OSs than BPs regarding their work being considered stressful, were more likely to report a lower perception of absenteeism due to stress.

General Comments Regarding These Findings

I somewhat predicted these results from review of the literature. I found no in-depth studies specifically relating to CPMs. Lingard's opinion in Yip and Rowlinson [12] that on-site CPMs faced more stress than office-based consultants was an important finding. However, my research revealed it was not so much the location of employment that predicted levels of stress as the type of work participants were doing. A Dutch study posited that men were less likely than women to be health-conscious and more likely than women to be competitive within the workplace [13]. In the predominately male Australian construction industry this was a possible explanation for CPMs' opinion their work was stressful.

There were relatively high means from all RP categories across all OSs for responses regarding participants' perception of the effects of stress on ability to perform at work, and these were of particular interest. Clearly, there was strong awareness of stress impacts on work performance, with greater significance of the issue found for CPMs.

Conclusions Regarding the Findings

Data analysis confirmed:

- CPMs believed stress was caused mainly by work-related factors while APs and BPs believed stress was mainly caused by non-work factors.
- CPMs considered their work to be stressful more so than did APs and BPs
- CPMs more than APs and BPs opined, regardless of the cause of stress, it could have a significant impact on their performance at work.

Discussion Regarding Staff Training and Attitudes to Assistance Programmes

I hypothesised, 'That opinions regarding stress avoidance training, stress management training and the use of Employee Assistance Programmes (EAPs) would differ substantially across role types', and posed one group of questions in the survey document to collect relevant data, which I analysed and presented in Chapter 3.

Salient Findings Regarding the Second Hypotheses

Percentages of 'unsure' responses regarding whether leaders were trained to recognise stress effects in employees differed across OS with the percentages of participants certain about whether their organisations had this training in place being 94.05, 81.45 and 67.62, respectively. Of those, 48.62 percent of CPMs reported their organisation did not train leaders in stress identification techniques, compared with 45.16 percent of APs and 59.82 percent of BPs. Given the prevalence of stress in modern workplaces, and its potential impacts of stress on productivity and other important work-related factors, these numbers were difficult to comprehend, and again raise the question, 'Is this shortcoming an indication of poor leadership, or of an attitude that stress is the individual's problems and not a matter in which workplaces need to become involved?' The question seemed relevant given only 24.51 percent of CPMs, 23.0 percent of APs, and 21.43 percent of BPs agreed or strongly agreed their organisation's attitude to this matter was effective.

Considering responses to the question regarding leaders being trained in stress identification, the figures relating to all staff being so trained should not come as a surprise. Specifically, 62.06 percent of CPMs reported their organisations did not train all staff in stress identification compared with 58.87 percent of APs and 66.96 percent of BPs. My previous question regarding lack of leadership or lack of concern applies equally to this topic.

CPMs and APs reported substantially higher levels of uncertainty than BPs regarding an EAP to deal with stress effects after they had manifested being all that was necessary for their business. Importantly, 83.33 percent of all participants from SOs, 38.71 percent from MOs and 40.21 percent from LOs disagreed an EAP was sufficient, and only 18.27 percent of CPMs, 26.61 percent of APs, and 16.06 percent of BPs agreed or strongly agreed their organisation's EAP was effective.

General Comments Regarding these Findings

Given the strong theme within the literature that work-related problems were frequent stressors for most people [14] and most stress was initiated at work, [10, 15–17] and given the stressful environment of many areas of construction, it is surprising training of managers and employees in stress identification is not regarded a more important priority. However, that well-entrenched industry culture built on strong competition and a reputation for toughness are hardly elements likely to motivate outspoken interest in stress amelioration activities.

An important finding was CPMs earned substantially more than their counterpart APs and BPs. The qualitative data analysis revealed one reason for this was top-level CPMs often had their salaries increased at times when management needed to distract them from moving to other jobs when the workload became overwhelming in a current position. While their salaries were generally good, and usually well in excess of those of APs and BPs, the expectations of CPMs by management were often extraordinarily high. In addition, it was commonplace for CPMs with families and children at school to have heavily committed their income to housing and education and participants saw this as preventing change to less stressful but lower paying work. This was definitely the case for our storyline couple, Will and Clare, but we'll spend more time discussing them later in this chapter.

It seems reasonable to expect management in the industry would want to ensure their best paid and best performing people were well looked after, and a long-term strategy for success would include training of all staff in stress symptoms identification and stress management techniques, and a well-promoted EAP or counselling service. This research did not find that to be the case at anywhere near the anticipated level.

Conclusions Regarding the Findings

The data analysis confirmed:

- The sub-hypothesis CPMs, more than APs and BPs would believe their organisations did not train leaders and managers to identify stress effects in their employees was not supported, because, contrary to expectations, more BPs than CPMs reported there was no such training in their organisations
- The sub-hypothesis CPMs, more than APs and BPs, would believe an EAP was all their organisation needed to address stress effects on personnel, was also not supported, because a higher percentage of APs than CPMs agreed that an EAP was all their organisation needed to address the effects of stress.

Given APs also work in construction organisations and taking a broader view of construction employees compared with other business professionals, it becomes arguably acceptable 'That opinions regarding stress avoidance training, stress management training and the use of EAPs would differ substantially across role types' was supported at that broader level.

Discussion About What Should Be Done in Relation to Stress Avoidance and Management

I hypothesised, 'That CPMs would express significantly different attitudes from APs and BPs regarding what they believed organisations should offer by way of stress avoidance and management'. Data collecting questions addressed whether CPMs would report stress should be a matter for individuals to address rather than organisations, and whether participants considered stress management programmes should involve training of leaders and all other personnel in stress symptoms recognition.

Salient Findings Regarding This Third Hypotheses

CPMs were more strongly of the opinion than APs and BPs organisations should be involved in stress avoidance and management within the workplace and stress should not be a matter for individuals to deal with without organisational assistance.

There was strong opinion across participants, particularly among CPMs and APs, that training of leaders in stress recognition was supported. Some 89.72 percent of CPMs, 81.45 percent of APs and 75 percent of BPs either agreed or strongly agreed that leaders should be trained in stress identification techniques.

Participants also strongly supported the proposition all staff should be trained in stress symptoms recognition. The percentages were 81.42, 79.84 and 66.97 for CPMs, APs and BPs, respectively. CPMs reporting the strongest support aligned with them experiencing high levels of the effects of stress.

General Comments Regarding These Findings

Organisational employees were not well versed regarding how debilitating stress effects can be on a person's health, but they were becoming better educated. This is largely the consequence of work by the Mates in Construction movement, which has achieved much in educating industry members, especially tradespersons, regarding the importance of discussing anxiety, depression and suicidal thoughts with a mate on site. The qualitative analysis revealed most interviewees knew of someone who had suffered or was suffering serious impacts of stress from work. Some even had friends who had suicided. It was probable this heightened awareness was behind the responses to this group of questions.

Participants might not have understood the psychological and physiological workings of stress, but many had experienced satisfying rewards from their hard work [19] to the point that situational pressure overcame the rewards they experienced [20] and it was probable they experienced heterostasis in the process. In addition, the popular media had published broadly regarding the serious effects of stress including depression, auto-immune disorders and coronary disease, and participants did not need to be familiar with double peer-reviewed published works [20–23] regarding the impacts of stress to understand they were at risk if they neglected stress in their work environment. It is common for stressed people to push on in the face of stress to the extent they risk burnout [17, 24–26]. It was refreshing participants responded to the questions in a manner which indicated an awareness of the problem and an awareness (at least on the part of CPMs) it was largely work-initiated and sustained, and in a manner which indicated they wanted to see something done about what caused stress impacts in their workplaces.

Conclusions Regarding These Findings

The data analysis confirmed:

- My hypothesis CPMs would report individuals and not employers should deal with stress more so than APs and BPs, was not strongly supported because CPMs more strongly confirmed organisations

should be involved in stress management training of leaders and employees
- The expectation all participants would report a stress management programme should involve training of all staff in stress symptoms recognition, was supported across RP types and OSs, with the strongest role support coming from CPMs.

On the strength of responses to each question, I concluded that the third hypothesis was, on balance, largely supported.

Discussion About Participants' Knowledge Regarding the Stress Avoidance/Management Programmes Their Organisations Had in Place

I hypothesised, 'That CPMs would be less knowledgeable than APs and BPs regarding what stress avoidance and/or management programmes their organisations had in place'. The survey sought information about participants' perceptions whether stress avoidance/management programmes existed in their organisations, and whether EAPs existed for their organisations.

Salient Findings Regarding the Fourth Hypothesis

There was high lack of certainty regarding the existence of various stress avoidance or management programmes in the workplace. CPMs recorded the highest levels of support for stress effects identification and stress avoidance and management techniques of all RP types, but also the highest lack of certainty regarding the existence of stress avoidance and/or management programmes in their organisations.

Some 14.22 percent of CPMs agreed or strongly agreed their organisation's stress avoidance programme was effective compared with corresponding percentages for APs and BPs of 20.16 and 15.18. In respect of stress management programmes, 17.78 percent of CPMs agreed or strongly agreed their organisation's was effective. The corresponding percentages for APs and BPs were 22.58 and 11.60. Regarding the effectiveness of EAPs or similar programmes, 27.27 percent of CPMs either agreed or strongly agreed they were effective compared with 25.0 percent of APs and 21.43 percent of BPs. In other words, CPMs had a lower rating of the effectiveness of stress avoidance programmes than both APs and BPs, a rating of stress management programmes effectiveness lower than APs but higher than BPs, and a higher rating of the effectiveness of EAPs than both APs and BPs.

General Comments Regarding These Findings

The CPMs considered Employee Assistance Programmes a more effective way to address stress than to use stress avoidance and stress management programmes. The qualitative analysis indicated this was because stress avoidance and stress management programmes were likely to take valuable time from people already stretched well beyond what could be regarded as a reasonable workload. The literature contained a substantial body of work that addressed the phenomenon of professionals who loved their work, and were effective at it, being overloaded because of perceived economic necessity and their own efficiency, to the point of burnout—or being 'broken' as some interviewees stated. High workload overlaid with high productivity expectations were prime contributors to burnout [17]. These were the circumstances faced by many CPMs, particularly senior members of the profession. Appreciation, acknowledgement by management and positive feedback partially alleviated the impacts of high work demands. The data indicated this was lacking in the tough-culture construction environment. In effect, even people who experienced positive eustress, if overburdened too much for too long, could quickly change to a state of distress, with all its negative attributes [10, 27] and eventually experience either aspects of a freeze response [27–30], burnout [17, 25, 26, 31] or the occupational stress disorder known as cumulative trauma [16, 32].

Participants in the pilot study described in Chapter 1 revealed some organisations attempted to ensure employees avoided stress by limiting driving and working hours each day, and restricting number of weekend days worked each month, a concept borrowed from the mining industry [33]. Those actions increased rather than reduced stress for the simple reason that completion dates were fixed by contract and heavy damages applied for late completion [33].

The circumstances for all semi-structured interview participants were almost the complete reverse of those in place at the time of the pilot study, due to the change in the economic circumstances for the construction industry. Most participants reported their organisations now required higher productivity regardless of hours worked and this gave rise to substantial stress, despite the fact most participants in those circumstances believed their organisation was acting to ensure the business survived and thrived in the current economic environment. Participants believed there was little time for stress avoidance and management training or activities and addressing stress via an EAP when required was a sensible approach. This misconception needed addressing at whole-of-industry level.

Another factor from qualitative data analysis that provided insight into the importance of having an effective stress avoidance and management strategy was many construction organisations either tendered for work at very low margins and then asked CPMs to push the project schedule and to engage cheap subcontractors to increase profit, or they offered to work six days per week to reduce delivery times and win work ahead of their competition. Both approaches maintained corporate financial health but placed the physical and mental health of employees at risk of overexposure to stress effects. Importantly, the stress effects of these seen-to-be-essential business strategies were felt by some of the organisations' most valuable human assets—their most experienced CPMs. These management actions gave rise to serious impacts including severe anxiety, depression, work–life balance challenges and even burnout for the senior CPMs affected, sometimes to the extent of relationship breakdown or feelings of lack of control over career and future. Some of the senior CPMs affected opined a more effective way of avoiding and managing stress was overdue.

These circumstances were not necessarily experienced only by CPMs, and the reality is APs and BPs also experienced high levels of workplace stress [34]. However, this study has contributed significantly to the knowledge in its important finding CPMs' stress was primarily caused by work-related factors while APs' and BPs' stress was primarily caused by non-work-related factors. In addition, the fact more CPMs stated their work was stressful than APs and BPs, and CPMs reported higher levels of stress than APs and BPs for the month prior to completing the survey supported claims more should be done about workplace stress in construction-related workplaces. It is essential to acknowledge the industry is well overdue for systemic change in work practices that heavily contribute to stress. It is also imperative to recognise the high level of uncertainty concerning what stress avoidance and/or management strategies were already in place in participants' organisations.

Conclusions Regarding These Findings

The data analysis confirmed:

- My expectation APs and BPs would be more aware of stress avoidance and/or management programmes in their workplaces than CPMs was not fully supported, because CPMs were less certain than APs and BPs in responses regarding this point.
- CPMs were less aware of the existence of an EAP in their organisations than were APs and BPs.

Accordingly, I concluded that the main fourth hypothesis was substantially, but not fully supported.

Discussion Regarding Participants Private Use of Stress Management Techniques

I hypothesised that, regardless of workplace programmes, participants would personally engage in some form of stress management activity, CPMs would be less likely to do so than APs and BPs, and CPMs would be more likely to rate their chosen technique as effective. Three separate questions in the online survey sought data in relation to this hypothesis, one regarding use of medication, one regarding use of other stress management techniques and one presenting a list of well-known stress avoidance/management techniques from which participants could select techniques they used.

Salient Findings Regarding This Fifth Hypotheses

The question regarding medication use was non-compulsory, yet 97.34 percent ($n = 476$) of all participants responded. The majority across all RP types did not take medication. Only 13.06 percent of CPMs took medication compared with 14.52 percent of APs and 17.86 percent of BPs. These figures were somewhat aligned with (but also higher than) statistics for the Australian population, among whom 14.40 percent suffer from anxiety (10.80 percent of males and 17.90 percent of females) and 7.80 percent took anti-depressant medication [35, 36]. Some 20.30 percent of CPMs considered their medication regime to be 70 percent or more effective, compared with 22.60 percent of APs and 17.00 percent of BPs.

The question regarding use of non-medication based stress avoidance and/or management techniques was also non-compulsory, but nonetheless 97.34 percent ($n = 476$) of all participants responded. Against expectations, some 50.20 percent of responding CPMs engaged in some form or stress avoidance or management, compared with 47.50 percent of APs and 45.95 percent of BPs.

General Comments Regarding These Findings

CPMs from SOs and LOs reported higher levels of effectiveness of chosen stress avoidance and/or management techniques than did their AP and BP counterparts, but those from MOs did not fit this pattern and there was no way of understanding why this was the case, apart from qualitative data that indicated senior CPMs from MOs were overloaded with work to the point they often had little or no time available for family time or self.

Conclusions Regarding the Findings

The data analysis confirmed:

- My hypothesis that, regardless of workplace programmes, CPMs would be less likely to engage in stress management than APs and BPs and would be less likely to rate their chosen technique as effective—was partially but not fully supported
- More CPMs than APs and BPs used forms of stress management other than medication
- Fewer CPMs rated technique effectiveness at higher than 70 percent than their AP and BP counterparts.

Accordingly, it was concluded this hypothesis was partially but not fully supported.

Summary of Discussion of Findings

Table 5.1 summarises this review of the study hypotheses and indicates the degree to which each hypothesis was supported.

Knowledge Gap Closure

Not all hypotheses were fully supported. However, salient information was obtained that helped close the knowledge gap as follows:

- Many organisations overload CPMs without affording them the authority to refuse additional work and CPMs often do not report stress experienced to management fearing they would look weak, or would risk losing their jobs
- The culture and processes of the construction industry contribute to the stress experienced by CPMs, and their stress is caused more by work-related factors than by home/personal factors. CPMs also report stress impacted performance at work

Table 5.1 Summary of conclusions from discussion of hypothesis

Hypothesis	Sub -hypothesis	Description	Conclusion
FIRST		**That CPMs would hold a different attitude towards the main causes of stress than would APs and BPs**	**Supported**
	First	That CPMs would believe stress was caused mainly by work-related factors and APs and BPs would hold the opinion that stress was mainly caused by non-work factors	Supported
	Second	That CPMs would consider their work to be stressful more than would APs and BPs	Supported
	Third	That CPMs more than APs and BPs, would hold the opinion that, regardless of the cause of stress, it could have a significant impact on their performance at work	Supported
SECOND		**That opinions regarding stress avoidance training, stress management training and the use of EAPs would differ substantially across role types and organisation sizes**	**Partially supported at level of general description**
	First	That CPMs, more than APs and BPs, would believe their organisations did not train leaders, managers and other personnel to identify stress effects in their employees	Not supported
	Second	That CPMs, more than APs and BPs, would believe an EAP was all their organisation needed to address stress effects on personnel	Not fully supported

(continued)

Table 5.1 (continued)

Hypothesis	Sub -hypothesis	Description	Conclusion
THIRD		**That CPMs would express significantly different attitudes from APs and BPs regarding what they believed organisations should offer by way of stress avoidance and management**	**On balance, supported**
	First	That CPMs would report that stress should be a matter for individuals to deal with, and not employers, more so than APs and BOs	Not strongly supported
	Second	That all participants would report a stress management programme should involve training of all leaders, managers and staff in stress symptoms recognition	Supported
FOURTH		**That CPMs would be less knowledgeable than APs and BPs regarding what stress avoidance and/or management programmes their organisations had in place**	**Substantially, but not fully supported**
	First	That APs and BPs would be more aware of the existence of stress avoidance and/or management programmes in their workplaces than would CPMs	Not supported
	Second	That CPMs would be less aware of the existence of an EAP in their organisations than would APs and BPs	Supported
FIFTH		**That, regardless of workplace programmes, participants would personally engage in some form of stress management activity**	**Partially but not fully supported**
	First	CPMs would be less likely to do so than APs and BPs	Unsupported
	Second	CPMs would be more likely than APs and BPs to rate their chosen technique as effective	Supported

- While attitudes appear to be changing, the construction industry has a long way to go in relation to establishing effective stress avoidance and management programmes
- Locus of control issues regarding work are a major source of stress for CPMs, and workplace-generated stressors impact the personal lives of many CPMs
- Several aspects of industry culture were important causative factors of CPMs' stress experience.

In addition to these key points I consider it important to reconcile research findings and to synthesise the findings from the quantitative and qualitative aspects of the study, comparing outcomes with research questions and objectives. Table 5.2 provides this synthesis.

The following were salient factors from the synthesis:

- Qualitative analysis outcomes endorse CPMs experience of stress and its causes differing from APs and BPs, while the quantitative analysis stood in partial support;
- Statistical analysis confirms CPMs experienced stress differently from APs and BPs and qualitative analysis emphasised lack of time prevented exercise and similar healthy stress avoidance/management pursuits;
- Both the statistical data analysis and the qualitative data analysis strongly support the experience of stress by CPMs does differ from that by APs and BPs on several dimensions;
- The qualitative analysis revealed a generally healthy attitude against use of maladaptive stress management, but a lack of time for engagement in much adaptive stress management;
- Regarding locus of control aspects of stress, both quantitative and qualitative analyses findings confirmed the difference between various role categories.

I now regard it essential to discuss other important findings from analysis of the research data. This is important not only for completeness of this work but also to ensure a foundation for essential ongoing work beyond this research.

Table 5.2 Synthesis of research questions, objectives and findings

Knowledge gap point	Research question/s	Related research objective/s	Key hypothesis point	Key qualitative findings	Key quantitative findings
Organisations might have overloaded CPMs without giving them authority to refuse additional work and protect their health, and CPMs were unlikely to report stress effects for fear of appearing weak	What was the attitude of CPMs and their employers to stress and its management and did it differ from the attitudes of APs and BPs?	To determine if findings of a pilot study (conducted prior to this research) represented the attitudes of a broader representation of CPMs	That opinions would differ across RPs regarding stress avoidance and management training and the use of EAPs to deal with stress after it had manifested	Senior managers lacked understanding of the CPM workload Work was won by margin reduction and 6-day week commitment—placing stress on CPMs Low-margin–no-margin tendering created stress for CPMs	Partially supported

Knowledge gap point	Research question/s	Related research objective/s	Key hypothesis point	Key qualitative findings	Key quantitative findings
CPMs might experience stress differently from APs and BPs	Was there a greater propensity for CPMs to use either adaptive or maladaptive stress avoidance and/or management techniques than APs and BPs?	To determine if attitudes to and management of stress among CPMs differed from those of APs, and To determine if attitudes to and management of stress among CPMs differed from those of BPs	CPMs would hold a different attitude to the main causes of stress than APs and BPs	CPMs were stressed by lack of time for family CPMs were stressed by lack of self time CPMs often believed they would lose their job if they complained about the stress CPMs had the sense they could not change a system that badly need changing	Substantially supported by the statistical analysis findings for this key hypothesis

(continued)

Table 5.2 (continued)

Knowledge gap point	Research question/s	Related research objective/s	Key hypothesis point	Key qualitative findings	Key quantitative findings
It was not clear whether stress experienced by CPMs was caused by culture and processes, by work factors generally or by home factors primarily	What strategies were in place to assist in avoidance or management of stress (for CPMs) and how did they compare with those for APs and BPs?	To determine if attitudes to and management of stress among CPMs differed from those of APs, and BPs	CPMs would be less aware of existence of organisational stress avoid-ance/management programmes in their workplace, and would report not having time to use these programmes	Cut-throat economy put great pressure on construction companies to cut prices and work longer hours, resulting in increased stress for senior CPMs in particular The 'tough' image of construction prevented many CPMs from speaking out about practices that were stressogenic, for fear of being ridiculed for appearing weak or soft	Supported by the statistical analysis findings in relation to the major sub-hypotheses for this key hypothesis
It was not clear to what extent CPMs used stress avoidance or management techniques, or maladaptive stress management approaches	Did CPM employers provide stress avoidance and/or management programmes, and did CPMs make use of any programmes provided?	To determine if findings of a pilot study (conducted prior to this research) represented the attitudes of a broader representa-tion of CPMs	CPMs would be less likely than APs or BPs to engage in some form of stress management activity, but would be more likely to consider it effective	Most semi-structured interview participants denied use of drugs or excess use of alcohol, but most also stated they had little time for exercise or other relaxation pursuits	Somewhat but not fully supported by the statistical analysis findings in relation to the main hypothesis

Knowledge gap point	Research question/s	Related research objective/s	Key hypothesis point	Key qualitative findings	Key quantitative findings
It was not clear if locus of control issues impacted on stress experienced by CPMs, or whether workplace-generated stress had an impact on their personal lives and relationships	Were the causes of stress the same for CPMs as for APs and BPs, and what were the effects of workplace-generated stress on the personal lives and relationships of CPMs?	To determine if findings of a pilot study (conducted prior to this research) represented the attitudes of a broader representation of CPMs	CPMs would express different attitudes from APs and BPs regarding what organisations should offer by way of stress avoidance and management	Cut-throat economy put great pressure on construction companies to cut prices and work longer hours, resulting in increased stress for senior CPMs in particular CPMs sensed they could not force required change	Substantially supported by the statistical analysis findings for this key hypothesis

Introduction to General Discussion

The study revealed a strong body of opinion, especially from semi-structured interviews, that people dealt with stress reasonably well provided they were given the appropriate information and tools to manage stressful situations. For example, referring to the way in which stress levels quickly rose and led to poor decision-making, one participant commented:

> *The one thing that should be added to university courses and corporate training is a deeper understanding of how this occurs and how to avoid it – a set of skills to manage stress when it is on the rise and (why it) must be kept under control to ensure the best decisions are made.*

I consider it necessary to further consider important findings from both qualitative and quantitative analysis, and I will now address that matter.

Addressing the Main Issues

The quantitative data analysis was invaluable in determining participants' opinions regarding a range of important points, and in gaining insight into how opinions varied between RP types and OSs. The qualitative analysis provided important insights regarding the depth of the stress problem, its main causes and its real impacts on the human capital of the construction industry. I present and discuss a salient example in the next section.

Problems at the Management—CPM Interface

Qualitative analysis findings included several themes under the category heading of 'specifically work/employer contributors to stress'. Those themes identified construction industry work practices requiring substantial, urgent and holistic adjustment as a fundamental component of any serious strategy to deal with the stress affecting CPMs. Without such a strategy, the industry cannot avoid substantial loss of productivity from its most senior and efficient operatives.

The most significant issues in this area include:

- Construction organisations continue to pursue work using practices effective for corporate survival, but changed from survival focus to a growth focus after winning work. This approach usually requires already-overburdened senior CPMs to adopt delivery strategies that place unreasonable stress upon themselves, their health, their colleagues, their families and, ultimately, their relationships;
- Senior management of construction organisations communicated too infrequently regarding their expectations of senior CPMs. Feedback showing appreciation for dedicated effort, shown in the literature to be effective at reducing stress effects, [17] was rare despite being much needed. I gained a strong sense the lack of such feedback could be the final straw in some CPMs dropping deeper into the grip of serious stress and its consequences; [10, 27]
- Management of some construction-related organisations include in their work-winning strategies in difficult economic circumstances, contractual undertakings to work six full-day weeks and to accept earlier completion dates than those defined in tender request documentation;
- The tendency of CPMs affected by these behaviours was to grin and bear it rather than initiate meaningful dialogue to decrease the extent of the problem, and even alleviate its effects substantially.

These are major issues and they require urgent attention. Attitudes to management strategies were mixed. Some participants believed without work, nobody could support their families and so everyone had to support management in whatever was necessary to continue winning work—at any cost. Others expressed a more cynical view management were focused only on profit and did not care about impacts of their actions on staff. This latter group tend to believe, because there are always people prepared to take their jobs if they caused trouble (for their busy, stressed and overworked managers) their jobs were never safe. I found no senior managers who appeared that cynical in regard to caring for their staff, but the data revealed even senior CPMs believed raising issues too strongly with senior management was seldom an advisable career move.

Construction has a reputation as a tough industry attracting tough people. To complain about the status quo, especially in relation to workload or stress problems, exposes the complainant to allegations of being weak and unsuited to the industry. Even seasoned industry professionals hold this belief. Despite unquestionable skills in leading those below them, they lack the leadership strength or knowledge to comprehend the necessity of communicating upwards about serious problems, such as the impacts of stress on personnel, notwithstanding outdated cultural dictates. This gave me the impression the tough industry culture might well be toughest at the top. The implications of this are potentially serious in terms of any stress management initiatives.

Fortunately, during the research period, a significant union and several major contractors announced an agreement whereby daily working hours would increase slightly but weekend work would cease. This provided CPMs with administration catch-up time on Saturday mornings (industry tradition for decades prior to the current stressogenic practices) and still spend time relaxing and rejuvenating for the week ahead. Importantly, this was a major improvement for CPMs with families, because working six-day weeks necessitated Sunday morning work for catch-up, leaving little time for relaxation and family.

Winning work through low-margin or no-margin bidding needs to be addressed. While many considered this an acceptable business practice for difficult economic times, the strategies often adopted after winning work are a different matter. For example, appointing already overworked senior CPMs to projects to increase profit from (say) one or two percent up to six to eight percent, was a significant contributor to much of the stress those CPMs experienced, and was ill-informed. On small to medium well-documented projects, there was little scope to increase profit except by engaging low-priced subcontractors, often insufficiently skilled or lacking the management ability to deliver on time, despite having technical competence. In either case it becomes necessary for a highly experienced CPM to manage the subcontractors' resources and this, more than most other factors, contributed to substantial distress of the level that could lead to burnout of key people.

Lack of Control and Stress Effects

Albeit some organisations are acutely aware of the importance of stress avoidance and management strategies, there remains a broader need for specifically designed strategies to effectively address the stressors faced by CPMs. Company-paid health and stress checks and stress awareness and management training were popular when offered. However, when stress (and general health) testing was made available, it usually was not compulsory, and it was commonly the more overworked (or remotely stationed) employees who did not become involved. When organisations provided work–life balance workshops, generally popular with staff, it was often people most in need of them who were least likely to have time to attend. Half the semi-structured interview CPMs spoke of long hours and weekend work on their health and/or families/relationships. Moreover, six survey respondents made nine unsolicited references to this issue.

EAPs drew mixed but generally positive comments. EAPs offered in isolation to stress avoidance and management education were seen to be indicative of probably *the* major stress management issue in the construction industry—dealing with problems after they manifest rather than reducing the likelihood the problem might arise. Another issue requiring attention is leaders and managers being expected to remain alert for signs of stress in subordinates, but not being given training in what those signs are.

Organisations that did invest in stress management specific to their people's needs were in the minority, but noted an unexpected benefit as the following demonstrates:

We have gained a reputation of being an employer of choice and we have got really good people through word-of-mouth. We found it costs a lot less to train good people so our investment in stress and health generally has paid off in areas we never would have anticipated.

The industry needs people aware of early signs of stress in themselves and others, and training in that area is crucial.

Discussion of General Observations

The purpose of this section is to make relevant brief comments on other important points:

- Many major construction organisations focussed on assisting those affected by stress after symptoms manifested. There was little emphasis on identifying workplace sources of stress and minimising them; [6]
- Issues that need to be addressed included assisting CPMs, especially if site-based, to become effectively involved in stress avoidance and management activities;
- Industry leaders need to be made aware their strategies, decisions and actions regarding winning work and growing their business have the potential to become major sources of stress for CPMs and other employees;
- The qualitative data analysis revealed most CPMs would not use an EAP for fear their use would be discovered and they would be considered weak. The need for culture change in this industry is glaringly obvious;
- CPMs salaries were substantially higher than those of APs and BPs within some age ranges, and those CPMs reported their work was stressful substantially more than did APs and BPs. It is therefore not surprising CPMs reported having experienced stress effects at a higher level than they would have liked over the month prior to completing the survey more than did APs and BPs. Qualitative data revealed management tended to deal with CPMs' threats of leaving due to stress by offering higher salaries, apparently oblivious to the potential negative impacts of this practice. While a salary increase might temporarily make stress worth tolerating, if stress continued to increase, not only did the CPMs feel more affected, they also felt less inclined to report that, or do anything about the problem within their workplace;
- The fact 52.59 percent of CPMs (compared with 43.55 percent and 41.07 percent of APs and BPs, respectively) reported doing something to manage stress was encouraging. However, that needed to be considered in light of 40.32 percent of CPMs (compared with 32.26 percent and 33.04 percent of APs and BPs, respectively) reporting they use alcohol to relax;

- The industry should no longer accept its leaders remaining oblivious to the stress placed upon CPMs by the practices adopted to win work at low margin in tight economic circumstances, and then to pressure CPMs to increase profit on work won by employing inefficient low-priced subcontractors;
- A clear lack of trust in management is of concern. Even participants who expressed respect for their organisation and its management often also stated that they had no doubt if they failed to perform at top level they would be quickly replaced, and the need to consistently perform at top level under high levels of stress constitutes a very stressful factor in itself.

I consider this research important to make an industry infamous for its tough culture and ingrained attitudes. Credit must be given to many organisations at various levels of the industry that continue to achieve relatively strong success, despite constantly changing economic and politico-legislative environments. However, the cost of success in terms of impact on human resources, and especially on the key drivers of performance, the industry's CPMs, was found to be now reaching the point where it should no longer be left unaddressed. I will now present my most important conclusions from this study, and provide recommendations for immediate action to be considered by governments and industry.

Conclusions Generally

Important findings from this study were:

- For CPMs, causes of stress were mainly work-related, while for APs and BPs, they were mainly non-work-related;
- Levels of stress for CPMs have been increasing over recent years and, unless some well-considered and formulated strategic actions are urgently taken, I expect stress impacts, including increases in serious illnesses and burnout for industry professionals, to develop;

- A recognition of need for focus on stress avoidance and management is becoming more common within the construction industry, and in some areas is already regarded as essential. However, use of an EAP or counselling service was all-too-often regarded as satisfactory management, despite the reality EAPs deal with stress after it manifests and its effects are felt by employees. In all probability, at this stage, stress has impacted the projects. A change of industry attitude is required to focus attention on avoidance of stress, and stress management from first signs of its manifestation, rather than dealing with effects of severe stress using an EAP after it had taken a toll;
- There is strong need for culture change throughout the industry regarding reporting of any aspect of stress, anxiety, depression and any other stress-related problem;
- The industry's tough culture needs to be microscopically identified, systematically addressed, and strategically replaced through education and example with healthier, and ultimately more-productive and profit-enhancing attitudes to open reporting of, and dealing with, all aspects of stress-related issues;
- Many stress impacts are exacerbated by lack of communication. Specifically, there is evidence of lack of communication from CPMs upwards to their senior management, especially concerning their workloads being increased to the point stress effects were experienced. Ideally, a renewed industry culture would see managers communicating downwards to check on the effects of high workloads on CPMs;
- It is important the management of construction-related organisations are made aware of the importance of:

  – Having their staff, and especially their senior staff, educated in stress avoidance and management techniques
  – Leadership in addressing the strongly-ingrained industry culture that one needed to be tough to work in the industry and to be affected by stress was a sign of weakness

- The apparent lack of awareness by senior management of many construction-related organisations concerning the stressogenic impacts of their strategies for winning work in tough economic climates needs to be brought to their awareness.

Conclusions—Important and Requiring Industry Attention

Some of the findings from this study demanded long consideration, which resulted in the strong conclusion that important steps for the construction industry need to be urgently taken in several specific areas.

Industry practices for winning and delivering work should be urgently reviewed. This would be difficult to achieve without the full engagement and active participation of both government and industry leaders. The quantity surveying profession is well aware the common approach of letting project work for construction using a lump-sum tendering approach was most effective only at times of the economic cycle where that cycle crossed its 'X' axis. At top of market, prices are usually well over budget because the best contractors have plenty of work and submitted high-profit prices despite probably not having resources currently on staff to adequately manage any additional work they win. At bottom of market, contractors 'bought' contracts by pricing work at low margin/no margin (or even at loss) to keep their people employed and their businesses operating, and often engaged incompetent subcontractors to deliver the work, thus placing immense stress on the CPMs charged with the responsibility of managing project performance.

This subcontractor aspect has quickly become one of the most significant problems in the construction industry. Left unresolved, it has capacity to increase an already prevalent fear and lack of trust between many CPMs and their senior management. Uncurbed, this issue presents a substantial risk to the industry continuing to operate at its traditional high standard of professionalism.

The industry urgently needs educational programmes, not only for delivery operatives in relation to strategies for avoiding and managing stress, but also for industry leaders at all levels of client, consultant and contractor organisations, in relation to systemic problems. These include problems triggered largely by contractual delivery systems designed decades ago for projects of a fraction of the size and complexity of those currently undertaken and/or planned. My closing comments to this chapter develop this concept further.

Recommendations for Future Research

I formulated the following recommendations for future research after considering the findings and conclusions presented above:

- This research should be extended to investigate stress levels of CPMs and other industry operatives who work in a range of project delivery systems, including Integrated Project Delivery, Design and Construction and Negotiated Contract approaches, among others. This information would be of particular use to senior industry personnel who might be engaged in revision of industry practices as proposed herein;
- Urgent research is needed regarding an effective stress education programme for the industry that included both stress avoidance and stress management components with which industry members were prepared to engage. The stress avoidance component should include education of industry leaders regarding stress effects on CPMs in particular of current work-winning protocols;
- It is essential the programme be focused on changing deeply ingrained tough-culture industry attitudes, and ridding the industry of the problem of members being embarrassed about facing mental health problems openly and confidently;
- A longitudinal study of the effects of any programme launched should be undertaken, with the intention early positive results might reinforce future continuation of positive change;
- Research is required into aspects of female involvement in construction project management. Important among the studies considered necessary are the following:
  - A comparison of perceptions of stress between male and female CPMs, inclusive of investigation into whether there is similarity regarding primary stress triggers, what those primary stress triggers might be, and how women and men who have successfully addressed and dealt with stressors managed the problem
  - Given various effects of female stress addressed in the literature review of this research, a study of female CPM fecundity, time to pregnancy and success/failure rates, especially for construction

professionals of 35 years of age and over, compared with women of similar age working in AP and BP environments

- Finally, while not directly associated with the work covered by this book, I consider there to be potential value for an extended comparison study of research triggers and effects as experienced by various professional groups associated with construction, including but not limited to development managers, property professionals, asset managers, funds managers, valuers and the like.

Study Weaknesses and Limitations

I considered it essential to emphasise, while the literature review covered aspects of literature from around the world, the data collection and analysis was undertaken specifically in respect of an Australia-based participants sample. Also, while the study might have been extended to include how different stress attitudes might have been developed/experienced by participants operating strictly within differing approaches to project delivery, that would have taken an already information and data dense body of work to an unmanageable level, given word count limitations for the work. The alternate approach of determining from this work what future studies would best benefit industry was adopted, and that future research was described in the previous section.

Implications of this Research

The implications of this research comprise both theoretical and practical aspects. These have largely been described in the conclusions and recommendations. From the practical perspective, the work contributes a sound and thorough platform from which approaches can be made to government and industry. One clear objective seen for such approaches was to garner support to initiate systemic change aimed at overcoming archaic cultural attitudes that encouraged male industry practitioners in particular to ignore mental health issues to the point of potential self-destruction. However, perhaps the most important practical aspect of the work is that it provides a firm basis for informing and motivating industry leadership groups towards a change in attitude from dealing with stress effects on people after they have manifested to changing ingrained cultural practices to substantially reduce the incidence of those stress effects manifesting.

There are two main aspects of theoretical implications of the study. The first is the strength obtained by the study using a mixed method approach, from both internal study triangulation and cross influence perspectives, and from employment of both positivist and constructivist epistemological approaches. By cross influence I refer to the capacity of findings from early responses to one aspect of the methodology to inform improvements in other aspects of the study. The second was the worrying reality that, despite the research findings so clearly indicating need for urgent industry cultural change, the strength of an industry culture ingrained for well over a century in this country might very well condemn findings to a life in the literature, with no prospect of a follow-up longitudinal research study of the positive effects of adoption of the recommendations made herein.

Hopefully, senior industry and government minds well practised in problem solving will become engaged, and take a deeply philosophical approach to recognising the extent of the problem, and to well-considered and long-term eradication, or at least amelioration of it.

Closing Thoughts

At the time of writing, it seemed a fortuitous opportunity might be forthcoming that leaders who agree with the issues raised in this book could exploit. That potential opportunity arises from the confluence of several factors, the most important being:

- There appears a high likelihood Brisbane, Australia will be named the host city for the 2032 Olympic Games (and this has been confirmed immediately prior to this monograph going to press);

- Market conditions in the construction industry in South East Queensland (where Brisbane is located) are already rapidly changing from being difficult for construction contractors to the point some contractors currently have more work to price than they have priced in the past several years;
- Over $200 billion (AUD) has been committed to infrastructure development by the governments of three eastern states of Australian over the coming five years or so, and the government of Queensland had decreed that all projects over $50 million must be completed using an innovative technology known as Building Information Modelling (BIM);
- Larger governments projects in Australia are increasingly being delivered using the Alliance Contracting approach, generally recognised as an Australian initiative which the Americans have raised to an art form and re-badged Integrated Project Delivery (IPD), a term now recognised throughout the western world;
- Another relatively modern construction innovation—Lean construction (Lean), adapted from the quality control movement and designed, *inter alia* to minimise wastage on construction and infrastructure projects for environmental benefit (as well as cost savings).

The earlier points above might appear to indicate many of the problems addressed in this book are about to become things of the past, but I strongly believe that if government and industry take that approach, they do so in naivety, and are likely to find their industry again facing the challenges addressed in this book when the economic cycle again changes from flow to ebb. Secondly, the implications of the latter points provide a basis for systemic change, if only industry and government leaders can see the potential and at least investigate the possibilities. Allow me to explain.

Academics and industry professionals alike agree the best possible results from the use of BIM, IPD and Lean, which are all relatively new and innovative technologies/methodologies expected to be used in construction and infrastructure for decades to come, are likely to be realised when all major contributors to project delivery are involved and work together from as early as possible in concept development until establishment of asset management operations; and that includes contractors and operations managers. This will require a change to the current contracting approach whereby the majority of projects are distributed by owners using lump-sum tendering processes. This is the case for government and private developers but for distinctly different reasons. Government uses that form of tendering approach to ensure probity in allocation of work paid for by the public while, for the most part, the motivator for developers is achieving the lowest prices possible, thereby enhancing profit potential of projects.

In tough economic times, appointing project participants within a mature industry using a reasonable, well-controlled but non-competitive approach would present distinct advantages. As an experienced construction professional with decades and billions of dollars of project experience, I am convinced the issues revealed by this research could be largely eradicated, in that a reasonable profit level could be experienced by any competent contractor appointed using the system I am about to propose to achieve the above, providing that contractor applied competence to the best of its ability on all projects won, and distributed work won to efficient subcontractors. The central success factors achieved would be contractors being offered reasonable profit on every project, and consequently, those contractors being able to cease the current practices of increasing profit from ridiculously low levels included in tender prices by using cheaper and often incompetent subcontractors, and subsequently overstressing their most experienced CPMs to manage project delivery.

This raises two important questions, those being, 'What would be a process of achieving this outcome' and, 'would such a process be workable across all phases of the economic cycle?'.

Let me first address the challenges of achieving the outcome mentioned above. The main one would be the natural zest (some might say greed) of any business to maximise profit. Indeed, many would argue that, for public companies in particular, maximisation of return to shareholders is and always will be a primary objective of company management. I would counter that modern attitudes and expectations of business are becoming more egalitarian and community-oriented, and corporate social responsibility (CSR) initiatives exemplify this.

For any organisation that accepts the relevance and importance of CSR, initiatives to protect the health and wellbeing of employees and avoid health care costs to the community, simply make sense, even without looking at the actual end cost and delivery time for projects let at a low tender prices and extended by endless disputes and negotiations regarding scope variations, time extensions and the like. In the case of government projects, accepting low prices that do not include a reasonable profit and so encourage engagement of lower price and sometimes incompetent subcontractors hardly achieves much in terms of ensuring best value for money for the taxpayer. Despite this, I recently learned from a senior government executive that another senior manager, who held a hierarchical position well beyond their competence and experience, lobbied strongly for adoption of a system for major projects tendering whereby a price would be sought from a competent contractor or quantity surveyor, and the department would then 'shop the market' seeking offers of lower price until the lowest price possible was attained, and companies refused to lower their prices further. In terms of the findings of this research, a senior government executive promoting such a reverse auction approach for major construction projects demonstrates precisely the mindset that qualifies them for little more than immediate dismissal.

The big issue, of course, is the likelihood that contractors would want to be involved in a scheme that promised reasonable profits in tough economic times but would probably prefer to chase the big profits rather than accept a reasonable margin, in a booming economy. That being the case, this would be a good time for me to state that my proposal is not presented as a definite solution, rather as a starting point for discussion about a topic that simply must be addressed for the benefit of the industry and those who work in it.

The reality is lump-sum tendering was effective for projects of low to medium cost, relatively simple in nature and with relatively low risk, fully documented and completed in a market with clearly delineated standards/competencies of contractors and a nice balance of government work during tough times and private work during boom times. However, the seventies are long gone, and it is time all industry leaders recognised that, and cooperated towards much needed the construction industry systemic change. I think that change should include, if not begin with, an adjustment of thinking regarding contracts awarding.

Here now is a proposal some might regard as radical, perhaps even unworkable. I cannot see any option other than government leading the initiative on this, as government has on so many construction and infrastructure delivery initiatives over decades. My proposal is for nothing more than commencement of an industry-wide discussion to address the issues raised in this work that are having such a substantial impact on the mental health of our most experienced construction professionals. To commence that discussion, I propose an adjustment in the manner in which at least 25 percent (to begin with) of government tenders are let to a process something along the lines of the following:

- Government maintains a register of contractors within project complexity/competency categories (most already do);
- For at least a percentage of major projects, but not those already done under Alliance negotiated arrangements, Government has project designs priced at reasonable current market rates, but by two independent quantity surveyors, preferably without each knowing which other firm is involved;
- Government determines 'next contractor/s in line' for an opportunity based on a range of factors including position in the Government register relative to the skills involved for the project, current work in progress, available resources, etc., and invites pricing, which could be done contemporaneously with the previous step;
- If the price/s provided falls within the range of the two QS prices, the contract is awarded. If it is not, a negotiation process could follow prior to offering the pricing opportunity to other contractors until a satisfactory price was agreed;
- Any contractor who does not accept an invitation to price a project offered under this arrangement might be required to miss another opportunity before being invited to be involved in the process again.

I am well aware such a simplistic sounding proposal will not resolve issues as it stands. I did not make it with that intent, but rather to present something around which much-overdue discussion can be commenced. I am well aware there is nothing in what I have proposed that might prevent contractors continuing with the very practices of increasing profit to maximum levels possible, regardless of the level of profit included in their tender prices, and regardless of the impact of that practice on their most experienced CPMs. That issue is most definitely one that would need to be addressed if the industry decides to take up my challenge to actively address the issues covered in this book.

I realise many construction professionals in Australia regard management contracting, so well understood and practised in the UK, as a potential solution to the problems described in this book. I would agree, if we had management contractors of the ilk of those in the UK, but in my experience, it is construction contractors who seek and usually win managing contractor roles. I am yet to see multiple examples of contractors well practised in competitive tendering and profit-enhancing practices adapt well (and to the client's benefit) to the essential client service focus of management contracting. Perhaps with the systemic industry change I have repeatedly stated is necessary, this attitude could also change for the better of all involved with construction, including clients.

I will now sign off with my best wishes the CPMs of Australia and the world realise better working and private lives because someone, somewhere, read and took positive action towards systemic construction industry change, because they read this work.

A Final Review of Will and Clare's Situation

In Chapter 4 I mentioned that while I presented Will and Clare as a 'metaphoric couple', I did not explain the context, and a more accurate description during earlier chapters might have been 'example couple'. However, I never intended they be so aligned with the business and private circumstances of many participants in my research. Rather I intended them to be a metaphor, not for industry members, but rather for the construction industry at large.

You are by now familiar with Will's and Clare's circumstances. In many ways the construction industry culture demonstrates many of the dysfunctional and ineffective characteristics of the manner in which they had been conducting their relationship. Clare, who tolerated Will's stress-driven behaviours without raising for discussion the impacts on her and the corrective action she might like to see taken, is not unlike the many CPMs who suffer the stressogenic effects of poor decisions by their managers and unreasonable practices of management of winning work at low margins and using their best and most heavily committed resources to increase profits after winning the jobs. Those CPMs often do this without complaining for fear of losing their job, or perhaps not wanting to earn the reputation of being a complainer, or being labelled a CPM who could not handle the pace and pressure of the job. Clare might have resisted complaining for fear of losing her relationship, or perhaps from feeling to do so would demonstrate her not being able to manage her share of the pressure of earning for and raising a family.

One common industry practice when top performing CPMs did report feeling high stress and asked for workload reduction was for their organisations to counter with an offer of a salary increase, a bonus, perhaps a trip or holiday—which often failed to eventuate, again due to pressure of work—but seldom with an adjustment of practices to help avoid, alleviate or manage stress. Indeed, Will experienced precisely this treatment. However, Will is very much a metaphor for management as much as for collective CPMs in this regard. He continued on with destructive practices in his own career, looking only at the benefits he was striving to deliver for his family without actually taking time to communicate with Clare and find out what her life priorities might have been. In a similar manner, many construction companies continue with practices which they see as essential to continue winning work, making profit and keeping people employed, without ever communicating with their employees, especially those carrying the bulk of the project delivery workload, to determine the impacts of the practices so employed, or discussing alternative arrangements.

It was refreshing during this research to hear one participant state their organisation had done the right thing, communicated with staff, and adopted a practice of expecting CPMs to deliver only the level of profit anticipated by the tender price; utterly refreshing!

It is time for this organisation, and not Will and Clare, to be the metaphor for the construction industry in Australia, and throughout the western world, into the future.

References

1. Australian Compensation and Safety Council 2006, *Work related mental disorders in Australia*, viewed 5th April 2017, <https://www.safeworkaustralia.gov.au/system/files/documents/1702/workrelated_mental_disorders_australia.pdf>.
2. Safe Work Australia 2006, *Work—Related mental disorders in Australia*. Australian Compensation and Safety Council, Canberra, viewed 13th October 2017 <https://www.safeworkaustralia.gov.au/system/files/documents/1702/work-related-mental-disorders-profile.pdf>.
3. Loss Prevention Council 1998, *Work Stress: a brief guide on its prevention and management*. Referenced in Safework Australia (2006) but no longer available.
4. Mohsin, S & Wahab, A 2013, 'Stress management and steps of managing stress', *Asia Pacific Journal of Management and Entrepreneurship Research*, vol. 2, no. 1, pp. 164–172.
5. Cook, M & Cripps, B 2005, *Psychological assessment in the workplace*, Wiley, New York.
6. Noblet, A & La Montagne, A 2006, 'The role of workplace health promotion in addressing job stress', *Health Promotion International*, vol. 21, no. 4, pp. 346–353.
7. Noblet, A & La Montagne, A 2006, 'The role of workplace health promotion in addressing job stress', *Health Promotion International*, vol. 21, no. 4, page 348.
8. Yip, B & Rowlinson, S 2009, 'Job burnout among construction engineers working within consultancy and contracting organisations', *Journal of Management in Engineering*, vol. 25, no. 3, pp. 122–130.
9. Lingard, H, 2003, in Yip, B & Rowlinson, S 2009, 'Job burnout among construction engineers working within consultancy and contracting organisations', *Journal of Management in Engineering*, vol. 25, no. 3, page 123.
10. Albertsen, K, Rugulies, R, Garde, A & Burr, H 2010, 'The effect of the work environment and performance-based self-esteem on cognitive stress symptoms among Danish knowledge workers', *Scandinavian Journal of Public Health*, vol. 38, no. 3, pp. 81–89.

11. Weinberg, A, Sutherland, V & Cooper, C, 2010, *Organisational stress management: a strategic approach*. Palgrave Macmillan Ltd., London.
12. Yip, B & Rowlinson, S 2009, 'Job burnout among construction engineers working within consultancy and contracting organisations' *Journal of Management in Engineering*, vol. 25, no. 3, page 123.
13. Verdonk, P, Seesing, H & de Rijk, A 2010, 'Doing masculinity, not doing health? A qualitative study among Dutch male employees about health beliefs and workplace physical activity', *BMC Public Health*, vol. 10, no. 712, viewed 21st January 2018, https://www.ncbi.nlm.nih.gov/pmc/articles/PMC2998494/
14. Nakao, M 2010, 'Work related stress and psychosomatic medicine', *BioPsycho Social Medicine*, vol. 4, no. 4.
15. Sparks, K, Faragher, B & Cooper, C 2001, 'Well-being and occupational health in the 21st century workplace', *Journal of Occupational and Organizational Psychology*, vol. 74, pp. 489–509.
16. Cox, T, Griffiths, A & Houdmont, J 2006. *Defining a case of work-related stress. Research Report 449*, United Kingdom, HSE Books, viewed 17th August 2016, <http://www.hse.gov.uk/research/rrpdf/rr449.pdf>.
17. Waite, A 2012, 'Battling workplace burnout', *OT Practice*, vol. 17, no.17, pp. 9–12.
18. Loosemore, M & Waters, T 2004, 'Gender differences in occupational stress in the construction industry', *Journal of Management in Engineering* vol. 20, no. 3, pp. 126–132.
19. Siegrist, J 2012, *Effort—reward imbalance at work—theory, measurement and evidence*. Department of Medical Sociology, University of Duesseldorf, Duesseldorf, viewed 30th January 2018, <http://www.uniklinik-duesseldorf.de/fileadmin/Datenpool/einrichtungen/institut_fuer_medizinische_soziologie_id54/ERI/ERI-Website.pdf>.
20. Cohen, S, Janicki-Deverts, D & Miller, G 2007, 'Psychological stress and disease', *The Journal of the American Medical Association*, vol. 298, no. 14, pp. 1685–1687.
21. Aronson, D 2009, 'Cortisol—its role in stress, inflammation and indications for diet therapy', *Today's Dietician*, vol. 11, no. 11, p. 38.
22. Burg, M 2014, 'Confluence of depression and acute psychological stress among patients with stable coronary heart disease: Effects on myocardial perfusion', viewed 22nd August 2016, <https://www.researchgate.net/publication/267746405_Confluence_of_Depression_and_Acute_Psychological_Stress_Among_Patients_With_Stable_Coronary_Heart_Disease_Effects_on_Myocardial_Perfusion>.

23. Yeung, A, Ivkovic, A & Friccione, G 2016, *The science of stress,* Ivy Press, Brighton UK.
24. Lingard, H, 2003, 'The impact of individual and job characteristics on 'burnout' among civil engineers in Australia and the implications for employee turnover', *Construction management and Economics,* vol. 21, no. 1, pp. 69–80.
25. Moore, H 2004, '10 Proven antidotes for workplace burnout', *Vibrant Life,* vol. 20, no. 2, pp. 12–15.
26. Ericson-Lidman, E & Strandberg, G 2007, 'Burnout: co-workers' perceptions of signs preceding workmates' burnout', *Journal of Advanced Nursing,* vol. 60, no. 2, pp. 199–208.
27. Colligan, T & Higgins, E 2008, 'Workplace stress', *Workplace Behavioural Health,* vol. 21, no. 2, pp. 89–97.
28. Taylor, C 2014, 'Workstress on the increase in Australia,' viewed 11th April 2017, www.hcamag.com/hr-news/workplace-stress-on-the-increase-in-australia-194165.aspx
29. Siegel, D 2010, *Mindsight: The New Science of Personal Transformation,* New York, Random House USA Inc.
30. Clark, H n.d., 'Adrenal fatigue—From chronic stress to complete burnout', viewed 13th October 2017 <https://www.vibrantagain.com/adrenal-fatigue-from-chronic-stress-to-complete-burnout/>.
31. Williams, P 2005, 'Design/construction consultant offers tips to prevent occupational burnout', *Daily Commercial News and Construction Record,* vol. 78, no. 22, p. 7.
32. Clarke, S & Cooper, C 2004, *Managing the risk of workplace stress,* New York, Routledge.
33. Patching, A. & Best, R 2014, 'An investigation into psychological detection and management in organisations operating in project an construction management', *Procedia—Social and Behavioural Sciences,* vol. 119, pp. 682–691.
34. Varvogli, L & Darviri, C 2011, 'Stress management techniques: evidenced-based procedures that reduce stress and promote health', *Health Science Journal,* vol. 5. No. 2, pp. 74–89.
35. ABS 2007, *National survey of mental health and wellbeing: summary of findings*—Cat. no. 4326.0. Australian Bureau of Statistics: Canberra.
36. Safe Work Australia 2017, *Australian Workers Compensation Statistics, 2014–2015,* viewed 16th October 2017, https://www.safeworkaustralia.gov.au/system/files/documents/1707/australian-workers-compensation-statistics-2014-15-revised_1.pdf

Index

A. Patching, *Attitudes to Psychological Stress Among Construction Professionals*, https://doi.org/10.1007/978-3-030-93776-8

The manufacturer's authorised representative in the EU is Springer Nature Customer Service Centre GmbH, Europaplatz 3, 69115 Heidelberg, Germany. If you have any concerns regarding our products, please contact ProductSafety@springernature.com

Printed and bound by CPI Group (UK) Ltd, Croydon, CR0 4YY
30/09/2026
02225246-0001